More Wiley Concise Guides to Mental Health

Books in the *Wiley Concise Guides to Mental Health* series feature a compact, easy-to-use format that includes:

- Vignettes and case illustrations
- A practical ⟨...⟩ ⟨...⟩er theory
- Resources f⟨...⟩ ⟨...⟩or patients

DATE DUE

MAY 1 0 2011			
FEB 1 8 2013			
JUL 25 2013			
SEP 2 1 2016			

Demco, Inc. 38-293

D1117848

The **Wiley Concise ⟨...⟩** ⟨...⟩ **to Mental Health: Health: Substance U**⟨...⟩ ⟨...⟩**der** is a handy you through the enti⟨...⟩ ⟨...⟩e that provides a addiction care and pr⟨...⟩ ⟨...⟩osis, treatment, entific understanding ⟨...⟩ ⟨...⟩trends, and other abuse. This compreh⟨...⟩ ⟨...⟩osttraumatic reference provides a ⟨complete overview⟩ Stress Disorder. The book is full of anecdotes, of diagnosis, treatment, research, emerg- sidebars, and self-test questions that both ing trends, and other critical information engage and inform, making this resource in- about chemical addictions. It covers some dispensable for busy professionals and of the most cutting-edge topics in the field, students alike. including innovative approaches, outcome demands, brain science, relapse-prevention 0-471-70513-6 • Paper • $34.95 • 304 pp. strategies, designer drugs, spirituality, and June 2006 other areas.

0-471-68991-2 • Paper • $34.95 • 336 pp.
February 2006

WILEY
Now you know.

The Wiley
Concise Guides
to Mental Health

Anxiety
Disorders

Larina Kase, PsyD
Deborah Roth Ledley, PhD

BICENTENNIAL
1807
WILEY
2007
BICENTENNIAL

John Wiley & Sons, Inc.

Published by John Wiley & Sons, Inc., Hoboken, New Jersey.

Published simultaneously in Canada.

For general information on our other products and services please contact our Customer Care Department within the United States at (800) 762-2974, outside the United States at (317) 572-3993 or fax (317) 572-4002.

Wiley also publishes its books in a variety of electronic formats. Some content that appears in print may not be available in electronic books. For more information about Wiley products, visit our web site at www.wiley.com.

Library of Congress Cataloging-in-Publication Data
Kase, Larina.
    Anxiety disorder / by Larina Kase and Deborah Roth Ledley.
      p. cm.—(Wiley concise guides to mental health)
    Includes bibliographical references.
    ISBN-13: 978-0-471-77994-0 (pbk.)
    1. Anxiety.   I. Ledley, Deborah Roth. II. Title. III. Series.
    [DNLM: 1. Anxiety Disorders—therapy—Case Reports.
    2. Cognitive Therapy—methods—Case Reports.   WM 172 K185a
    2007]
    RC531.K38 2007
    616.85'22—dc22

                                                2006023190

Printed in the United States of America.

10 9 8 7 6 5 4 3 2 1

To Gary and Jenna
−D.R.L.

To Moraima and John, for fostering my creativity and interest
in writing, and serving as wonderful role models
−L.K.

CONTENTS

SERIES PREFACE

The *Wiley Concise Guides to Mental Health* are designed to provide mental health professionals with easily accessible overview of what is currently known about the nature and treatment of psychological disorders. Each book in the series delineates the origins, manifestations, and course of a commonly occurring disorder and discusses effective procedures for its treatment. The authors of the *Concise Guides* draw on relevant research as well as their clinical expertise to ground their text both in empirical findings and in wisdom gleaned from practical experience. By achieving brevity without sacrificing comprehensive coverage, the *Concise Guides* should be useful to practitioners as an on-the-shelf source of answers to questions that arise in their daily work, and they should prove valuable as well to students and professionals as a condensed review of state-of-the-art knowledge concerning the psychopathology, diagnosis, and treatment of various psychological disorders.

Irving B. Weiner

ACKNOWLEDGMENTS

We would both like to thank, first and foremost, the numerous patients that we have treated with anxiety disorders. We have enjoyed our work immensely and have learned something new in our interactions with each and every patient.

We would also like to thank the entire faculty and staff of the Center for the Treatment and Study of Anxiety at the University of Pennsylvania where we met, and both worked. Special thanks to Edna Foa, Shawn Cahill, Kelly Chrestman, Marty Franklin, Lib Hembree, Jonathan Huppert, Pat Imms, Miles Lawrence, Kate Muller, Sheila Rauch, Simon Rego, Dave Riggs, and Elna Yadin for their valuable teaching, clinical insights, and friendships. We were also so lucky at the CTSA to supervise many fabulous interns—we would like to extend a special thank you to Joelle McGovern who taught us more than we taught her about working with kids. More recently, we have also enjoyed peer supervision with Lynn Siqueland and Tamar Chansky.

We appreciate our editor, David S. Bernstein, at Wiley. We would also like to thank the Series Editor of *Wiley Concise Guides to Mental Health*, Irving B. Weiner, for his suggestions and enthusiastic support for this book.

Deborah would also like to thank Marty Antony, who first got her interested in anxiety disorders and Rick Heimberg, who has been an excellent mentor and collaborator for years. Larina would also like to thank her many wonderful supervisors, particularly those from her internship, Nancy Talbot, Sharon Gordon, Deborah King, Dennis Foley, and Mark Larson who encouraged her to pursue her dream of specializing in the cognitive behavioral treatment of anxiety disorders.

Conceptualization
and Assessment

CHAPTER 1

Overview of the Anxiety Disorders

Description of the Anxiety Disorders

The Diagnostic and Statistical Manual of Mental Disorders, fourth edition (*DSM-IV;* American Psychiatric Association, 1994) includes six anxiety disorders: Panic Disorder, Specific Phobia, Social Phobia (also known as Social Anxiety Disorder), Obsessive-Compulsive Disorder (OCD), Posttraumatic Stress Disorder (PTSD), and Acute Stress Disorder. In this chapter, these disorders will be described and a case description of each will be introduced. These cases will be used in later chapters of the book to demonstrate treatment techniques. The chapter will conclude with a discussion of differential diagnosis (how to differentiate one anxiety disorder from another anxiety disorder, and from other disorders), comorbidity (which disorders tend to co-occur with each anxiety disorder), and prevalence of the anxiety disorders.

Panic Attacks, Agoraphobia, and Panic Disorder
Panic Attacks
Panic Disorder is characterized by recurrent, unexpected ("out of the blue") panic attacks. Prior to describing panic *disorder* in more detail, it is important to define panic *attacks*. A panic attack is an *experience*, not a psychiatric disorder. The experience of panic attacks is most associated with panic disorder, but in fact, panic attacks are seen across the anxiety disorders. A *panic attack* is characterized by a period of fear or discomfort during which a person experiences at least four panic symptoms. These symptoms come on abruptly and peak within ten minutes. This does not mean that a panic attack completely goes away within ten minutes; rather, the symptoms reach their peak severity and intensity very rapidly, and then recede gradually. The symptoms of panic attacks are listed in Table 1.1. Panic attacks can include cardiovascular and respiratory symptoms like heart palpitations and shortness of breath; gastrointestinal symptoms like nausea or abdominal distress; and

TABLE 1.1.

Symptoms of Panic Attacks

A discrete period of intense fear or discomfort, in which *at least four of the following symptoms develop abruptly* and *reach a crescendo within 10 minutes:*
1. Racing or pounding heart
2. Sweating
3. Trembling or shaking
4. Shortness of breath
5. Feeling of choking
6. Chest pain or discomfort
7. Nausea or abdominal distress
8. Feeling dizzy, unsteady, or faint
9. Feeling unreal or detached
10. Tingling or numbness (usually in the hands and/or feet)
11. Chills or hot flashes
12. Fear of going crazy or losing control
13. Fear of dying

Source: DSM-IV (American Psychiatric Association, 1994).

cognitive symptoms like fear of losing control or going crazy. For some patients who experience panic attacks, the main symptom is a sense of derealization (feelings of unreality) or depersonalization (feeling detached from oneself). Clinicians should be aware that panic attacks can be quite variable from patient to patient since only four of 13 symptoms are required for a person to be considered to have panic attacks.

Agoraphobia
Like panic attacks, Agoraphobia is included in the anxiety disorders section of the *DSM*, but is not a diagnosable disorder. Agoraphobia is defined as anxiety about being in particular places or situations where escape might be difficult or help might not be available, should a panic attack or panic-like symptoms arise. Commonly feared situations include using public transportation, going to movie theatres, being away from home, and being in crowds. Agoraphobia leads to avoidance of these situations, or great distress when in these situations if they cannot be avoided.

Panic Disorder
With panic attacks and Agoraphobia defined, it is appropriate to return to the diagnostic criteria for *Panic Disorder*–the disorder most associated with these

experiences (see Table 1.2 for a summary of the diagnostic criteria). Panic Disorder is characterized by recurrent, unexpected panic attacks. The *DSM* defines "recurrent" as two or more unexpected panic attacks. When patients have had panic attacks for quite some time, they might deny the experience of unexpected attacks. This is because unexpected attacks usually happen early on in a patient's experience with the disorder. Gradually, patients come to associate panic attacks with specific situations. For example, a patient might have an "out of the blue" panic attack at the supermarket and then come to fear having additional panic attacks at the supermarket. This expectation can actually bring on attacks, as patients enter a situation already feeling anxious and being hypervigilant to their internal, physical state. Often, by the time a patient presents for treatment, he will report that all of his panic attacks are cued or expected (e.g., "I always have panic attacks in line at the supermarket and the bank."). The clinician should inquire if they *ever* experienced an "out of the blue" attack–particularly when they first started experiencing panic. Most will report that their first few attacks were indeed unexpected or surprising.

The *DSM* also requires that at least one panic attack has been accompanied by one month or more of concern about having additional attacks, worry about the consequences of having attacks (e.g., worrying about having a heart attack or going crazy), or change in behavior due to the attacks (e.g., avoiding the supermarket). Some of these behavioral changes can be subtle, like no longer drinking caffeine, having sex, or watching scary movies simply because they bring on the same physical sensations as those experienced during a panic attack.

TABLE 1.2

Summary of the Diagnostic Criteria for Panic Disorder

- **Defining characteristic:** Recurrent, unexpected panic attacks (see Table 1.1)
AND:
  - One of the following (for one month or more):
    — Worry about having additional attacks.
    — Worry about the implications of having attacks (e.g., having a heart attack, going crazy).
    — Change in behavior related to the attacks (e.g., will not exercise, see scary movies, have sex, drink caffeinated beverages, etc.).
  - Not due to organic factors (e.g., medical problems, substance use).
  - Not better accounted for by another disorder.

Source: DSM-IV (American Psychiatric Association, 1994).

It is also essential to rule out any physiological cause for panic symptoms. Panic symptoms can be brought on by various medical problems, like hyperthyroidism, or by the use of substances, like caffeine or marijuana. Particularly for patients who have never had problems with anxiety, it is advisable that they see their physician for a thorough medical evaluation to rule out any medical problems. When patients with panic disorder present for an evaluation by a mental health professional, it is often the case that they have already undergone medical evaluation—typically many times. Since patients often think that they are having a heart attack when they first experience panic attacks, it is not unusual for them to first present to emergency rooms. Once cardiac problems have been ruled out, many savvy physicians will suggest that anxiety might be the cause of the patients' difficulties and will recommend that they see a mental health professional.

Panic Disorder can be diagnosed with or without Agoraphobia. Clinicians should keep in mind that Panic Disorder with Agoraphobia would be diagnosed if (a) patients avoid situations because of their fear of having a panic attack while in them; (b) endure such situations with a great deal of distress; and/or (c) enter such situations but only with a safe person or by engaging in some other safety behavior such as carrying anti-anxiety medication, sitting near exits, or always having a cell phone available. Not surprisingly, most patients with Panic Disorder have at least mild Agoraphobia (White & Barlow, 2002).

Case Example: Panic Disorder with Agoraphobia

Susan was a 30-year old mother of a baby boy. She experienced her first panic attack a few months after her baby was born. She was alone at home with him at the time, and it was a particularly stressful day. The baby was inconsolable and would not eat or sleep. Susan was exhausted, frustrated, and worried. She suddenly became very dizzy, felt her heart racing, and experienced chest pain and pressure. She was terrified that she was "going crazy." Her brother was schizophrenic and she worried that she was developing the disorder too. Susan called her husband at work, and he came home and took her to the emergency room. After a thorough workup, Susan was deemed healthy. It was recommended that she cut back on caffeine and smoking (she was drinking many pots of tea and smoking up to two packs of cigarettes per day) and try to get some more rest and help around the house.

About a week later, Susan took the baby to the supermarket. She found the fluorescent lights to be very annoying and she started to feel anxious. Before she knew it, she was having another panic attack and had to leave her cart of food and rush from the store. Over the next few months, Susan had panic attacks in more and more places and even started to have them at home. She was so scared of "going crazy" when home alone with the baby that her mother had to come over while her husband was at work. By the time she presented for treatment, she was totally housebound and was experiencing multiple panic attacks each day. Even once a panic attack had subsided, Susan was left with a chronic, low-level of anxiety throughout the day.

Specific Phobia and Social Phobia
Specific Phobia
The *DSM-IV* includes two types of phobias: Specific Phobia and Social Phobia. *Specific Phobia* is characterized by a "marked or persistent fear ... of a specific object or situation" (American Psychological Association, 1994, p. 410; see Table 1.3 for a summary of the diagnostic criteria). To be diagnosed with a simple phobia, patients must realize that their fears are excessive or unreasonable; this criterion is not applied to children, although they must exhibit symptoms of the specific phobia for at least 6 months in order to differentiate a clinically significant phobia from

TABLE 1.3

Summary of the Diagnostic Criteria for Specific Phobia

- **Defining characteristic:** Marked and persistent fear that is excessive or unreasonable, cued by the presence (or anticipation) of a specific object or situation.
- Must experience anxiety almost every time the feared stimuli is confronted.
- Must recognize that the fear is excessive or unreasonable.
- Must avoid the feared object, or endure exposure to it with intense anxiety.
- Must experience significant distress or impairment in functioning because of the fear/avoidance.
- Must have had the fear for more than 6 months.
- Not better accounted for by another disorder.

Subtypes of specific phobia:
- — Animal type (e.g., fear of spiders, dogs).
- — Natural environment type (e.g., fear of lightening/thunder, water).
- — Blood-injection-injury type (e.g., fear of injections, having blood drawn).
- — Situational type (e.g., fear of flying, driving).
- — Other type (e.g., fear of choking, vomiting).

Source: DSM-IV (American Psychiatric Association, 1994).

TABLE 1.4

Lifetime Prevalence of Common Specific Phobias

Stimuli	Prevalence (%)
Storms	2.9
Water	3.4
Flying	3.5
Enclosed places	4.2
Blood	4.5
Heights	5.3
Animals	5.7

Source: Curtis et al. (1998).

the transient fears that are common during childhood. Specific Phobia is only diagnosed when patients report that their fear causes them significant distress or impairment in functioning. The *DSM-IV* includes five specific phobia subtypes: animal type, natural environment type (e.g., fear of storms, water, heights), blood-injection-injury type, situational type (e.g., flying, driving, bridges), and other type (e.g., fear of choking or vomiting, etc.). Common phobias include fear of heights, flying, being in enclosed places, storms, animals, blood, and water (see Table 1.4; Curtis, Magee, Eaton, Wittchen, & Kessler, 1998).

Social Phobia

Social Phobia shares similar diagnostic criteria with Specific Phobia, but the focus of concern is on social and/or performance situations (see Table 1.5 for diagnostic criteria). The core concerns of patients with Social Phobia are doing or saying something embarrassing (or exhibiting anxiety symptoms such as blushing, shaking, or sweating) that will lead to negative evaluation from others. Situations commonly feared by patients with Social Phobia include initiating and maintaining conversations, speaking up in groups, doing things in front of other people (e.g., eating, filling in a form), making requests of others, and asking others to change their behavior (see Table 1.6). The *DSM-IV* requires clinicians to specify if the social fears are "generalized," meaning that the individual fears most social situations. In contrast, some individuals with Social Phobia have very discrete social fears, such as a circumscribed fear of public speaking. Patients with generalized Social Phobia tend to experience more severe Social Phobia symptoms and suffer greater impairment in functioning (Mannuzza et al., 1995) than those with more discrete fears.

TABLE 1.5

Summary of Diagnostic Criteria for Social Phobia

- Defining characteristic: A marked and persistent fear of one or more social or performance situations in which the person is exposed to unfamiliar people or to possible scrutiny by others. The individual fears he or she will act in a way (or show anxiety symptoms) that will be humiliating or embarrassing.
- Must experience anxiety almost every time the feared social or performance situations are confronted.
- Must recognize that the fear is excessive or unreasonable.
- Must avoid the feared situations, or endure exposure with intense anxiety.
- Must experience significant distress or impairment in functioning because of the fear/avoidance.
- Must have had the fear for more than 6 months.
- Not due to organic factors (e.g., medical problems, substance use).
- Not better accounted for by another disorder.

Source: DSM-IV (American Psychiatric Association, 1994).

TABLE 1.6

Situations Commonly Feared by Individuals with Social Phobia

- Public speaking (e.g., making a speech, making a toast at a wedding, doing a reading in church/synagogue, making a presentation in class).
- Being the center of attention (e.g., telling a story or a joke, receiving a compliment).
- Initiating and/or maintaining casual conversations.
- Meeting new people (e.g., introducing self, breaking into conversations, etc.).
- Eating, drinking, writing, working in front of others.
- Being assertive—asking others to change their behavior or refusing unreasonable requests.
- Voicing opinions, especially if they are controversial.
- Talking to authority figures.
- Interviewing for a job.
- Dating.
- Talking on the telephone.
- Going to the gym or participating in sports.
- Performing in front of an audience (e.g., playing an instrument, acting in a play).

Case Example: Specific Phobia

Felicia was a 19-year-old college student who had recently developed a terrible fear of pigeons. According to Felicia, she was walking through campus with a friend about six months prior to her evaluation when a pigeon suddenly landed on her friend's head, becoming entangled in her hair. Since that time, Felicia became terrified each time she saw a pigeon, which was many times a day around campus and the city where it was located. She feared that a pigeon would land on her head, just as had happened to her friend. When Felicia presented for treatment, she was not avoiding being outside, but was taking great pains to avoid pigeons. She would cross to the other side of the street each time she saw one (sometimes necessitating "multiple crossings" on a single block!) and often walking with an umbrella covering her head on a perfectly sunny day. She was prompted to enter treatment when a cousin invited her to visit him in Venice. The patient, knowing how common pigeons are in Venice, could not imagine going despite very much wanting to visit Italy and getting to know her extended family.

Case Example: Social Phobia

Jeff was a 27-year-old young man who had been working as a paralegal since finishing his undergraduate degree. He presented for treatment a few weeks before beginning law school. He had been accepted to law school many times since he graduated, but kept turning down his admission offers because of his social anxiety. Jeff dreaded being called on in law school classes. He worried that he would get questions wrong and embarrass himself in front of his classmates and professors. He was even more nervous, however, about having to argue cases in court. He could not imagine being able to speak coherently with all eyes on him in the courtroom. Jeff imagined stumbling over his words, or even completely forgetting what he had meant to say. Meeting with new clients also made him anxious. He worried about saying the wrong thing and making mistakes, and he also felt uncomfortable with the casual conversations that typically happened at the beginning of meetings.

Jeff felt at ease at his paralegal job. He interacted with a couple of lawyers with whom he felt very comfortable and all of his work happened "behind the scenes," doing research and preparing documents. Jeff felt he could stay in this job forever, but also recognized that he was not living up to his potential. He finally decided to enroll in law school and seek treatment for his social anxiety so that he could succeed at this life-long goal.

Obsessive-Compulsive Disorder
Obsessive-Compulsive Disorder (OCD)

This anxiety disorder is characterized by the presence of obsessions and/or compulsions (see Table 1.7). Typically, obsessions and compulsions occur together and are functionally related. Obsessions are defined as "recurrent and persistent thoughts, impulses, or images that are experienced ... as intrusive and inappropriate and that cause marked anxiety or distress" (American Psychiatric Association, 1994, p. 422). Common obsessions include fear of contamination, fear of acting on unwanted sexual or aggressive impulses, fear of throwing things away, and fear of making mistakes. In response to the anxiety caused by obsessions, patients with OCD engage in compulsions or rituals. Rituals are meant to

TABLE 1.7

Summary of Diagnostic Criteria for OCD

- **Defining characteristic:** OCD is characterized by the presence of obsessions and/or (but, most typically AND) compulsions.
- **Obsessions** are defined as:
  (1) Thoughts, impulses, or images that persist, are intrusive, and cause distress.
  (2) These thoughts, impulses, or images have different content than "every day worries."
  (3) The person attempts to get rid of the thoughts, impulses, or images.
  (4) The person recognizes that the thoughts, impulses, or images are a product of his or her own mind
- **Compulsions** are defined as:
  (1) Repetitive behaviors or mental acts that the person feels that they need to perform in response to an obsession.
  (2) Compulsions are meant to reduce anxiety brought on by obsessions or prevent feared outcomes.
- At some point during the disorder, the person must realize that the obsessions/compulsions are excessive or unreasonable.
- Obsessions and/or compulsions must cause distress or take up more than one hour per day or lead to interference in functioning.
- Not due to organic factors (e.g., medical problems, substance use).
- Not better accounted for by another disorder.

Source: DSM-IV (American Psychiatric Association, 1994).

decrease or prevent the experience of anxiety and prevent the occurrence of feared consequences. Rituals can be overt behaviors (e.g., washing hands after touching something contaminated to prevent sickness) or mental acts (e.g., saying a prayer to ward off the possibility of stabbing a loved one while making dinner). Common obsessions and compulsions are listed in Table 1.8.

A few important points regarding the diagnostic criteria should be highlighted. First, obsessions are not simply excessive worries about every day problems. The content of obsessions tends to be slightly more unusual or less reality-based than "every day worries" which are the defining feature of generalized anxiety disorder. This distinction can be challenging since there is great overlap in the themes of obsessions and worries. For example, worry about the health and safety of loved ones is seen in OCD and GAD (Generalized Anxiety Disorder). In GAD, patients might worry that their spouse will be in a terrible car crash on the way home from work. Clearly, this *could* happen (although the probability is very low). A patient with OCD, on the other hand, might worry that he will pass contaminants onto his wife if he doesn't shower after coming home from working from his office in the city. His carelessness will then cause his wife to get a rare illness and die a quick and tragic death. This outcome is highly unlikely, lending the feared consequence an "OCD feel" rather than a "GAD feel."

Another important point to keep in mind when considering a diagnosis of OCD is that patients must recognize that their obsessions are a product of their own mind. The content of obsessions is sometimes so bizarre that clinicians might question whether a patient in fact has schizophrenia or some other psychotic

TABLE 1.8

Common Obsessions and Compulsions

Obsessions	Compulsions
Harm-related obsessions	Checking rituals (can include reassurance seeking)
Contamination obsessions	Washing/cleaning rituals
Symmetry/Exactness	Repeating; ordering and arranging
Fear of throwing things away	Hoarding/acquiring rituals
Religious obsessions	Mental rituals (e.g., praying)
Sexual obsessions	Mental rituals (e.g., mental checking and reassuring self)

disorder. Patients should be asked where they believe their thoughts are coming from. Patients with OCD must recognize that the thoughts are their own and not being placed in their minds by some other force.

As in the case of Specific Phobia, patients with OCD must recognize at some point during the course of the disorder that their fears are excessive and unreasonable (this criterion does not apply to children). Clinicians should be aware that a broad range of insight is exhibited by patients with OCD. By the time patients present for treatment, 5 percent report *complete* conviction that their obsessions and compulsions are realistic, and an additional 20 percent report a strong, but not entirely fixed conviction (Kozak & Foa, 1994). When patients hold so strongly to their beliefs about the consequences of confronting their feared object that they seem to be delusional, they are considered to have overvalued ideation (OVI; Kozak & Foa, 1994). Determining whether clients have OVI is important because poor insight is predictive of poor treatment outcome (Foa, Abramowitz, Franklin, & Kozak, 1999).

Case Example: OCD

Phillip was an 18-year-old young man, just about to leave home for college, when he presented for treatment. For as long as he could remember, Phillip had been concerned about contamination. His obsessions were provoked by public bathrooms, like many patients with OCD, but also by many other stimuli. He feared walking by homeless people, touching old books in the library, and picking things up off the ground (like the ball during a baseball game). Phillip's greatest fear was breathing in particles of contaminants that would make him sick. He did not have a clear idea of what kind of illness he might contract, but he was sure that it would come on very quickly after the ingestion (e.g., within 24 hours) and result in death. In response to these concerns, Phillip engaged in a number of rituals and subtle avoidance behaviors. He would frequently spit to rid his mouth of contaminants and would often hold his breath when walking by a street person or bending down to get a baseball. He also engaged in elaborate hand-washing rituals to make sure that contaminants would not get from his hands into his mouth.

In general, Phillip was functioning quite well when he came in for treatment. He had done well in his senior year of high school and was attending college on a baseball scholarship. However, he found his obsessions and rituals terribly annoying and wished he could stop doing them. He also expressed concern about experiencing an exacerbation of his OCD in the college dorm, which he predicted would not be as pristinely clean as his parents' home! Phillip's parents, at times, seemed more distressed by his OCD than he was. They reported that he spent at least an hour at the end of the day washing up after baseball practice, delaying their family dinner, and wasting a lot of water and soap. Phillip demanded a clean house but refused to help out with house cleaning, worrying that he would get sick either from germs and dirt in the house or from the cleaning products used to get rid of them. They also wondered how Phillip was going to be able to function in the dorms, particularly since he could not clean up the very germs and dirt that triggered his OCD symptoms.

Generalized Anxiety Disorder
Generalized Anxiety Disorder (GAD)

The core feature of Generalized Anxiety Disorder (GAD) is excessive worry about a number of events or activities that occurs more days than not, for six months or more. Typical areas of worry include health of self and others, relationships, minor matters (e.g., getting to places on time, fixing things around the house), and world affairs. Patients with GAD find it difficult to control their worry and experience accompanying somatic and affective symptoms like muscle tension, irritability, and sleep disturbance (American Psychiatric Association, 1994; see Table 1.9).

TABLE 1.9

Summary of Diagnostic Criteria for GAD

- **Defining characteristic:** Excessive anxiety and worry occurring more days than not for at least six months about a number of events and activities.
- Difficulty controlling worry.
- The anxiety and worry is associated with three or more of the following symptoms:
  — Feeling restless, keyed up, or on edge
  — Being easily fatigued
  — Difficulty concentrating or mind going blank
  — Irritability
  — Muscle tension
  — Sleep disturbance
- The anxiety, worry, or physical symptoms causes distress or impairment in functioning.
- Not due to organic factors (e.g., medical problems, substance use).
- Not better accounted for by another disorder.

Source: DSM-IV (American Psychiatric Association, 1994).

Case Example: GAD

For as long as she could remember, Rose was a "worry wart." As a child, she always worried about getting her schoolwork done on time and doing well in school. She worried that something bad was going to happen to her parents and sister. In college, these worries continued, but added to them were significant concerns about meeting the "right" person. Even at 20, years before she wanted to get married, she worried that she would never meet "the one," never have children, and grow old all by herself. At 30, Rose did get married, and a few years later had children. When she presented for treatment at age 40, her worries had become increasingly severe. Rose constantly worried about the health and safety of her husband and children, her performance at work, and the state of the world. She always worried about being on time and getting all the things done that she needed to accomplish. Ironically, Rose was typically quite unproductive. She worried so much about doing things well that she often procrastinated, spending all of her time making lists and planning how she was going to do her projects. Her worry also caused interpersonal problems. She called her husband many times a day to see if he was okay, which irritated him. She noticed that her children were "worriers," despite being just 5 and 8 years old! It seemed that she had taught them to worry.

When Rose began worrying, she found it impossible to stop. Not even the most engaging activity could get her mind onto something else. She had frequent migraines, terrible muscle tension in her back, shoulders, and neck, and often lay awake at night thinking of all of the things that could go wrong. Not surprisingly, Rose was always exhausted. She knew she had to do something to become a calmer person.

Posttraumatic Stress Disorder (PTSD)

PTSD will be described only briefly here because a whole volume of this series is dedicated to the disorder. Posttraumatic Stress Disorder is the only anxiety disorder with a required precipitant. In order to be diagnosed with PTSD, patients must have been exposed to a traumatic event that "involved actual or threatened death or serious injury, or a threat to the physical integrity of self or others" that the person responded to with "intense fear, helplessness, or horror" (American Psychiatric Association, 1994, p. 427–428). It is interesting to note that most people who experience a trauma do not go on to develop PTSD. In one study of rape survivors, for example, 94 percent of victims exhibited full PTSD symptoms 2 weeks post-trauma, but only 47 percent continued to exhibit symptoms 3 months post-trauma (Rothbaum & Foa, 1993). This suggests that many people who experience a trauma naturally recover without any specific intervention.

Some traumatic experiences seem to put people at elevated risk for the development of PTSD. In two studies using large, nationally representative samples, physical abuse, sexual abuse, and combat exposure were much more likely to lead to the development of PTSD than natural disasters and accidents (Kessler, Sonnega, Bromet, Hughes, & Nelson, 1995; Resnick, Kilpatrick, Dansky, Saunders, & Best, 1993). For example, in Resnick et al.'s study, 39 percent of women who experienced a physical assault and 30 percent of women who experienced a rape or other sexual assault developed PTSD, while only 9 percent of women developed PTSD following a natural disaster or accident.

For a diagnosis of PTSD to be made, patients must exhibit symptoms from three major categories: (1) re-experiencing symptoms; (2) avoidance and numbing symptoms; and (3) hyper-arousal symptoms. With respect to re-experiencing, patients might experience intrusive thoughts, distressing dreams or nightmares, and intense emotional upset or physical symptoms about the trauma. Some patients also experience flashbacks, during which they lose touch with reality and actually act or feel as if the trauma were re-occurring.

To be diagnosed with PTSD, patients must also experience three or more avoidance/numbing symptoms. These include concerted efforts to avoid thoughts or feelings associated with the trauma (i.e., trying very hard to *not* think about what happened); avoidance of activities, places, or people that remind patients of the trauma; inability to recall some parts of the trauma memory; loss of interest in previously enjoyed activities; feeling detached or cut off from others (often described as people not understanding what the client has been through); difficulty experiencing the whole range of emotion; and a sense of a foreshortened future. These criteria would only be met if the patient did not have these experiences before the trauma. For example, if a patient who lived in a dangerous neighborhood was mugged and beat up and reported feeling that he might not live until age 25, it would be important to ask if he felt this way before being attacked. Many clients who live in dangerous neighborhoods have *always* felt a sense of a foreshortened future. This, then, would not be coded as a symptom of PTSD.

Finally, to be diagnosed with PTSD, individuals must experience two or more symptoms of increased arousal; again, these must not have been present prior to the trauma. These symptoms include: difficulties with sleep; irritability or problems with anger; difficulty concentrating; hypervigilance (e.g., always being on the lookout for what is going on around you); and an exaggerated startle response.

PTSD is only diagnosed when symptoms have been present for one month or more. The *DSM-IV* also includes a diagnosis of *Acute Stress Disorder* for patients who have experienced a trauma and have had trauma symptoms for at least two days, but less than a month. This diagnosis can only be made within a month of the occurrence of the trauma. If a patient experiences a trauma, but his or her symptoms persist past one month, the diagnosis switches from acute stress disorder to PTSD.

Case Example: PTSD

John was a 50-year-old man who worked at a restaurant located just off the interstate highway. The restaurant was open until 11 PM, at which time most of the other staff left and John was in charge of the final evening cleanup. One evening, as John was vacuuming, he felt cold metal on the back of his neck. He turned around to find a man much larger than him, pointing a revolver right at him. Clearly, the employee in charge of locking the doors had not done so and the perpetrator had easily slipped into the restaurant. John quickly told the man that all of the deposits had already been taken to the bank by another employee, and that there was no cash at all in the restaurant. That was the last thing he remembered. John had been shot in the neck.

After a difficult recovery in the hospital, John felt like a changed person. He took a leave of absence from his job that continued long past his physical recovery had occurred. Throughout the day, he found himself continually thinking about the attack. He tried not to remember the horrifying incident but it continuously popped up in his mind. Everything he tried to do to distract himself, like reading or watching TV, ended up reminding him of the trauma. Every time he saw a crime scene on TV, his heart raced and he felt short of breath. John spent his days checking the locks and windows to ensure that no one could get in his house or trying to catch up on the sleep he was not able to get the night before.

John's wife of 30 years tried to be as supportive as possible. But John felt that she could just not understand what he was going through. He was constantly irritable, and often yelled at her. This was very out of character for such a mild-mannered man. Another major change in John was his social withdrawal. John no longer attended his weekly bowling game with his buddies, and simply could not get interested in any of the other activities he used to enjoy. He felt that life as he knew it had ended on the night that he was shot.

Differential Diagnosis

There is a great deal of overlap across the anxiety disorders, not only in terms of what patients fear, but also in terms of the symptoms that they experience (e.g., panic attacks can occur in all of the anxiety disorders). This makes differential diagnosis among the anxiety disorders both challenging and important. The key to proper differential diagnosis is to go beyond *what* the patient is afraid of, and gain a clear understanding of *why* patients fear a specific object or situation. The *why* that underlies the fear will help clinicians make an accurate diagnosis and an appropriate treatment plan.

Fear of flying is an excellent way to demonstrate how important it is to gain a clear understanding of the nature of a patient's fears. When a clinician hears that a patient has a fear of flying, the immediate assumption is that the client has a specific phobia. The client fears that the plane will crash. This is probably a correct diagnosis for most patients with a fear of flying.

Yet, there are many other possibilities. Some patients fear flying because they are scared of having a panic attack on the plane. The idea of not being able to escape from that situation is terrifying. This would point to a diagnosis of panic disorder. Although less likely, patients might fear flying because they are anxious about making casual conversation with a seatmate (Social Phobia), because they had a traumatic experience in the past while on an airplane (PTSD), or because they worry about contracting germs from being in such close proximity to so many people (OCD).

By asking patients detailed questions about the nature of their fears, clinicians can make accurate diagnoses and devise appropriate treatment plans. Clinicians can say, "What specifically do you fear could happen if you were to take a flight on a plane?" If a patient responds with a vague response such as "I would become nervous," the clinician can probe further to see what exactly the patient would be nervous about. If the patient is unable to articulate his fears, the clinician can provide examples such as those described previously to see which scenario the patient fears most.

While it is very important to correctly differentiate one anxiety disorder from another, it is also important to recognize that comorbidity (the co-occurrence of two or more disorders) among the anxiety disorders is very common. It is also very common to see comorbidity between anxiety disorders and other disorders, including mood disorders, substance-use disorders, and personality disorders.

Prevalence of Anxiety Disorders

Anxiety disorders are highly prevalent. Our most useful information on the prevalence of psychiatric disorders comes from The National Comorbidity Survey (NCS). The NCS was conducted in the early 1990s to assess the prevalence of psychiatric disorders in a representative sample of the U.S. population aged 18 years and older. The NCS was based on *DSM-III-R* criteria for psychiatric disorders. The NCS was then replicated (NCS-R) between 2001 and 2003 using a new sample of respondents in order to assess prevalence of psychiatric disorders based on *DSM-IV* criteria. The NCS-R also afforded the opportunity to examine the prevalence of disorders not included in the original NCS.

The NCS-R data (see Kessler et al., 2005; see also http://www.hcp.med.harvard.edu/ncs for the most up-to-date data) show that anxiety disorders are the most prevalent class of disorders, with 31.2 percent of the population meeting criteria for at least one anxiety disorder at some time in their lives and 18.7 percent of the population meeting criteria for at least one anxiety disorder in the previous year. Phobias are particularly common, with 12.5 percent of the population meeting criteria for a specific phobia at some time in their lives and 12.1 percent meeting criteria for Social Phobia. The prevalence rates (both lifetime and 12-month) for all of the anxiety disorders are shown in Table 1.10.

The NCS-R also provides important data on the median age of onset of the anxiety disorders (Kessler et al., 2005). The median age of onset for all anxiety disorders is 11, much earlier than for substance use (median age 20) or mood disorders (median age 30). This suggests that anxiety disorders might be a risk factor for the later development of other disorders. This is not surprising—after years of avoidance and distress, it is easy to see how patients can become depressed or resort to alcohol and/or drugs as a means of self-medication. The median age of onset for anxiety disorders is diverse, with specific phobias having a very early age of onset (age 7) and other anxiety disorders (like GAD, age 31 and Panic Disorder, age 24) beginning much later. The median ages of onset for the anxiety disorders are shown in Table 1.10.

As has been shown repeatedly in the literature, including in the NCS-R, anxiety disorders are significantly more common in women than in men. This is also demonstrated in Table 1.10.

TABLE 1.10

Lifetime Prevalence and Median Age of Onset of *DSM-IV* Anxiety Disorders

Disorder	Total (%)	Female (%)	Male (%)	Median age of onset
Panic Disorder	4.7	6.2	3.1	24
Specific Phobia	12.5	15.8	8.9	7
Social Phobia	12.1	13.0	11.1	13
GAD	5.7	7.1	4.2	31
PTSD	6.8	9.7	3.6	23
OCD	1.8	2.6	1.0	19
Any anxiety disorder	31.2	36.3	25.3	11

Source: Table reproduced from http://www.hcp.med.harvard.edu/ncs and Kessler et al., 2005.

References

American Psychiatric Association. (1994). *Diagnostic and statistical manual of mental disorders* (4th ed). Washington, DC: Author.

Curtis, G. C., Magee, W. J., Eaton, W. W., Wittchen, H. U., & Kessler, R. C. (1998). Specific fears and phobias: Epidemiology and classification. *British Journal of Psychiatry, 173,* 212–217.

Foa, E. B., Abramowitz, J. S., Franklin, M. E., & Kozak, M. J. (1999). Feared consequences, fixity of belief, and treatment outcome in OCD. *Behavior Therapy, 30,* 717–724.

Kessler, R. C., Berglund, P., Demler, O., Jin, R., Merikangas, K., & Walters, E. E. (2005). Lifetime prevalence and age-of-onset distributions of *DSM-IV* disorders in the national comorbidity survey replication. *Archives of General Psychiatry, 62,* 593–602.

Kessler, R. C., Sonnega, A., Bromet, E., Hughes, M., & Nelson, C. (1995). Posttraumatic stress disorder in the National Comorbidity Survey. *Archives of General Psychiatry, 52*(12), 1048–1060.

Kozak, M. J., & Foa, E. B. (1994). Obsessions, overvalued ideas, and delusions in obsessive-compulsive disorder. *Behaviour Research and Therapy, 32,* 343–353.

Mannuzza, S., Schneier, F. R., Chapman, T. F., Liebowitz, M. R., Klein, D. F., & Fyer, A. J. (1995). Generalized Social Phobia: Reliability and validity. *Archives of General Psychiatry, 52,* 230–237.

Resnick, H. S., Kilpatrick, D. G., Dansky, B. S., Saunders, B. E., & Best C. L. (1993). Prevalence of civilian trauma and posttraumatic stress disorder in a representative national sample of women. *Journal of Consulting and Clinical Psychology, 61,* 984–991.

Rothbaum, B. O., & Foa, E. B. (1993). Subtypes of posttraumatic stress disorder and duration of symptoms. In J. R. T. Davidson & E. B. Foa (Eds.), *Posttraumatic Stress Disorder: DSM-IV and beyond* (pp. 23–35). Washington, DC: American Psychiatric Press.

White, K. S., & Barlow, D. H. (2002). Panic Disorder and Agoraphobia. In D. H. Barlow (Ed.), *Anxiety and its disorders: The nature and treatment of anxiety and panic* (2nd ed., pp. 328–379). New York: Guilford.

CHAPTER 2

CBT for the Anxiety Disorders: Description and Research Findings

The major goal of this book is to help readers learn to use the core cognitive-behavioral therapy techniques to treat patients with anxiety disorders. In this chapter, these core techniques will be briefly introduced. While some techniques are common to all of the anxiety disorders, techniques that are unique to specific disorders will also be introduced.

Once readers have a sense of what constitutes CBT, research on the efficacy of these techniques will be reviewed. It is beyond the scope of this book to thoroughly review all of the relevant literature. Rather, for each disorder, major treatment outcome studies will be summarized and discussed, paying attention to the most recent, cutting-edge research.

Components of Cognitive Behavioral Therapy

Many treatment techniques fall under the CBT umbrella. Common to most treatments for anxiety disorders are psychoeducation, cognitive restructuring, and exposure to feared situations (called *in vivo* exposure).

Psychoeducation, described in much greater detail in Chapter 5, is integral to CBT. Rather than the clinician being "all-knowing," the goal of CBT is to teach patients to be their own therapists. In the initial portion of therapy, clinicians educate patients about the nature of the problems they are having and how to best treat them. As patients are asked how particular concepts apply to them, clinicians also become "educated" about the client's unique difficulties. This openness to learning from the client facilitates the process of formulating the case and making an appropriate treatment plan. Psychoeducation sets a unique tone in therapy, where the clinician and client are working together to help the client achieve symptom reduction and improved functioning.

Cognitive restructuring (CR), outlined in Chapter 6, involves a four-step process. Anxious thoughts tend to come fast and furiously and are taken as fact. In CR, patients first are taught to be aware of what they are thinking–in essence to "catch" their thoughts as one would catch a butterfly in a net. They are then taught to label the thought, assigning a name to what is "wrong" with the thought. Next, they are taught to question the thought and consider whether there is a different way to view the situation that is causing the anxiety. Finally, in the process of answering the questions, patients come up with a more rational and adaptive way of viewing the situation. The goal with cognitive restructuring for anxiety disorders is to help patients to learn (a) that they overestimate the probability that bad events will happen and (b) that they overestimate the cost of these bad events, were they to happen.

In Chapter 1, the case of Felicia was described. Felicia had a specific phobia of pigeons. She feared that a pigeon would land on her head and become entangled in her hair, as had happened to her friend. The process of CR would help Felicia to question her beliefs about the danger of pigeons. For example, she would be taught to question her belief: "Pigeons land on people's heads." The therapist would help Felicia to see that she has only one piece of evidence to support this belief–what happened to her friend. She must have confronted thousands of other pigeons in her life–none of which landed on her head, calling into question whether it is rational to fear *all* pigeons. Through CR, Felicia learned that the *probability* of this event happening again was very low and if it were to happen, that the *cost* would be quite low. When this bizarre event happened to her friend, the pigeon landed for just a few seconds and then flew off without causing injury. In the very unlikely event that this would happen to Felicia too, she also could expect just a few moments of discomfort and no injury or pain.

In vivo exposure, discussed in Chapter 7, involves helping patients to confront the very situations that cause them anxiety and distress. The goals of exposure are two-fold. First, it is believed that with repeated exposure, anxiety habituates. In other words, the more that a person confronts a feared situation, the less anxiety that situation causes. Related to this, as patients repeatedly confront feared situations, they learn the same two lessons accomplished via CR: that the probability and cost of feared outcomes is much lower than they think. Often, the lessons learned via exposure are even more powerful than those learned via CR since it takes place with direct experience rather than through dialogue.

In the case of Felicia, exposure involved confronting pigeons. Felicia was so avoidant when she first came in for treatment that early exposures simply involved looking at pictures of pigeons and scenes of movies with pigeons in them. Gradually, Felicia went to a science lab to see pigeons in cages and then started to go to various parts of the city where there were a lot of pigeons. Over the course of treatment, Felicia did not grow to like pigeons, but did learn that they are very unlikely to land on people's heads. This change in her belief system greatly improved Felicia's functioning.

Homework is also an essential part of CBT for the anxiety disorders (see Roth, Ledley, & Huppert, 2007). Assignments can include thought records, CR exercises, *in vivo* exposures, imaginal exposures, and other CBT techniques. The purpose of homework is two-fold. First, the more patients practice their new skills, the more ingrained they will become. Second, patients often see therapists as safe people and clinics/hospitals as safe places. As such, they may discount exposures that happen during sessions. If a patient with social phobia makes a speech to the clinic staff and receives good feedback for it, she might assume that people are going out of their way to be nice because they know she has social phobia. It is extremely important that patients complete the same exposures that they did during sessions outside of sessions to learn that there is nothing magical about the therapy environment. Engaging in exposures in the "real world" shows patients that they have learned valuable skills in therapy and that they can cope with feared stimuli without the help of the clinician.

Various other CBT techniques are used in the treatment of anxiety disorders. These will be introduced throughout this chapter, and will be covered in much more detail later in the book.

Reviewing the Treatments

It is difficult in limited space to review *all* of the literature on the effectiveness of CBT for the anxiety disorders. For each disorder, we will try to answer four important questions:

1. What does CBT for this disorder consist of?
2. How does CBT work relative to no treatment or to control/placebo treatments?
3. How does CBT work relative to medication?
4. Is there any advantage of combining CBT and medication over using each treatment alone?

Panic Disorder

CBT for Panic Disorder

Many different CBT protocols for Panic Disorder have been developed (e.g., Barlow & Craske, 2000; Zuercher-White, 1998). In addition to psychoeducation, cognitive restructuring, and *in vivo* exposure, interoceptive exposure is also commonly used in the treatment of Panic Disorder. *Interoceptive exposure* is a component unique to the treatment of Panic Disorder that involves confrontation of feared physical sensations. For example, if patients fear the racing heart that they experience during panic attacks, they would do exercises to bring on this symptom like jogging on the spot. The goal of doing such exercises is to show patients that it will not result in feared consequences, even if they feel uncomfortable.

Some panic protocols (e.g., Zuercher-White, 1998) also include breathing retraining to help patients stop hyperventilating. Patients are taught to practice diaphragmatic breathing *when they are not anxious* so that they can learn the difference between this and the shallow breathing that can bring on the symptoms of panic. Unfortunately, some patients use breathing retraining as an avoidance strategy, using it in anxiety provoking situations to avoid feeling short of breath (Taylor, 2001). This had led some to question whether breathing retraining can actually lead to poorer treatment outcome. One study that systematically examined this issue showed that breathing retraining does not add to the benefit of CBT without breathing retraining (Schmidt et al., 2000). Taken together, it seems that breathing retraining is not a necessary component of CBT for panic, but that if it is taught, explicit instructions about its use must be given.

CBT for Panic Disorder Compared with No Treatment or Control/Placebo Treatments

Research on the use of CBT for Panic Disorder has a long and successful history. Meta-analytic findings show that CBT is significantly more effective than no treatment and placebo psychotherapies (Mitte, 2005). Craske and Barlow (2001) computed summary statistics for numerous studies of CBT for panic and concluded that 76% of patients are free of panic attacks at post-treatment; this number jumps to 78% at a follow-up assessment up to two years after the completion of treatment. Using more stringent criteria, 52% of patients were free of panic *and* excessive anxiety following CBT for Panic Disorder. Even with these more stringent criteria, these numbers might still be somewhat inflated since research studies tend to exclude the most severe cases, particularly those with such severe Agoraphobia that they are not able to participate (see Craske & Barlow, 2001). Most studies on the efficacy of CBT for the anxiety disorders are performed in research settings with expert clinicians. This calls into question whether CBT is as effective in community-based clinics. One study suggests that CBT for Panic Disorder in a community-based clinic was as effective as treatment carried out in research clinics (Wade, Treat, & Stuart, 1998).

CBT for Panic Disorder Compared with Medication

There is a rich body of literature showing that many medications are effective in the treatment of Panic Disorder, including tricyclic antidepressants, selective serotonin reuptake inhibitors, and other antidepressants like venlafaxine (see Antony & Swinson, 2000 for a succinct summary). Meta-analyses have allowed for the comparison of CBT to medication to combined treatments. Older meta-analyses suggest that all three approaches are equally effective (see Bakker, van Balkom, Spinhoven, Blaauw, & van Dyck, 1998; van Balkom et al., 1997), but a more recent publication suggests that CBT is slightly more effective than medication and that there is no clear advantage of combined treatment over CBT alone (Mitte, 2005).

There is some controversy about the comparative long-term efficacy of these treatment approaches. The most comprehensive study to date for the treatment of Panic Disorder compared CBT, imipramine, CBT plus imipramine, CBT plus pill placebo, and pill placebo (Barlow, Gorman, Shear, & Woods, 2000). Immediately post-treatment, all active treatment groups showed greater improvement than pill placebo and the four active treatments did not differ from one another. However, at the 6-month follow-up, patients who received imipramine either alone or with CBT showed a greater return of symptoms than patients who received CBT alone. That medication alone was associated with greater risk of relapse than CBT alone was not surprising—similar results have been found across the anxiety disorders. However, the finding that combined CBT and imipramine was associated with greater risk of relapse than CBT alone was surprising. The researchers suggested that patients might have different beliefs about their improvement when they receive combined treatment. They might attribute their improvement to the medication, rather than to the effort that they made in CBT. Once medication was discontinued (as it was at the end of the acute phase of this study), they might have expected a return of their symptoms, setting up a self-fulfilling prophecy.

Specific Phobia

CBT for Specific Phobia

Treatment for specific phobia typically includes psychoeducation, CR, and exposure. Whenever possible, *in vivo* exposure should be used rather than imaginal exposure. Imaginal exposure can be helpful early in treatment with patients who are too fearful to confront the phobic stimuli and in situations where it would be difficult to set up repeated exposures (e.g., thunder and lightening storms; flying). *Virtual reality* is also being used to aid with exposure to feared stimuli.

An interesting technique is used in the treatment of one specific phobia—fear of blood, injections, and injury. Individuals with this type of phobia who tend to faint at the sight of blood or needles are taught *applied muscle tension* (Öst & Sterner, 1987). Tensing all muscles during exposure to these stimuli is effective in preventing fainting.

CBT for Specific Phobia Compared with No Treatment or Control/Placebo Treatments

CBT is an excellent "stand-alone" treatment for phobias. Recent studies have shown that many phobias can be treated in a single two- to three-hour session (e.g., Öst, Brandberg, & Alm, 1997; Öst, Salkovskis, & Hellstrom, 1991). In fact, these brief treatments yield significant improvement in up to 90 percent of patients. Brief treatments for specific phobias have also been shown to be effective with children (e.g., Öst, Svensson, Hellstrom, & Lindwall, 2001). Researchers have also begun to study the use of virtual reality in the treatment of phobias, with promising initial results (see Wiederhold & Wiederhold, 2004).

CBT for Specific Phobia Compared with Medication

In contrast to the other anxiety disorders, medication is generally not used in the treatment of specific phobia.

Social Phobia

CBT for Social Phobia

As with the other anxiety disorders, various treatments for social phobia have been developed (Heimberg & Becker, 2002; Hope, Heimberg, Juster, & Turk, 2000; Clark, 2005). The most studied treatment for social phobia is Heimberg's cognitive behavioral group therapy for social phobia (Heimberg & Becker, 2002). This protocol includes psychoeducation, cognitive restructuring, *in vivo* exposure, and homework.

Some treatments for social phobia also include *social skills training* (e.g., Davidson et al., 2004; see Chapter 9 of this book). Controversy exists about whether or not patients with social phobia in fact have social skills deficits, with some researchers maintaining that many patients with social phobia do have such deficits and others proposing that anxiety interferes in patients' ability to use their social skills (e.g., Clark, 2005). A recent study (Herbert et al., 2005) showed that adding social skills training to cognitive behavioral group therapy yielded better outcomes than cognitive behavioral group therapy alone. Further research is still needed to learn more about this important issue.

Recently, novel treatments for social phobia have been developed (e.g., Clark, 2005) that include unique components. Clark's cognitive therapy for social phobia utilizes *video feedback* (see Chapter 7; see also Clark, 2005). Individuals with social phobia tend to come away from situations basing their judgments on how they *felt* in a situation ("I *felt* nervous, so I must have looked nervous."), rather than on what actually happened. To counter this tendency, patients are shown videos of exposures that they have engaged in. They are instructed to view the video as an objective observer, rather than through their own self-critical eyes. The purpose of video feedback is to show patients that their self-image is much worse than how they actually come across to others.

Another novel treatment, Comprehensive Cognitive Behavioral Therapy (CCBT; see Huppert, Roth, & Foa, 2003), is based on Clark's cognitive therapy but includes optional modules to be used with patients with specific symptom presentations. One module is social skills training. Another module is *imaginal exposure*. This technique has been used extensively in the treatment of OCD (Foa & Wilson, 2001) and PTSD (Foa & Rothbaum, 1998), but is used for social phobia for the first time in the CCBT protocol. Imaginal exposure is used when patients have catastrophic predictions of specific outcomes that are not easily testable. For example, a patient might fear doing public speaking in front of a large audience. The therapist helps the patient to create a script depicting this situation, articulating the client's most feared outcomes. The idea is not simply to imagine a scenario of speaking in public, but rather to spell out in great detail the most negative possible outcome. The patient might imagine many members of the audience nodding off, and others simply getting up and walking out of the auditorium until he is lecturing to ten or fifteen snoring individuals! While this script might sound ridiculous, it is what the patient with social phobia fears most. The idea of imaginal exposure is to have the patient confront this imaginary scene repeatedly by listening to a tape of the story until it no longer evokes anxiety (see Chapter 8). Furthermore, after many repetitions, patients often come to see the scenario as boring, ridiculous, or even funny.

CBT for Social Phobia in Individual or Group Treatment

An interesting issue that arises in the treatment of social phobia is whether to conduct treatment individually or in a group format. While group treatment has been used to treat other anxiety disorders including OCD (see Whittal & McLean, 2002) and Panic Disorder (Telch et al., 1993), clinicians who treat social phobia have a particular interest in it because the group format itself serves as an excellent exposure for patients. Meta-analyses (Gould, Buckminster, Pollack, Otto, & Yap, 1997) done some years ago suggested that group treatment is as effective as individual treatment. More recently, however, there is growing evidence that individual treatment might yield better outcomes than group treatment (Stangier, Heidenreich, Peitz, Lauterbach, & Clark, 2003; see also Coles, Hart,& Heimberg, 2005). Given the logistical difficulties of carrying out group treatment, and the fact that many patients with social phobia reject group treatment, individual treatment seems ideal in most situations.

CBT for Social Phobia Compared with No Treatment or Control/Placebo Treatments

The most researched psychosocial treatment for social phobia is Heimberg's cognitive behavioral group therapy (CBGT; see Heimberg & Becker, 2002). CBGT yields superior outcomes to no treatment and to control psychotherapies; individual versions of the CBGT protocol have yielded similar results (see reviews by Rodebaugh, Holaway, & Heimberg, 2004, and Zaider & Heimberg, 2003).

CBT for Social Phobia Compared with Medication

There is ample evidence suggesting that pharmacological treatments yield good outcomes in the treatment of social phobia. These treatments include the monoamine oxidase inhibitors, the SSRIs, other antidepressants like venlafaxine, and benzodiazepines (again, there is an excellent summary of studies in Antony & Swinson, 2000). Studies have also examined the differential efficacy of CBT and medication in the treatment of social anxiety disorder. Two major studies deserve mention. In a large multisite study (Heimberg et al., 1998), CBGT was compared to the monoamine oxidase inhibitor, phenelzine. The study included two control treatments, educational supportive therapy (a control psychotherapy) and pill placebo. At the end of the 12-week study, CBGT and phenelzine had both yielded superior outcomes to the control treatments and did not differ from one another. Although patients who received phenelzine improved somewhat more quickly than those who received CBGT, the CBGT group was less likely to relapse during a 6-month follow-up period (Liebowitz et al., 1999). More recently, Clark (2005) developed a cognitive therapy for social phobia that includes behavioral experiments, video feedback, and some cognitive work. Clark and colleagues (2003) compared cognitive therapy to fluoxetine and pill placebo. The group who received CT had better outcomes than the other two groups, which did not differ from one another. This was the first study to find that CBT was superior to medication immediately following treatment for social phobia. This might be explained by the fact that Clark's cognitive therapy yields better outcomes than those found in studies using other forms of treatment for social phobia.

Meta-analyses have also shed light on the relative efficacy of CBT and pharmacotherapy for social anxiety disorder (Federoff & Taylor, 2001; Gould et al., 1997). In both meta-analyses, CBT and pharmacotherapies were roughly equivalent in the treatment of social anxiety disorder. Interestingly, in the meta-analysis by Federoff and Taylor (2001), the benzodiazepines were the only class of drug significantly superior to CBT, but there have been only a few studies of this class of drug in the treatment of social phobia. Furthermore, the decision to utilize benzodiazepines as a sole treatment must be weighed against their limitations (e.g., potential for abuse).

Combined CBT and Medication Treatment for Social Phobia

One study has been published that explored the question of whether combined treatment confers more advantage in the treatment of social phobia than either medication or CBT alone. Davidson, Foa, and colleagues (2004) compared fluoxetine, CBT, CBT plus fluoxetine, CBT plus placebo, and placebo alone. This study found that all active treatments outperformed placebo. Another study, as yet unpublished, found some preliminary support for the use of combined treatment over monotherapies (Heimberg, 2002). The final conclusions from this study are still pending, but will certainly inform the debate over whether combined treatment should be used for patients with social phobia.

At the present time, however, there is not yet compelling evidence to support the use of combined treatments for social phobia. However, in both of these studies, patients started medication and therapy at the same time. It is possible that combined treatments might confer more advantage when delivered sequentially. For example, patients might show more improvement if they began medication and allowed it to take its effect, and then added therapy. A study is currently underway at Temple University and Columbia University (by the team led by Drs. Heimberg and Liebowitz) that explores just this question.

Obsessive-Compulsive Disorder

CBT for OCD

The most studied psychosocial treatment for OCD is called exposure and response (ritual) prevention therapy (EX/RP; Foa & Kozak, 1997). As its name implies, EX/RP involves two main components: exposure to feared stimuli (via both *in vivo* and imaginal exposure) and abstinence from rituals. The purpose of the treatment is to show patients that their most feared consequences of exposure to stimuli will not happen, even without the use of rituals. In Chapter 1, the case of Phillip was described. When Phillip engaged in EX/RP, a major component of his treatment was to play baseball without engaging in his spitting and breath-holding rituals, and without washing his hands. The purpose was for Phillip to learn that he would not contract an illness after playing baseball, even without these elaborate rituals.

CBT for OCD Relative to No Treatment or Control/Placebo Treatments

EX/RP has been studied extensively. Combining the results of many EX/RP outcome studies, an average of 83% of patients responded to treatment acutely (Foa & Kozak, 1996). Furthermore, 76% of patients tended to maintain their gains at long-term follow-up (Foa & Kozak, 1996). EX/RP has been found to be more effective than control psychotherapies (Fals-Stewart, Marks, & Schafer, 1993; Lindsay, Crino, & Andrews, 1997) and pill placebo (Foa et al., 2005).

CBT for OCD Relative to Medication

In terms of medication, both the tricyclic antidepressant, clomipramine, and the SSRIs have been found to be more effective than placebo in the treatment of OCD (see Franklin, Riggs, & Pai, 2005). However, Foa and Franklin (1999) point out that in most trials, patients experience only a 5 to 8-point reduction on the Yale-Brown Obsessive Compulsive Scale (Y-BOCS; Goodman et al., 1989 a, b) following medication treatment. In contrast, patients who receive EX/RP typically experience a 14 to 15 point drop on the Y-BOCS. A recent meta-analysis of studies in pediatric populations also suggests that EX/RP might have some advantage over medication in the treatment of OCD (Abramowitz, Whiteside, & Deacon, 2005).

Combined CBT and Medication Treatment for OCD

As we have just noted, medication does lead to improvement in OCD symptoms. However, many patients complete treatment exhibiting symptoms of great enough severity that they would still be eligible for the exact treatment study that they just participated in (see Franklin, Riggs, & Pai, 2005). This calls into question whether there is an advantage of combining EX/RP with medication. Foa and colleagues (2005) compared EX/RP, clomipramine, and their combination, finding that the EX/RP alone yielded superior outcomes to the other two groups. In other words, combined treatment did not yield better outcomes than EX/RP alone. Studies with similar design have found some advantage of combined treatment for OCD, but none provide compelling support for using combined treatment (see Franklin, Riggs, & Pai, 2005). As with the social phobia studies we already discussed, the combined treatment studies in OCD have also generally started medication and therapy at the same time. In a typical 12–20 week treatment study, this might mean that the medication is just starting to have an effect when the study is almost complete. It is certainly possible that combined treatment could yield better results if administered sequentially. Like the ongoing social phobia study described, a study of sequential treatment in OCD patients has just recently been completed at the University of Pennsylvania and Columbia University (led by Drs. Foa and Liebowitz). In this study, patients had been on an SSRI for at least 12 weeks prior to starting therapy. Patients were randomly assigned to either EX/RP or a control psychotherapy. If EX/RP leads to greater decreases in OCD symptoms than the control therapy, this would suggest that EX/RP added to existing SSRI treatment is superior to taking SSRIs alone.

Generalized Anxiety Disorder

CBT for Generalized Anxiety Disorder

Of all the anxiety disorders, treatment for GAD is still in a relatively early stage of development, as researchers seek to understand the nature of the disorder (for an excellent resource on GAD, see Heimberg, Turk, & Mennin, 2004). Commonly used treatments generally include psychoeducation, CR, breathing retraining and other relaxation exercises, and some form of exposure to worry or worry triggers.

CBT for GAD Relative to No Treatment or Control/Placebo Treatments

Borkovec and Ruscio (2001) reviewed 13 GAD treatment outcome studies. Their review suggested that CBT for GAD is more effective than no treatment and control treatments. More recently, Gould and colleagues (2004) did a meta-analysis of CBT studies for GAD. Their analysis also suggested that CBT is more effective than no treatment or control treatments. Studies that included follow-up assessments suggest that gains are generally maintained over time.

It is important to note that there is a great deal of variability in the components included in GAD treatment packages; which components are most effective and/or important is still unclear. Furthermore, compared to the efficacy of CBT for other anxiety disorders, success rates in GAD studies have been disappointing (see Brown, Barlow, & Liebowitz, 1994). In GAD studies, clinical improvement rates range from 38 to 63% of patients. In contrast, between 80 and 85% of patients who do CBT for Panic Disorder improve (see Waters & Craske, 2005).

These disappointing figures might be because our understanding of GAD has lagged behind our understanding of the other anxiety disorders. Recently, a number of research groups have started to explore different models for the maintenance and treatment of GAD. For example, Borkovec's avoidance theory of worry posits that patients use worry as a means of avoiding thoughts of future bad events and more emotional topics like past trauma and interpersonal relationships. Based on this theory, Borkovec's treatment for GAD includes both classic CBT techniques like worry exposure at a set time each day and worry outcome monitoring, as well as identifying and working through the core fears that patients are avoiding through worry (see Borkovec, Alcaine, & Behar, 2004). Roemer & Orsillo (2002), following Borkovec's theory of experiential avoidance, suggest integrating mindfulness and acceptance-based treatments (see Chapter 11 of this volume) into GAD treatment. Mennin and his colleagues (e.g., Mennin, Heimberg, Turk, & Fresco, 2005) propose that GAD is a disorder of emotion regulation and suggest that treatment should involve helping patients to identify, label, and process emotion (Mennin, 2004).

CBT Relative to Medication for GAD

Benzodiazepines (BZs) are the most commonly studied drugs for GAD and the most commonly prescribed anxiety drugs by physicians in general practice (Waters & Craske, 2005). Many studies show the BZs are more effective than placebo for treating anxiety (see Waters & Craske, 2005). While they might be a good choice for the treatment of acute (short-term) anxiety, GAD is a chronic condition and there are many reasons why BZs should not be used over the long-term. The most important reason is that BZs have abuse potential. This makes them particularly problematic for patients with current substance use disorders, or a history of these disorders, as well as for patients at risk of suicide. Given the high rates of comorbidity between depression and GAD, this might exclude many GAD patients.

A superior first-line pharmacological treatment for GAD are the tricyclic antidepressants and SSRIs. Both have been found to be more effective than placebo in patients with GAD (see Waters & Craske, 2005).

Very few studies have compared CBT, medication, and combined treatment for GAD. Power et al. (1990) found that CBT, either alone or in combination with a BZ, yielded superior outcomes to a BZ alone or pill placebo. Patients who received combined treatment showed improvements most quickly, and those who received CBT (either alone or with BZs) showed the greatest long-term maintenance of gains. Clearly, more research in this area is needed and clinicians should not base treatment decisions on one study.

Summary

To summarize, there is compelling evidence to support the use of CBT for anxiety disorders. CBT is more effective than no treatment and control therapies. In general, CBT alone is equally as effective as medication. In some studies, CBT has been shown to be more effective than medication (e.g., Clark's social phobia study) and in some cases, seems to have greater long-term efficacy than medication (e.g., Liebowitz et al.'s (1999) social phobia study). The jury is still out on combined treatments. Taken as a whole, compelling evidence to support combined treatment is lacking with a few studies actually showing that combined treatment can yield poorer outcomes than CBT alone (e.g., Barlow's panic study). Further research is most definitely needed to learn if the way in which combined treatments are administered is important (e.g., concurrent versus sequential treatment) and whether combined treatment might in fact be indicated for specific groups of patients (e.g., those who obtain only limited response from any one treatment alone).

References

Abramowitz, J. S., Whiteside, S. P., & Deacon, B. J. (2005). The effectiveness of treatment for pediatric obsessive-compulsive disorder: A meta-analysis. *Behavior Therapy, 36,* 55–63.

Antony, M. M., & Swinson, R. P. (2000). *Phobic disorders and panic in adults: A guide to assessment and treatment.* Washington, DC: American Psychological Association.

Bakker, A., van Balkom, A. J. L. M., Spinhoven, P., Blaauw, B. M. J. W., & van Dyck, R. (1998). Follow-up on the treatment of Panic Disorder with or without Agoraphobia: A quantitative review. *Journal of Nervous and Mental Disease, 186,* 414–419.

Barlow, D. H., & Craske, M. G. (2000). *Mastery of Your Anxiety and Panic: Client workbook for Anxiety and Panic (MAP-3).* San Antonio, TX: Graywind/Psychological Corporation.

Barlow, D. H., Gorman, J. M., Shear, M. K., & Woods, S. W. (2000). A randomized controlled trial of cognitive-behavioral treatment vs. imipramine and their combination for Panic Disorder: Primary outcome results. *Journal of the American Medical Association, 283,* 2529–2536.

Borkovec, T. D., Alcaine, O., & Behar, E. (2004). Avoidance theory of worry and Generalized Anxiety Disorder. In R. G. Heimberg, C. L. Turk, & D. S. Mennin (Eds.), *Generalized anxiety disorder: Advances in research and practice* (pp. 77–108). New York: Guilford.

Borkovec, T. D., & Ruscio, A. M. (2001). Psychotherapy for Generalized Anxiety Disorder. *Journal of Clinical Psychiatry, 62*(Suppl. 11), 37–42.

Brown, T. A., Barlow, D. H., & Liebowitz, M. R. (1994). The empirical basis of Generalized Anxiety Disorder. *American Journal of Psychiatry, 151,* 1272–1280.

Clark, D. M. (2005). A cognitive perspective on social phobia. In W. R. Crozier & L. E. Alden (Eds.). *The essential handbook of social anxiety for clinicians* (pp. 193–218). Hoboken, NJ: Wiley.

Clark, D. M., Ehlers, A., McManus, F., Hackmann, A., Fennell, M., Campbell, H., Flower, T., Davenport, C., & Louis, B. (2003). Cognitive therapy vs fluoxetine in generalized social phobia: A randomized placebo controlled trial. *Journal of Consulting and Clinical Psychology, 71,* 1058–1067.

Coles, M. E., Hart, T. A., & Heimberg, R. G. (2005). Cognitive-behavioral group treatment for social phobia. In W. R. Crozier & L. E. Alden (Eds.), *The essential handbook of social anxiety for clinicians (pp. 265–286).* Hoboken, NJ: Wiley.

Craske, M. G., & Barlow, D. H. (2001). Panic disorder and Agoraphobia. In D. H. Barlow (Ed.), *Clinical handbook of psychological disorders* (3rd ed.). New York: Guilford.

Davidson, J. R., Foa, E. B., Huppert, J. D., Keefe, F. J., Franklin, M. E., Compton, J. S., Zhao, N., Connor, K. M., Lynch, T. R., & Gadde, K. M. (2004). Fluoxetine, comprehensive cognitive behavior therapy, and placebo in generalized social phobia. *Archives of General Psychiatry, 61,* 1005–1013.

Fals-Stewart, W., Marks, A. P., & Schafer, J. (1993). A comparison of behavior group therapy and individual behavior therapy in treating obsessive-compulsive disorder. *Journal of Nervous and Mental Disease, 181,* 189–194.

Fedoroff, I. C., & Taylor, S. T. (2001). Psychological and pharmacological treatments of social phobia: A meta-analysis. *Journal of Clinical Psychopharmacology, 21,* 311–324.

Foa, E. B., & Franklin, M. E. (1999). Obsessive compulsive disorder: Behavior therapy. In M. Hersen & Bellack (Eds.), *Handbook of comparative interventions for adult disorders* (2nd ed., pp. 359–377). New York: Wiley.

Foa, E. B., & Kozak, M. J. (1996). Psychological treatment for obsessive-compulsive disorder. In M. R. Mavissakalian & R. F. Prien (Eds.), *Long-term treatments of anxiety disorders* (pp. 285–309). Washington, DC: American Psychiatric Press.

Foa, E. B., & Kozak, M. J. (1997). *Therapist's guide for the mastery of your obsessive compulsive disorder.* New York: Psychological Corporation.

Foa, E. B., Liebowitz, M. R., Kozak, M. J., Davies, S., Campeas, R., Franklin, M. E., Huppert, J. D., Kjernisted, K., Rowan, V., Schmidt, A. B., Simpson, H. B., & Tu, X. (2005). Randomized, placebo-controlled trial of exposure and ritual prevention, clomipramine, and their combination in the treatment of obsessive-compulsive disorder. *American Journal of Psychiatry, 162,* 151–161.

Foa E. B., & Rothbaum, B. O. (1998). *Treating the trauma of rape: Cognitive-behavioral therapy for PTSD.* New York: Guilford.

Foa E. B., & Wilson, R. (2001). *Stop obsessing: How to overcome your obsessions and compulsions* (2nd ed.). New York: Bantam.

Franklin, M. E., Riggs, D., & Pai, A. (2005). Obsessive Compulsive Disorder. In M.M. Antony, D. Roth Ledley, & R. G. Heimberg (Eds.), *Improving outcomes and preventing relapse in cognitive behavioral therapy* (pp. 128–173). New York: Guilford.

Goodman, W. K., Price, L. H., Rasmussen, S. A., Mazure, C., Delgado, P., Heninger, G. R., & Charney, D. S. (1989a). The Yale-Brown Obsessive Compulsive Scale. II. Validity. *Archives of General Psychiatry, 46,* 1012–1016.

Goodman, W. K., Price, L. H., Rasmussen, S. A., Mazure, C., Fleischmann, R. L., Hill, C. L., Heninger, G. R., & Charney, D. S. (1989b). The Yale-Brown Obsessive Compulsive Scale. I. Development, use, and reliability. *Archives of General Psychiatry, 46,* 1006–1011.

Gould, R. A., Buckminster, S., Pollack, M. H., Otto, M. W., & Yap, L. (1997). Cognitive-behavioral and pharmacological treatment for social phobia: A meta-analysis. *Clinical Psychology: Science and Practice, 4,* 291–306.

Gould, R. A., Safren, S. A., O'Neill Washington, D., & Otto, M. W. (2004). A meta-analytic review of cognitive-behavioral treatments. In R. G. Heimberg, C. L. Turk, & D. S. Mennin (Eds.). *Generalized anxiety disorder: Advances in research and practice* (pp. 248–264). New York: Guilford.

Heimberg, R. G. (2002). Cognitive-behavioral therapy for social anxiety disorder: Current status and future directions. *Biological Psychiatry, 51*, 101–108.

Heimberg, R. G., & Becker, R. E. (2002). *Cognitive-behavioral group therapy for social phobia: Basic mechanisms and clinical applications.* New York: Guilford.

Heimberg, R. G., Liebowitz, M. R., Hope, D. A., Schneier, F. R., Holt, C. S., Welkowitz, L., Juster, H. R., Campeas, R., Bruch, M. A., Cloitre, M., Fallon, B., & Klein, D. F. (1998). Cognitive-behavioral group therapy versus phenelzine in social phobia: 12-week outcome. *Archives of General Psychiatry, 55*, 1133–1141.

Heimberg, R. G., Turk, C. L., & Mennin, D. S. (Eds.). (2004). *Generalized anxiety disorder: Advances in research and practice.* New York: Guilford.

Herbert, J. D., Gaudiano, B. A., Rheingold, A. A., Myers, V. H., Dalrymple, K., & Nolan, E. M. (2005). Social skills training augments the effectiveness of cognitive behavioral group therapy for Social Anxiety Disorder. *Behavior Therapy, 36*, 125–138.

Hope, D. A., Heimberg, R. G., Juster, H. R., & Turk, C. L. (2000). *Managing social anxiety: A cognitive-behavioral therapy approach.* San Antonio, TX: Psychological Corporation.

Huppert, J. D., Roth, D. A., & Foa, E. B. (2003). Cognitive behavioral treatment of social phobia: New advances. *Current Psychiatry Reports, 5*, 289–296.

Liebowitz, M. R., Heimberg, R. G., Schneier, F. R., Hope, D. A., Davies, S., Holt, C. S., Goetz, D., Juster, H. R., Lin, S.-L., Bruch, M. A., Marshall, R., & Klein, D. F. (1999). Cognitive-behavioral group therapy versus phenelzine in social phobia: Long-term outcome. *Depression and Anxiety, 10*, 89–98.

Lindsay, M., Crino. R., & Andrews, G. (1997). Controlled trial of exposure and response prevention in obsessive-compulsive disorder. *British Journal of Psychiatry, 171*, 135–139.

Mennin, D. S. (2004). An emotion regulation treatment for Generalized Anxiety Disorder. *Clinical Psychology and Psychotherapy, 11*, 17–29.

Mennin, D. S., Heimberg, R. G., Turk, C. L., & Fresco, D. M. (2005). Preliminary evidence for an emotion regulation deficit model of Generalized Anxiety Disorder. *Behaviour Research and Therapy, 43*, 1281–1310.

Mitte, K. (2005). A meta-analysis of the efficacy of psycho- and pharmacotherapy in Panic Disorder with and without Agoraphobia. *Journal of Affective Disorders, 88*, 27–45.

Öst, L-G., Brandberg, M., & Alm, T. (1997). One versus five sessions of exposure in the treatment of flying phobia. *Behaviour Research and Therapy, 35*, 987–996

Öst, L-G., Salkovskis, P. M., & Hellstrom, K. (1991). One-session therapist-directed exposure vs. self-exposure in the treatment of spider phobia. *Behavior Therapy, 22*, 407–422.

Öst, L-G., & Sterner, U. (1987). Applied tension: A specific behavioral method for treatment of blood phobia. *Behaviour Research and Therapy, 25*, 25–29.

Öst, L-G., Svensson, L., Hellström, K., & Lindwall, R. (2001). One-session treatment of specific phobias in youths: A randomized clinical trial. *Journal of Consulting and Clinical Psychology, 69*, 814–824.

Power, K. G., Simpson, R. J., Swanson, V., Wallace, L. A., Feistner, A. T. C., & Sharp, D. (1990). A controlled comparison of cognitive-behavior therapy, diazepam, and placebo, alone and in combination, for the treatment of Generalized Anxiety Disorder. *Journal of Anxiety Disorders, 4*, 267–92.

Rodebaugh, T. L., Holaway, R. M., & Heimberg, R. G. (2004). The treatment of social anxiety disorder. *Clinical Psychology Review, 24*, 883–908.

Roemer, L., & Orsillo, S. M. (2002). Expanding our conceptualization of and treatment for Generalized Anxiety Disorder: Integrating mindfulness/Acceptance-based approaches with existing cognitive-behavioral models. *Clinical Psychology: Science and Practice, 9,* 54–75.

Roth Ledley, D., & Huppert, J. D. (2007). Behavior therapy. In N. Kazantzis & L. L'Abate (Eds.), *Handbook of homework assignments in psychotherapy: Research, practice, and prevention* (pp. 19–34). New York: Springer.

Schmidt, N. B., Woolaway-Bickel, K., Trakowski, J., Santiago, H., Storey, J., Koselka, M., & Cook, J. (2000). Dismantling cognitive-behavioral treatment for Panic Disorder: Questioning the utility of breathing retraining. *Journal of Consulting and Clinical Psychology, 68,* 417–424.

Stangier, U., Heidenreich, T., Peitz, M., Lauterbach, W., & Clark, D. M. (2003). Cognitive therapy for social phobia: Individual versus group treatment. *Behaviour Research and Therapy, 41,* 991–1007.

Taylor, S. (2001). Breathing retraining in the treatment of Panic Disorder: Efficacy, caveats and indications. *Scandinavian Journal of Behaviour Therapy, 30,* 49–56.

Telch, M. J., Lucas, J. A., Schmidt, N. B., Hanna, H. H., LaNae Jaimez, T., & Lucas R. A. (1993). Group cognitive-behavioral treatment of Panic Disorder. *Behaviour Research and Therapy, 31,* 279–287.

van Balkom, A. J. L. M., Bakker, A., Spinhoven, P., Blaauw, B. M. J. W., Smeenk, S., & Ruesink, B. (1997). A meta-analysis of the treatment of Panic Disorder with or without Agoraphobia: A comparison of psychopharmacological, cognitive-behavioral, and combination treatments. *Journal of Nervous and Mental Disease, 185,* 510–516.

Wade, W. A., Treat, T. A., & Stuart, G. L. (1998). Transporting an empirically supported treatment for Panic Disorder to a service clinic setting: A benchmarking strategy. *Journal of Consulting and Clinical Psychology, 66,* 231–239.

Waters, A. M., & Craske, M. G. (2005). Generalized anxiety disorder. In M. M. Antony, D. Roth Ledley, & R. G. Heimberg (Eds.), *Improving outcomes and preventing relapse in cognitive behavioral therapy* (pp. 77–127). New York: Guilford.

Whittal, M. L., & McLean, P. D. (2002). Group cognitive behavioral therapy for obsessive compulsive disorder. In R. O. Frost & G. Steketee (Eds.), *Cognitive approaches to obsessions and compulsions: Theory, assessment, and treatment* (pp. 417–433). Amsterdam, Netherlands: Pergamon/Elsevier Science.

Wiederhold, B. K., & Wiederhold, M. D. (2004). *Virtual reality therapy for anxiety disorders: Advances in evaluation and treatment.* Washington, DC: American Psychological Association.

Zaider T. I., & Heimberg R. G. (2003). Non-pharmacologic treatments for social anxiety disorder. *Acta Psychiatrica Scandinavica, 108*(Suppl. 417), 72–84.

Zuercher-White, E. (1998). *End to panic* (2nd ed.). Oakland, CA: New Harbinger Publications.

CHAPTER 3

Assessment of the Anxiety Disorders

The Role of Clinical Evaluation

Prior to beginning treatment with any patient, it is essential to carry out a thorough evaluation. The purpose of doing so is twofold. First, the process of assessment allows the clinician to arrive at a diagnosis to describe the patient's symptoms. Giving a formal name to a patient's problems is important for practical reasons such as completing insurance forms or collecting data on a clinic's patient population, for example.

Establishing a diagnosis also aids in the process of case conceptualization and treatment planning. Embarking on these tasks without having first thoroughly assessed the patient would be like leaving for a road trip without a map! Rather than risk getting lost, it is essential that clinicians spend time reaching a thorough understanding of the factors that are likely maintaining a patient's problems, and making a plan for how to change these maintaining factors and improve quality of life.

Setting the Stage

The assessment interview is often the first time a clinician meets a new patient. It is important to consider each party's role during the assessment process. The task of the patient is to educate the clinician about the kinds of problems that she is having. The patient tells the clinician when the problem began, whether it has changed over time, and with some directed questions from the clinician, can likely articulate some factors that might be maintaining the problem. The patient can express the difficulty or impairment that the anxiety is creating in her life and describe her goals for anxiety reduction. The patient can also provide the clinician with some personal and interpersonal history so that the problem can be understood within the context of the patient's life.

As the clinician learns from the patient, he or she has some important tasks as well. A particularly important one, and one that is often forgotten, is to use the assessment as an opportunity to begin establishing a strong rapport with the patient. When patients feel at ease with the clinician, they will find it easier to be honest and open about their thoughts, feelings, and behaviors. When patients feel that they can share their feelings and experiences with the clinician, the information gathered during the assessment yields a more accurate diagnosis and a more thorough case conceptualization.

How should a clinician establish a strong rapport with a client? Unfortunately, there is no set of rules or guidelines for establishing a good rapport, but the work of Carl Rogers (1957) describes many crucial components to rapport-building. Rogers emphasized the importance of demonstrating empathy (seeing the patients' world from their point of view), genuineness (allowing what we say and how we behave to be congruent with what we think and feel), and non-possessive warmth (treating patients with care and respect). He also encouraged a stance of unconditional positive regard in which patients are accepted and valued for who they are. This idea of unconditional positive regard fits well with the stance of cognitive behavioral therapists who do not place blame on patients for their symptoms. These Rogerian qualities have been found quite reliably to predict good treatment outcome in many forms of therapy, including CBT (see review by Keijsers, Schaap, & Hoogduin, 2000).

How do these clinician qualities translate into actual behavior in the room with a patient? There are a number of behaviors clinicians can use to accomplish the goal of setting a strong rapport. These are shown in Table 3.1.

TABLE 3.1

Tips for Establishing Rapport

- Review confidentiality at the beginning of the assessment so that patients feel comfortable discussing personal matters.
- Educate patient about the assessment process so that they know what to expect. Tell them what is going to happen, how long it is going to take, and what the purpose is. Invite them to take a break and ask questions as needed.
- Normalize patients' problems—without "downplaying" the seriousness of their own problems, let them know that you have "heard it all" and you are comfortable discussing even uncomfortable things.
- Use patients' language (e.g., if they call a panic attack a "stress attack," refer to it as such so that they feel understood).
- React appropriately to everything a patient tells you.
- Provide psychoeducation about the nature and treatment of anxiety so patients feel that they are active participants in their treatment.

Special Issues Specific to Each Anxiety Disorder

Panic Disorder

Some patients with Panic Disorder have such severe Agoraphobia that they are rarely able to leave their houses. More mobile patients also have fears that can be triggered by coming to a clinician's office for an assessment: using various modes of transportation, driving into the city, using elevators, being on high floors of buildings, and being in small enclosed rooms. In other words, simply coming for an assessment appointment can trigger a great deal of anxiety for patients, and certainly can trigger full-blown panic attacks.

For a clinician, such experiences serve as important fodder for the assessment process. When patient are in the throes of anxiety, they often do a better job of explaining the situations that bring on their panic attacks and the thoughts, feelings, and behaviors that they experience during them. If patients reveal to clinicians that they had a panic attack while coming to the appointment, or if they are having a panic attack during the appointment, the clinician can be supportive, but also frame it positively, "I'm sorry you're having a rough time. But, this really helps me to better understand what you've been experiencing. Why don't you tell me about what you're experiencing right now?" It is unusual for patients to be so debilitated by a panic attack that they cannot proceed with the evaluation. Sometimes, patients can go right ahead and other times, a brief break can help them get back on track.

A greater problem occurs when patients call to book an appointment, but cannot leave the house to come to it. Few clinicians will go the patient's home to carry out the evaluation, and even if they did, this simply prolongs the inevitable fact that patients will need to muster up the strength to come to sessions. Patients can be encouraged to ask a trusted family member or friend to accompany them to the assessment. Clinicians can also provide some brief psychoeducation by phone to help them see that even if they have a panic attack on the way to the session, the consequences of this are typically minimal. In fact, successfully arriving at the assessment *despite feeling anxious* can set a very positive tone for exposure-based treatment. Since clinicians have limited time to discuss these issues by phone, and do not want to enter into a therapeutic relationship with a patient until consent for assessment and treatment is obtained in person, they can also recommend self-help books to clients that might provide them with enough information to get them to a session.

Specific Phobia and Social Phobia

Specific Phobias occasionally get in the way of the assessment process. For example, consider a patient who had a severe phobia of the sun. She was terrified of leaving her house during daylight hours. After discussing this with a clinician by phone, she agreed that she would come for her session toward the end of the day so that it would at least be dark on her way home. However, she was also concerned about the sun beaming into the clinician's office. While the clinician spent some time explaining to her how important it would be to directly confront these concerns, she did agree for the initial assessment and the first few treatment sessions, to keep her blinds drawn. This arrangement made it possible for the patient to come in. While clinicians always want to be mindful of not facilitating a client's avoidance, it is sometimes the case that doing so is the only way to get the client to come in for an assessment and the first few sessions of treatment. So long as clients understand that confronting feared stimuli will be the cornerstone of treatment, the benefits of making clients feel comfortable initially certainly outweighs the costs. It also presents a nice benchmark for treatment progress—at the end of treatment, the clinician can remind the patient, "When you first came in to meet with me, the blinds were drawn and we faced away from the window. Now we're sitting in the sunlight looking out the window—what progress you have made!"

While Specific Phobias rarely prevent people from seeking treatment, Social Phobia can pose a significant barrier. Coming in to speak with a complete stranger about highly personal issues presents the exact type of situation that patients with social phobia typically fear and avoid. This can make it very difficult for patients to come to an assessment appointment, or might make it very hard for them to discuss their difficulties once there. The best way for clinicians to deal with this is to be direct. When introducing the process of assessment to patients with social phobia, it is very beneficial to reinforce patients for coming in and to normalize their concerns—even if they do not bring them up. For example, a clinician can say, "I am really glad that you came to speak to me today about social anxiety. I know it's really difficult for many patients with fears like yours to do this. I just want you to know that I work with socially anxious patients all the time and really understand the types of concerns that they experience. I hope you will feel comfortable sharing your own experiences with me today. I just want you to know that I am not here to judge you—my goal is to listen to what you have to say and figure out how we can best help you. Okay?"

Keeping with the general theme of openness, it can also be very helpful for the clinician to specifically tell socially anxious patients that they should feel free to ask questions or to ask for a break should they need one. Some patients with social anxiety feel uncomfortable making requests, so if clinicians are conducting a lengthy evaluation, it may be a good idea to offer a break directly.

Obsessive-Compulsive Disorder

OCD can show up in all sorts of interesting ways during assessments. Sometimes, clinicians get a clear view of a patient's OCD symptoms. For example, patients with contamination concerns might refuse to shake hands, touch pieces of paper or pens, or sit in a waiting room or office chair. Patients who desire symmetry and exactness have been known to straighten pictures on office walls or express distress over a cluttered, messy desk. And patients who are concerned about making mistakes or saying "just the right thing" might frequently correct themselves or check that the clinician understands them, might speak very slowly and deliberately or have a hard time being concise. All of these "in session" behaviors help the clinician to see how the patient's OCD symptoms are expressed and are very useful in conceptualizing the case and planning treatment.

At times, rituals and avoidance behaviors can make the assessment process very difficult. Some patients get "stuck" and have a hard time moving from one topic to another. Other patients fear saying certain things and might not be able to share all the details of their difficulties with the clinician. Patients may be embarrassed by the content of their OCD concerns and find it troublesome to express their thoughts. In these cases, the clinician should ask the patient if OCD is getting in the way and help them to move on in any way that they can. For example, if a patient keeps answering the same question over and over again to make sure they say it "just right," the clinician can say, "I sense your OCD is making it hard for you to move on from this question. I am pretty sure I understand what you're saying. How about we move on, and if at the end of the assessment I have any questions about that issue, we can come back to it?" Patients are often reassured to have a clinician recognize their problematic behaviors as part of their OCD and are often relieved to have assistance getting themselves out of a ritual.

Generalized Anxiety Disorder

GAD does not typically interfere a great deal with the assessment process. However, there are times when the content of the patient's worries leads to difficulties in coming in for the evaluation. For example, a GAD patient whose worries center on time, job performance, and money may feel that she cannot miss several hours of work and pay the fee for the evaluation.

Current understanding of GAD proposes that it is a disorder of emotional regulation (e.g., Mennin, Heimberg, Turk, & Fresco, 2005). Specifically, patients with GAD have a hard time labeling and managing their emotions. During the assessment and process of therapy, these patients may avoid dealing with issues of emotional significance. Often, patients with GAD come across as very chatty, but in essence, do not say much. They often talk about a lot of "surface" concerns like being on time or completing work assignments. Yet, it is often the case that they are bothered by more difficult issues, like childhood trauma and the quality of their current interpersonal relationships. Because of their emotional regulation deficits, they often will not reveal such difficulties during an assessment, focusing instead on the aforementioned "surface" concerns. During a single assessment session, there is not much that can be done to remedy this problem since it really is the root of their disorder. Rather, clinicians should listen closely to what patients are saying and begin to formulate hypotheses about what might be underlying patients' worry. Clinicians should focus on using Rogerian skills to build rapport, engage patients in the process of treatment, and inspire hope that patients can indeed gain control over their problematic worries and emotional processes.

Assessment Tools

To gather the most detailed information during an assessment, information should be gathered from multiple sources. Most clinicians will use some sort of interview during an assessment to gather most of the pertinent details from the client, but other sources of information can also be useful. In this section, the clinical interview will be discussed first and then other assessment tools will be introduced.

The Clinical Interview

The method by which clinicians perform assessments depends on the setting in which they work, the orientation to which they ascribe, and their own personal style. Regardless of these factors, one of the most commonly used assessment techniques is the clinical interview.

Interview Methods

Semi-structured interviews are used in many settings, particularly those in which research is carried out. Interviews of this type include the Structured Clinical Interview for *DSM-IV* (SCID-IV; First, Spitzer, Gibbon, & Williams, 1997) and the Anxiety Disorders Interview Schedule for *DSM-IV* (ADIS-IV; Brown, DiNardo, & Barlow, 1994). These interviews consist of scripted questions based on *DSM* criteria that allow clinicians to arrive at a diagnosis (or diagnoses). They are referred to as "semi-structured" because they require skill beyond simply reading a question and getting a "yes" or "no" response from a respondent (as would be the case with the highly structured interviews used in epidemiological studies, for example). After reading scripted questions, clinicians ask follow-up questions to obtain the information that they need to make an accurate diagnosis.

In addition to broad semi-structured interviews that cover most *DSM* categories, interviews are also available to gather information on specific disorders. These interviews are extremely useful for case conceptualization and treatment planning. Rather than simply helping the clinician to establish a diagnosis, they facilitate the gathering of more detailed and useful information that assists with treatment planning. For example, the Liebowitz Social Anxiety Scale (LSAS) inquires about the degree to which patients fear and avoid particular social and performance situations. By completing this interview, the clinician gets a clear sense of the exact types of situations that the patient has difficulties with, as well as providing a metric of the severity of the social phobia. Knowing the specific situations that pose problems for the client aids in the planning and process of treatment. As will be outlined in Chapter 7, the LSAS proves very useful when creating a hierarchy of feared situations that the client wishes to work on over the course of treatment. Furthermore, since the LSAS quantifies severity of social phobia, it serves as an excellent way to measure progress over the course of treatment. Table 3.2 lists commonly used interviews for the specific anxiety disorders.

TABLE 3.2

Disorder Specific Interviews for the Anxiety Disorders

Disorder	Interview	Purpose	Description	Number of Items, Scoring, and Range of Score	Mean Score in Clinical Group
Panic Disorder	Panic Disorder Severity Scale (PDSS; Shear et al., 1997).	Assesses severity of panic symptoms over the past month.	Patients are asked seven questions about their panic symptoms.	7 items; total score is average of the scores for each of the seven items.	**1.59;** Other information: data are from patients with mild or no Agoraphobia (Shear et al., 1997).
Social Phobia	Liebowitz Social Anxiety Scale (LSAS; Liebowitz, 1987)	Assesses fear and avoidance of social and performance situations.	Clients rate the degree to which they have feared each situation and the degree to which they have avoided each situation over the past week.	24 items (11 items pertain to social interactions; 13 pertain to performance situations); yields a total score and a number of subscale scores (see Antony et al., 2001).	**67.2;** Other information: a cut-off of 30 distinguished individuals with social phobia from nonclinical controls; a cut-off of 60 distinguished individuals with discrete social fears from those with the generalized subtype of Social Phobia (Mennin et al., 2002).
OCD	Yale-Brown Obsessive Compulsive Scale (Y-BOCS; Goodman et al., 1989a, 1989b)	Identifies obsessions and compulsions that patients experience and also assesses severity of OCD	Includes a checklist of commonly experienced obsessions and compulsions; also includes 10 items, 5 that assess for the severity of obsessions and 5 that assess for severity of compulsions, yielding a Y-BOCS total score	10 items (plus checklist); yields a total score (range = 0–40) and an obsession and compulsion subscale score	**21.9;** Other information: 16 is typical cut-off for entry into clinical trials

Note: At the present time, there are no interviewer-rated measures available for assessing specific phobias or GAD.

Some clinicians prefer to use unstructured interviews, rather than the structured or semi-structured ones described above. While these interviews can also help clinicians arrive at a diagnosis, they are more focused on gaining an understanding of how patients are functioning and dealing with difficulties in their lives. Each clinician develops his or her own interviewing style. It can be helpful to have a rough set of guidelines to follow to ensure that all of the important areas are covered. These guidelines are shown in Table 3.3 and described briefly below.

TABLE 3.3

Summary of Topics for an Unstructured Clinical Interview

DEMOGRAPHICS

- Name
- Date of birth/age
- Ethnic/religious background
- Current work status/educational status
- Current relationship status/family structure
- Current living arrangements

PRESENTING PROBLEM

- Description of problem
- Onset and course of problem; frequency of symptoms/episodes
- Antecedents of the problem (e.g., situational triggers, life events, etc.)
- Thoughts associated with the problem (e.g., automatic thoughts, beliefs)
- Reactions to the triggers/life events (e.g., emotional, physiological, and behavioral reactions)
- Intensity and duration of the problem
- Previous treatment for the problem
- Additional problems

FAMILY BACKGROUND

- Ages of parents and siblings
- Upbringing and family relations
- Parents' marital history
- Parents' occupations; socioeconomic status
- Family medical and psychiatric history

TABLE 3.3 *(continued)*

PERSONAL HISTORY

- Developmental milestones
- Early medical history
- Adjustment to school and academic achievement
- Presence of acting out
- Peer relations
- Hobbies/interests
- Dating history

Gathering Demographic Information

Prior to delving into all the intricacies of a client's presenting problem, clinicians should spend some time getting to know the client. These details include the client's age, relationship status, living arrangements, employment status, and so on. By soliciting this type of information, clinicians can begin to get a sense of the degree to which patients' current difficulties are impacting their functioning. The best way to get at this information is to ask patients whether their functioning has changed from a previous level.

Take for example a patient who is a dentist, but has been struggling for years with Obsessive-Compulsive Disorder (OCD). Ever since dental school, he has worried about contracting illnesses from his patients and engaged in rituals ranging from wearing two or three sets of latex gloves to taking lengthy showers after work. Despite these obsessions and compulsions, the patient had been able to function quite effectively for years and had built a successful practice. Over the past year, however, his OCD had become much more severe. After seeing his first morning patient, his washing rituals had become so extreme that he was hours behind seeing subsequent patients. His evenings were spent "de-contaminating" from the day, both through long showers and praying rituals. His earnings fell significantly and he began to have trouble paying both his business and personal expenses. By the time the patient presented for treatment, he was in the process of selling his practice and was going through a painful divorce. Learning about these major changes in his functioning helped the clinician to understand how severe his OCD had become.

The Presenting Problem and History of the Presenting Problem

With the demographic information covered, it is appropriate to ask the client about his or her presenting problem. Often, this will come up even earlier in the interview (as demonstrated in the example of the dentist with OCD), but if it has not, a good way to ask this question is "What brings you here today?" or "Can you tell me about the problem that you've been having?"

Once a patient gives an initial overview, the clinician should get a sense of the history of the disorder. Clinicians should ask the patient when the problem began and whether anything in particular was going on in the patient's life when the problem started (e.g., a patient who begins to get panic attacks when caring for her dying mother in the hospital). The clinician can also assess whether particular stimuli trigger the symptoms at the current time (e.g., experiencing panic attacks at the supermarket and on the subway).

It is also important to learn about the course of the problem. Has the problem gone away at any point and then come back? If so, does the patient have a sense of why the problem went away and why it came back again? The clinician should also inquire about how frequently the symptoms currently occur (e.g., how many panic attacks does the client have each week, or how much of the client's day is taken up by obsessions and compulsions).

Cognitive-behavioral therapists move beyond symptoms to gather information about the thoughts, emotions, and behaviors (particularly escape and avoidance behaviors) that patients experience when their symptoms are triggered. This knowledge helps the clinicians to begin piecing together a cognitive-behavioral framework for understanding the patient's problems. Returning to the case of the dentist, his symptoms were clearly brought on by coming in contact with germs during his day at work. As he examined a patient, he began to think, "I wonder if they have any illnesses?" "I'm going to get sick," and "I can't wait for this to be over." As the exam continued, the patient would experience escalating anxiety (emotion). He would rush through the exam because he was so uncomfortable and then spend an inordinate amount of time scrubbing his hands with harsh cleansers, despite having worn two sets of gloves and a protective mask (behaviors).

Obtaining this sort of information is essential to conceptualizing the case and making a plan for treatment. To the clinician, it is clear that the patient's anxiety is being maintained by his avoidance behaviors. By taking excessive precautions against getting sick, the dentist never learned that he likely had an equal chance of getting sick by following the much simpler precautions mandated by his profession. Clearly, treatment would entail helping the dentist to discontinue his rituals, become accustomed to taking "normal precautions" at work, and learn that his work was not nearly as dangerous as he believed.

It is quite common for patients to present with more than one problem. For example, the dentist with OCD also had significant depression that had recently worsened with the loss of his business and marriage. After discussing the presenting problem, patient should be asked what other difficulties they are having, including difficulties with mood, other types of anxiety, eating, sleep, substance use, somatic concerns (e.g., hypochondriasis, body dysmorphic disorder), relationships, and sexual/gender identity concerns. If there is suspicion of psychotic symptoms, these should also be explored. It is certainly appropriate to also screen for "problems of living" (rather than just *DSM* diagnostic categories) including anger problems, perfectionism, and body image concerns. When specific problems are identified, clinicians should again use the cognitive model as a guide to adequately gather information for cognitive-behavioral case conceptualization and treatment planning.

Psychiatric History

Once the clinician feels confident that he understands the scope of the patient's current problems, it is also appropriate to ask if the patient has received treatment for these problems and to discuss the adequacy of the treatment. Clinicians should inquire about both pharmacological and psychosocial approaches to treatment and get a sense of the adequacy of each; both in terms of dose (e.g., dose of medication, frequency of therapy) and duration (e.g., how long the client stayed on medication or stayed in therapy).

When clients are given feedback at the end of the assessment, it can be useful to return to this information. For example, a patient might be averse to trying therapy after a previous treatment. Yet, if clinicians have learned that the prior attempt at therapy was not appropriate, they can educate the patient and encourage him to try again. The dentist with OCD had indeed had previous treatment—he had seen a psychoanalyst every other day for years, with no decrease in his OCD symptoms. When the clinician suggested he try CBT, he was not enthused, explaining that he had already thrown enough money away on therapy. The clinician was then able to educate the patient about CBT for OCD, telling him about major treatment trials showing it to be effective. He also described the process of CBT so that the client would see that this mode of therapy was very different from what he had experienced before. After this discussion, the patient decided that he would indeed try CBT. He went into his initial treatment session with an optimistic attitude that it might help him where other treatments had failed.

Family Background

CBT clinicians do not tend to delve deeply into the past during the assessment process. Yet, inquiring about a patient's family background can help round out the CBT case conceptualization. Family factors can certainly play a role in the etiology of patients' problems, as well as in the way they currently think, feel, and behave. Patients can be asked about their family's socioeconomic status, parents' occupations, and their relationships with their families both in the past and present. It is also very useful to ask about family psychiatric and medical history since this information can aid in making an appropriate diagnosis. For example, some patients with OCD believe so strongly in their beliefs that they seem to be psychotic. It can be challenging to differentiate OCD from a psychotic disorder. Knowing whether or not patients have a family history of psychotic disorders can provide important information (albeit one piece) in arriving at a correct diagnosis.

Other Assessment Tools

In the assessment of anxiety disorders, other tools in addition to the clinical interview can help to round out the assessment and provide further information for diagnosis, case conceptualization, and treatment planning.

Using the Assessment as a Window into Clients' Lives

Before moving on to more formal assessment tools, it is important to note that much can be learned by how clients behave during the assessment. Even during the initial assessment, the interaction between patient and clinician serves as a window into the patient's world. It permits the clinician to see how the patient typically relates to others. This knowledge can help establish diagnoses. For example, most patients with Social Phobia will be quite shy and reticent during an assessment. It also helps the clinician to begin to understand the kinds of interpersonal difficulties the client might be having. A client who repeatedly interrupts the clinician probably does this in "real life" too, and probably suffers because of it.

Self-Report Questionnaires

Questionnaires should never be relied on as the sole means of making a diagnosis or formulating a case. Yet, they can certainly be a useful component of the overall assessment process. Some clinicians might want to send questionnaire packets in advance to individuals who are scheduled to come in for assessments. By completing questionnaires in advance of the assessment, the clinician can review them with the patient at the assessment appointment and use the information as part of the case conceptualization. Alternatively, patients can be given questionnaire packets to complete in the clinic either before or after their assessment appointment. Patients can be told in advance to arrive early, or prepare to stay a bit late in order to complete the packets. A drawback of sending patients home with packets to complete and send or bring back is that often the packets are not returned.

What do self-reports contribute to the assessment that is not captured by the clinical interview? In some cases, patients are more likely to reveal very personal or sensitive information in written format than when they are posed questions directly. For example, a patient might deny suicidal thoughts during an interview, but endorse the item about such thoughts on the Beck Depression Inventory (BDI-II; Beck, Steer, & Brown, 1996). When clinicians carefully review self-reports, they can identify these inconsistencies and inquire about them in a sensitive way.

Another clear advantage of self-reports is that these measures have norms. This allows the clinicians to evaluate how the patient compares to similar patient populations and to non-clinical controls. Finally, self-reports provide an easy measure of progress during treatment. It is much easier to have a patient complete a BDI every few weeks during treatment than to re-administer portions of clinical interviews.

What measures should be administered to patients with anxiety disorders? A general measure of anxiety like the Spielberger State-Trait Anxiety Scale can reveal the client's general level of anxiety (Usually....) and current level of anxiety (Right now...). Given the high comorbidity of mood and anxiety disorders, it is also important to give a measure of depression, like the Beck Depression Inventory. Alternatively, patients can complete a single measure like the Depression, Anxiety, Stress Scale (DASS) that captures both depression and anxiety. A summary of these general measures is given in Table 3.4.

It is beyond the scope of this book to review every possible measure that can be used with patients with specific anxiety disorders. An excellent resource for this purpose is the *Practitioner's Guide to Empirically Based Measures of Anxiety* (Antony, Orsillo, & Roemer, 2001). In Table 3.5, we have listed some useful measures for each anxiety disorder, described each, and provided information on how to obtain them.

Behavior Tests

When assessing clients with anxiety disorders, behavior tests can be particularly helpful. As with simple observation of the patient's behavior during the assessment, setting up a formal behavior test provides clinicians with a window into the patient's world. In the behavior test, patients are exposed to the exact stimuli that they fear. This allows the clinician to observe the thoughts, feelings, and behaviors that clients experience when faced with their feared stimuli. The behavior test can also serve as a very useful tool for treatment planning and measuring progress over the course of treatment.

Behavior tests will vary widely, depending on a patient's fears. Consider a patient with a fear of spiders. This patient might be presented first with line drawings of spiders to look at, followed by more realistic pictures, and then moving images in a documentary or movie. Then, the patient can be asked to enter a room where a spider is housed in a closed container. The clinician can then assess how close the patient can get to the spider (e.g., entering the room, touching the closed container, putting one's hand in the container, touching the spider with a ruler or pen, touching a spider directly, allowing a spider to walk in one's hand).

At the end of this test, the clinician has a few pieces of valuable information. First, the patient can be asked for a Subjective Units of Discomfort (SUDS) rating at each step. The SUDS scale asks patient to quantify from 0–100 (or 0–10) how anxious they feel, with 0 being not at all anxious and 100 being extremely anxious. This standard scale provides a convenient way for the patient to communicate just how anxious he or she feels. The SUDS scale is described in more detail in Chapter 7. Second, the clinician will know how far up the hierarchy the patient can get prior to treatment. If the patient cannot even look at a line drawing of a spider, treatment should begin at this step of the hierarchy. If the patient

TABLE 3.4

Self-Report Measures for Anxiety and Depression

Construct	Measure	Description	Number of Items and range of scores	Guidelines for interpretation of scores
Anxiety	Beck Anxiety Inventory (BAI; Beck, Epstein, Brown, & Steer, 1988)	Assesses anxiety symptoms within the past week	21 items	0–7 = minimal anxiety; 8–15 = mild anxiety; 16–25 = moderate anxiety; 26–63 = severe anxiety
	State-Trait Anxiety Inventory (STAI; Spielberger, Gorsuch, Lushene, Vagg, & Jacobs, 1983)	Assesses both trait (how people *generally* feel) and state (how people feel *right now*) levels of anxiety	40 items (20 for trait anxiety and 20 for state anxiety)	Manual provides percentile ranks for various populations
Depression	Beck Depression Inventory–II (BDI-II; Beck, Steer, & Brown, 1996)	Assesses the intensity of depression over the past two weeks	21 items	0–13 = minimal depression; 14–19 = mild depression; 20–28 = moderate depression; 29–63 = severe depression
Anxiety and Depression	Depression Anxiety Stress Scales (DASS; Lovibond & Lovibond, 1995)	Assesses for depression, anxiety, and stress over the past week	42 items (21 items, short-form scale also available; total and subscale scores are multiplied by 2 to form equivalence with original scale)	Normal: 0–9 (depression), 0–7 (anxiety), 0–14 (stress); Mild: 10–13 (depression), 8–9 (anxiety), 15–18 (stress); Moderate: 14–20 (depression), 10–14 (anxiety), 19–25 (stress); Severe: 21–27 (depression), 15–19 (anxiety), 26–33 (stress); Extreme: 28+ (depression), 20+ (anxiety), 34+ (stress)

TABLE 3.5

Self-Report Measures for Specific Anxiety Disorders

Disorder	Measure	Description	Number of Items and Scoring Instructions	Mean Score in Clinical Group	Mean Score in Nonclinical/ Comparison Group
Panic Disorder	Agoraphobic Cognitions Questionnaire (ACQ)	Measures fearful cognitions associated with panic attacks and Agoraphobia	15 items, scored by calculating the means for items 1–14	**2.32**	1.60 (Bibb, 1988)
	Body Sensations Questionnaire (BSQ; Chambless, Caputo, Bright, & Gallagher, 1984)	Assesses for the intensity of fear associated with physical symptoms of panic	18 items, scored by calculating the means for items 1–17	**3.05**	1.80 (Bibb, 1988)
	Anxiety Sensitivity Index (ASI; Reiss, Peterson, Gursly, & McNally, 1986)	Assesses the construct of anxiety sensitivity, which is defined as fear of symptoms associated with anxiety.	16 items, scored by summing all 16 items	Among patient with Panic Disorder with mild or no Agoraphobia, mean score = **36.4;** Panic Disorder with moderate or severe Agoraphobia = **32.1** (Rapee, Brown, Antony, & Barlow, 1992; see p. 102 of Antony, Orsillo, & Roemer (2001) for means in other anxiety disorder groups)	19.1 (Peterson & Reiss, 1993)

continued

TABLE 3.5 (continued)

Disorder	Measure	Description	Number of Items and Scoring Instructions	Mean Score in Clinical Group	Mean Score in Nonclinical/ Comparison Group
Specific Phobia	Fear Survey Schedule (FSS-II; Geer, 1965; and FSS-III; Wolpe & Lang, 1964)	Measures degree of fear associated with particular objects and situations	FSS-II, 51 items; FSS-III, 72 items	Total score should not be used, rather items should be used clinically to identify patients' fears; numerous measures exist to assess for fears of specific objects/situations (see Antony, Orsillo, & Roemer (2001) for additional information)	
Social Phobia	Social Phobia and Anxiety Inventory (SPAI; Turner, Beidel, Dancu, & Stanley, 1996)	Assesses somatic, cognitive, and behavioral aspects of social phobia	45 items (2 subscales, social phobia and Agoraphobia; difference score derived by subtracting Agoraphobia scale from Social Phobia scale	Generalized social phobia = **96.5;** Speech phobia = **75.8** (Ries et al., 1998)	32.7 (Turner, Beidel, Dancu, & Stanley, 1989)
	Social Phobia Inventory (SPIN; Connor et al., 2000)	Assesses symptoms of social phobia	17 items, items are summed for total score; also yields three subscales	**41.1**	12.1
	Social Phobia Scale (SPS; Mattick & Clarke, 1998)	Assesses for degree of fear experienced in situations where one is observed by others	20 items, items are summed for total score	**32.8**	12.5 (Heimberg et al., 1992)
	Social Interaction Anxiety Scale (SIAS; Mattick & Clarke, 1998)	Assesses for cognitive, affective, and behavioral aspects of social interaction anxiety	20 items, items are summed for total score	49	19.9 (Heimberg et al., 1992)

TABLE 3.5 (*continued*)

Disorder	Measure	Description	Number of Items and Scoring Instructions	Mean Score in Clinical Group	Mean Score in Nonclinical/ Comparison Group
GAD	Generalized Anxiety Disorder Questionnaire–IV (GADQ-IV; Newman et al., 2002)	Can be used for diagnosing GAD and as a continuous measure of GAD severity	9 items (for detailed scoring rules, see Antony, Orsillo, & Roemer, 2001)	**19.93**	2.34
	Penn State Worry Questionnaire (PSWQ; Meyer, Miller, Metzger, & Borkovec, 1990)	Assesses tendency to worry excessively	16 items, items are summed for total score	**67.66**	44.27
OCD	Obsessive Compulsive Inventory–Revised (Foa et al., 2002)	Measures obsessive–compulsive symptoms	18 items, items are summed for total score; also yields six subscales	**28**	11.95 in one sample and 18.91 in another sample (Hajcak, Huppert, Simon, & Foa, 2004)
	Y-BOCS–self report version (see Baer, 2000)	Same as Y-BOCS (see Table 3.4)	Same as Y-BOCS	**21** (Steketee, Frost, & Bogart, 1996)	4.6 in one sample and 9.2 in another sample
	Maudsley Obsessive Compulsive Inventory (MOCI; Hodgson & Rachman, 1977)	Measures obsessive-compulsive symptoms	30 true/false items; yields a total score and four subscale scores; complex scoring (see Antony et al., 2001)	**13.67** (Richter, Cox, & Direnfeld, 1994)	6.32 (Dent & Salkovskis, 1986)
	Padua Inventory – Washington State University Revision (Burns et al., 1996)	Measures obsessive-compulsive symptoms	39 items, items are summed for total score; also yields subscale scores	**54.93**	21.78

is fine looking at pictures, but refuses to enter the room in which the spider was housed, the clinician will know that treatment should begin at this point. Finally, by being with the patient in the presence of the feared stimuli, the clinician can ask the patient "in the moment" what they are thinking and feeling, and can observe how they are behaving. This information then serves as fodder for cognitive restructuring and behavioral change during treatment. It should also be noted that behavior tests can be redone at the end of treatment to measure a patient's progress.

The major advantage of behavior tests is that they let clinician's see patients as they confront their most feared stimuli. This is particularly useful for patients who are poor at reporting their own symptoms and even more so, for patients who are so avoidant of their feared stimuli that it is difficult for them to explain what they would think and feel and how they would behave if they indeed confronted them. For example, a patient who is fearful of flying, but has not done so in 20 years might have a difficult time articulating the "ins and outs" of his fear.

The major disadvantage of behavior tests is their time-consuming nature. Because feared stimuli vary so widely across patients with anxiety disorders, it would be impossible to carry out behavior tests with every patient. Certainly, clinicians who specialize in particular anxiety problems can be set up to carry out behavior tests appropriate to the type of patients that they most often see (e.g., clients with animal/insect phobias). As technology evolves, clinicians might also be able to rely more heavily on virtual reality technology to carry out behavior tests (and for treatment, see Chapter 7).

Self-monitoring

Self-monitoring is another excellent way to gather information from patients with anxiety disorders. With this technique, the patient keeps a record of the occurrence of target behaviors or symptoms (e.g., hand washing, panic attacks, etc.). Such recording often includes the date and time of the occurrence, the situation during which the symptom was present, and the thoughts, feelings, and behaviors that the client experienced at the time that the symptom occurred. This information helps the clinician assess the nature and the severity of the problem (e.g., how much time per day is taken up by the symptom). Furthermore, a well-completed self-monitoring sheet contains the exact information that is necessary for a cognitive-behavioral case formulation. Clinicians can complete a self-monitoring sheet with a patient during the assessment interview by reflecting back on what the client has experienced in the last few days. Alternatively, a client can take a self-monitoring sheet home, complete it, and bring it back for a second assessment appointment or for the first session of therapy. Information will be most accurate if patients maintain records on an ongoing basis as symptoms occur, rather than reflecting back on experiences that they have already had. Self-monitoring is described in more detail, and a sample self-monitoring sheet is shown, in Chapter 7.

Speaking to Other Professionals and to Significant Others

It can also be useful to gather information from other professionals with whom a patient has worked and from family members, who might have a unique perspective on the patient's difficulties. Before doing either, it is essential to obtain permission from the client. While verbal consent that is documented in the chart is acceptable, it is advisable to get written consent whenever possible.

There are a number of scenarios in which speaking to other professionals is helpful. Perhaps the most common is the case of patients who obtain medication from a psychiatrist or general practitioner. It is good practice to contact the prescribing physician so that medical and psychosocial treatments can be coordinated. For example, during CBT for anxiety disorders, patients should not take benzodiazepines as a means of managing their anxiety during assigned exposures. It is helpful to have the prescribing physician support this instruction, and as patients begin to feel less anxious, psychiatrists and psychologists can work together effectively to help patients discontinue medication. Clinicians who specialize in the treatment of anxiety disorders can also discuss medication options with prescribing physicians. While clinicians without prescription privileges cannot make treatment decisions, physicians are often open to discussing these choices. Physicians who work with many different kinds of patients may not be as well-versed in the literature on the treatment of anxiety disorders as clinicians who specialize in this area. Thus, it can be helpful to let physicians know about recent studies that can inform treatment choices.

Clinicians might also want to contact physicians who are monitoring their patient's physical health. This is pertinent when ruling out possible medical causes for anxiety (e.g., thyroid problems), as well as to ascertain whether patients are in good enough physical health to endure the rigors of some CBT activities. For example, in the case of hoarding (a sub-type of OCD), treatment involves helping the patient to throw away accumulated materials. For some patients who have engaged in hoarding behaviors for years, their homes are full of material, requiring physical strength to "de-bulk." If a patient's physical health is in doubt, it is always best to check with his or her physician prior to initiating physically taxing treatment.

Finally, it can be helpful to speak to other clinician's with whom a patient has worked. This is particularly important when a patient has done CBT in the past. Some patients did well initially with CBT, but seek out additional CBT after a relapse or simply because they desire a few "booster" sessions. Other patients might not have had success with past CBT and it can be helpful to ask both the patient and the previous clinician why that was the case. While there are all sorts of reasons why previous CBT might not have been effective, it can be very useful to know whether the patient refused to make changes that were necessary for symptom reduction (e.g., exposure, discontinuation of rituals, etc.). In a non-accusing way, the clinician can then discuss with the patient why this attempt at CBT might be different. This includes inquiring about whether patients have experienced any changes in their own attitudes and behaviors, as well as what the clinician can do to increase the likelihood of success of this course of treatment.

As noted above, it can also be helpful to discuss cases with significant others in patient's lives. Most patients with anxiety disorders are honest and open during assessments and the purpose of seeking out the input of others is not to have a "tattletale" provide the real scoop on the patient's symptoms. Rather, significant others sometimes have a unique insight into a patient's symptoms. For example, patients with OCD often have a difficult time quantifying how much time they spend engaging in rituals each day. A spouse might be able to shed some light on this question. It is ideal to try to discuss these issues in the presence of the patient so that he/she does not feel as if the inquiries are accusatory in nature. Rather, the idea is to gather as much information as possible to understand the patient's situation and develop an appropriate treatment plan.

References

Antony, M. M., Orsillo, S. M., & Roemer, L. (Eds.). (2001). *Practitioner's guide to empirically based measures of anxiety.* New York: Klumer Academic/Plenum Publisher.

Baer, L. (2000). *Getting control: Overcoming your obsessions and compulsions* (Revised ed.). New York: Plume.

Beck, A. T., Epstein, N., Brown, G., & Steer, R. A. (1988). An inventory for measuring clinical anxiety: Psychometric properties. *Journal of Consulting and Clinical Psychology, 56,* 893–897.

Beck, A. T., Steer, R. A., & Brown, G. K. (1996). *Beck Depression Inventory Manual* (2nd ed.). San Antonio, TX: The Psychological Corporation.

Beidel, D. C., Turner, S. M., & Cooley, M. R. (1993). Assessing reliable and clinically significant change in social phobia: Validity of the Social Phobia and Anxiety Inventory. *Behaviour Research and Therapy, 31,* 331–337.

Bibb, J. L. (1988). *Parental bonding, pathological development, and fear of losing control among agoraphobics and normals.* Unpublished doctoral dissertation, American University, Washington, DC.

Brown, T. A., DiNardo, P. A., & Barlow, D. H. (1994). *Anxiety Disorders Interview Schedule for DSM-IV, Lifetime Version.* San Antonio, TX: The Psychological Corporation.

Burns, G. L., Keortge, S. G., Formea, G. M., & Sternberger, L. G. (1996). Revision of the Padua Inventory of Obsessive Compulsive Disorder Symptoms: Distinctions between worry, obsessions, and compulsions. *Behaviour Research and Therapy, 34,* 163–173.

Chambless, D. L., Caputo, G. C., Bright, P., & Gallagher, R. (1984). Assessment of fear in agoraphobics: The Body Sensations Questionnaire and the Agoraphobic Cognitions Questionnaire. *Journal of Consulting and Clinical Psychology, 52,* 1090–1097.

Connor, K. M., Davidson, J. T., Churchill, E., Sherwood, A., Foa, E., & Weisler, R. H. (2000). Psychometric properties of the social phobia inventory. *British Journal of Psychiatry, 176,* 379–386.

Dent, H. R., & Salkovskis, P. M. (1986). Clinical measures of depression, anxiety, and obsessionality in non-clinical populations. *Behaviour Research and Therapy, 24,* 689–691.

First, M. B., Spitzer, R. L., Gibbon, M., & Williams, J. B. W. (1997). *Structured clinical interview for* DSM-IV *Axis I disorders (SCID-I), clinician version*. Washington, DC: American Psychiatric Publishing.

Foa, E. B., Huppert, J. D., Leiberg, S., Langner, R., Kitchik, R., Hajcak, G., & Salkovskis, P. M. (2002). The Obsessive-Compulsive Inventory: Development and validation of a short version. *Psychological Assessment, 14*, 485–496.

Geer, J. H. (1965). The development of a scale to measure fear. *Behaviour Research and Therapy, 3*, 45–53.

Goodman, W. K., Price, L. H., Rasmussen, S. A., Mazure, C., Delgado, P., Heninger, G. R., & Charney, D. S. (1989a). The Yale-Brown Obsessive Compulsive Scale. II. Validity. *Archives of General Psychiatry, 46*, 1012–1016.

Goodman, W. K., Price, L. H., Rasmussen, S. A., Mazure, C., Fleischmann, R. L., Hill, C. L., Heninger, G. R., & Charney, D. S. (1989b). The Yale-Brown Obsessive Compulsive Scale. I. Development, use, and reliability. *Archives of General Psychiatry, 46*, 1006–1011.

Hajcak, G., Huppert, J. D., Simons, R. F., & Foa, E. B. (2004). Psychometric properties of the OCI-R in a college sample. *Behavior Research and Therapy, 42*, 115–123.

Heimberg, R. G., Mueller, G. P., Holt, C. S., Hope, D. A., & Liebowitz, M. R. (1992). Assessment of anxiety in social interaction and being observed by others: The Social Interaction Anxiety Scale and the Social Phobia Scale. *Behavior Therapy, 23*, 53–73.

Hodgson, R. J., & Rachman, S. (1977). Obsessive compulsive complaints. *Behaviour Research and Therapy, 15*, 389–395.

Keijsers, G. P. J., Schaap, C. P. D. R., & Hoogduin, C. A. L. (2000). The impact of interpersonal patient and therapist behavior on outcome in cognitive-behavioral therapy: A review of empirical studies. *Behavior Modification, 24*, 264–297.

Liebowitz, M. R. (1987). Social phobia. *Modern Problems of Psychopharmacology, 22*, 141–173.

Lovibond, S. H., & Lovibond, P. F. (1995). *Manual for the Depression Anxiety Stress Scales* (2nd ed.). Sydney, Australia: The Psychology Foundation of Australia.

Mattick, R. P., & Clarke, J. C. (1998). Development and validation of measures of social phobia scrutiny fear and social interaction anxiety. *Behaviour Research and Therapy, 36*, 455–470.

Mennin, D. S., Fresco, D. M., Heimberg, R. G., Schneier, F. R., Davies, S. O., & Liebowitz, M. R. (2002). Screening for social anxiety disorder in the clinical setting: Using the Liebowitz Social Anxiety Scale. *Journal of Anxiety Disorders, 16*, 661–673.

Mennin, D. S., Heimberg, R. G., Turk, C. L., & Fresco, D. M. (2005). Preliminary evidence for an emotion regulation deficit model of Generalized Anxiety Disorder. *Behaviour Research and Therapy, 43*, 1281–1310.

Meyer, T. J., Miller, M. L., Metzger, R. L., & Borkovec, T. D. (1990). Development and validation of the Penn State Worry Questionnaire. *Behaviour Research and Therapy, 28*, 487–495.

Newman, M. G., Zuellig, A. R., Kachin, K. E., Constantino, M. J., Przeworski, A., Erickson, T., & Cashman-McGrath, L. (2002). Preliminary reliability and validity of the Generalized Anxiety Disorder questionnaire-IV: A revised self-report diagnostic measure of Generalized Anxiety Disorder. *Behavior Therapy, 33*, 215–233.

Peterson, R. A., & Reiss, S. (1993). *Anxiety Sensitivity Index revised test manual*. Worthington, OH: IDS.

Rapee, R. M., Brown, T. A., Antony, M. M., & Barlow, D. H. (1992). Response to hyperventilation and inhalation of 5.5% carbon dioxide-enriched air across the *DSM-III-R* anxiety disorders. *Journal of Abnormal Psychology, 101,* 538–552.

Reiss, S., Peterson, R. A., Gursky, D. M., & McNally, R. J. (1986). Anxiety sensitivity, anxiety frequency and the prediction of fearfulness. *Behaviour Research and Therapy, 24,* 1–8.

Richter, M. A., Cox, B. J., & Direnfeld, D. M. (1994). A comparison of three assessment instruments for obsessive-compulsive symptoms. *Journal of Behavior Therapy and Experimental Psychiatry, 25,* 143–147.

Ries, B. J., McNeil, D. W., Boone, M. L., Turk, C. L., Carter, L. E., & Heimberg, R. G. (1998). Assessment of contemporary social phobia verbal report instruments. *Behaviour Research and Therapy, 36,* 983–994.

Rogers, C. R. (1957). The necessary and sufficient conditions of therapeutic personality change. *Journal of Consulting Psychology, 21,* 95–103.

Shear, M. K., Brown, T. A., Barlow, D. H., Money, R., Sholomskas, D. E., Woods, S. W., Gorman, J. M., & Papp, L. A. (1997). Multicenter collaborative Panic Disorder severity scale. *American Journal of Psychiatry, 154,* 1571–1575.

Spielberger, C. D., Gorsuch, R. L., Lushene, R., Vagg, P. R., & Jacobs, G. A. (1983). *Manual for the State-Trait Anxiety Inventory (form y): Self evaluation questionnaire.* Palo Alto, CA: Consulting Psychologists Press.

Steketee, G., Frost, R., & Bogart, K. (1996). The Yale-Brown Obsessive Compulsive Scale: Interview vs. self-report. *Behaviour Research and Therapy, 34,* 675–684.

Turner, S. M., Beidel, D. C., Dancu, C. V., & Stanley, M. A. (1989). An empirically derived inventory to measure social fears and anxiety: The Social Phobia and Anxiety Inventory. *Psychological Assessment, 1,* 35–40.

Wolpe, J., & Lang, P. J. (1964). A Fear Survey Schedule for use in behaviour therapy. *Behaviour Research and Therapy, 2,* 27–29.

CHAPTER 4

Case Conceptualization and Treatment Planning

A s we mentioned in Chapter 3, beginning treatment without first doing a thorough assessment is like leaving for a road trip without a map! You may or may not end up where you are trying to go when you do not have a map and plan. With your comprehensive evaluation and conceptualization in place, you will get there much more efficiently and effectively. The process will be clear and predictable for the clinician and the patient.

Doing an evaluation and then putting together all the pieces of information that have been gathered to establish a diagnosis is an essential part of building this map. The other part is forming a case conceptualization. The diagnosis is simply a name assigned to a cluster of symptoms. If a patient fears negative evaluation and meets various other criteria, he is assigned the diagnosis of Social Phobia. However, this diagnosis tells the clinician nothing about why the social anxiety symptoms are maintained, or what needs to be done to decrease the symptoms and improve functioning. In other words, if the clinician embarked on treatment after having only given the patient a diagnosis, he might still get lost!

Case conceptualization is a task that involves thinking–it is an intellectual process. There is no set way to do it, although some authors have written very helpful works on it (e.g., Roth Ledley, Marx, & Heimberg, 2005; Persons, 1989). For the purposes of this book, we will keep it simple, but we refer readers to these other works for more detail.

The Major Question

The major question clinicians should ask themselves following an evaluation with a patient with anxiety is: *What is maintaining this person's anxiety?* While clinicians who come from other orientations might be interested in the under-lying causes of anxiety, clinicians who practice cognitive behavior therapy focus on the "here and now." Anxiety is aversive and people who experience anxiety try all sorts of things to make their anxiety go away. Despite their best efforts (and wishes), their anxiety "sticks." It is the job of the CBT therapist to figure out why.

Behavioral Maintaining Factors

The likeliest culprit for the maintenance of anxiety is *avoidance.* While avoid-ance works in the short-term, giving patients temporary relief of anxiety, it tends to backfire in the long-term. Patients never learn that their feared outcomes are unlikely to occur. Furthermore, they never get the opportunity to see that they could cope even in the unlikely event that something bad indeed happened.

Let's return again to the case of Felicia. Felicia left her house everyday and, liv-ing downtown in a major city, confronted pigeons every day. So, why did her fear of pigeons "stick"? While Felicia was technically coming in contact with pigeons many times a day, she was engaging in both overt and subtle forms of avoidance. She refused to travel to Italy where she perceived there to be many more pigeons than in her hometown. She crossed to the other side of a street when she saw pigeons. More subtly, she had taken to always wearing a hat or tying her hair into a tight ponytail, figuring that if a pigeon did land on her head, this would pre-vent it from getting tangled. She even contemplated a new, short, cropped hair-cut so that pigeons could not get entangled in her hair. Felicia had class during her lunch hour and knew that she should have a snack while walking from class to class. Yet, she was so afraid of the crumbs attracting pigeons that she often went without eating at all. If she walked or sat with someone eating snacks outside, she would remain far away from them or make an excuse to leave.

Felicia's avoidance prevented her from learning that pigeons are quite differ-ent than she thought. Had she *directly* confronted pigeons, she would see that the likelihood of one landing on her head (or anyone else's head) was extremely slim. Cognitive behavior therapists sometimes relish unusual experiences though. What if, in the course of treatment, a highly unlikely event occurred–a pigeon actually landing on Felicia's head? This could actually be a life changing event for Felicia because she would see that her most feared outcome was man-ageable. It might be unpleasant and a little scary when it was happening, but probably not nearly as bad as Felicia had imagined. Once she had this direct experience, her fear might lose its power and no longer affect her day-to-day life.

Clinicians must spend time with patients to figure out their avoidance behav-iors. It is easy to find out what they overtly avoid by asking, "What won't you do because of your anxiety?" or "What would you like to be able to do, but can't because of your anxiety?" The more subtle forms of avoidance are more diffi-cult to get at. Helpful questions include, "When you do find yourself in the feared situation, what do you do to feel less anxious?" and "When you do find yourself in the feared situation, what do you do to make sure X (feared outcome) doesn't happen?" Experience also helps with these questions. When clinicians have seen multiple patients with the same fears, they come to possess a laundry list of possible avoidance strategies that patients might employ. It can be very reassuring to patients to have the clinician ask them if they engage in certain behaviors (e.g., "Do you carry water with you that you can sip if your mouth gets dry?" or "Do you hold your breath when you walk past a street person who you fear contracting an illness from?"). Patients are often very surprised that clinicians understand the subtleties of their disorder.

Cognitive Maintaining Factors

Cognitive maintaining factors are intricately tied to behavioral maintaining factors. Patients avoid feared stimuli because of their beliefs about them. The problem with these beliefs is that they tend to be negative and distorted. Coming to understand a patient's difficulties involves finding out their automatic thoughts and uncovering the errors inherent in these thoughts.

Finding the Automatic Thoughts

When patients are confronted with feared stimuli, or even when they think about feared stimuli, anxious patients experience *automatic thoughts*. These thoughts come fast and furiously, are negative, and tend to be taken as truths by patients. Felicia avoided pigeons because she believed with great certainty that they would land on her head and become entangled in her hair. Every time Felicia saw a pigeon (or any bird, in fact), she thought, "That bird is going to land on my head," "It will get tangled in my hair," and "It's swooping down." Furthermore, she believed that were this outcome to occur, it would be terrible. Felicia's thoughts included, "I won't be able to cope," "I'll die from anxiety," and "The anxiety will go on forever." These thoughts popped into Felicia's mind any time she confronted a bird and she just accepted them and let them drive her behavior (e.g., avoidance) and emotions (e.g., she felt anxious). Clinicians can help patients to spot the automatic thought by asking, "What was the first thought that popped into your mind when you thought about X (feared stimulus)?" or simply, "What were you thinking?"

Uncovering Cognitive Errors

Upon closer inspection, automatic thoughts are frequently fraught with cognitive errors. They can also serve as windows into underlying core beliefs that the patient may possess about being inadequate or unable to cope. Felicia's automatic thoughts showed many cognitive distortions. First, the probability of a pigeon landing on a person's head is very small. Second, if it were to happen, the pigeon would probably be more uncomfortable than Felicia and would fly away quickly.

In other words, the discomfort would be momentary and no long-term harm would be done. Because Felicia was not able to challenge her own thoughts to arrive at these more rational conclusions, her fear of pigeons was maintained.

Across the anxiety disorders, these two types of cognitive errors are consistently important. They are referred to as probability overestimation and catastrophizing (see Craske & Barlow, 2001). Because people believe that their feared outcomes are very likely to occur (probability overestimation), and to be very costly if they do occur (catastrophizing), their fear and avoidance is maintained over time.

Underlying automatic thoughts (those thoughts that quickly pop to mind in anxiety-provoking situations) are *core beliefs*. Core beliefs are defined as "one's most central beliefs about the self" (Beck, 1995, p. 166). Beck goes on to explain that core beliefs develop in childhood based on interactions with significant others and various life experiences. Unlike automatic thoughts that are typically specific to the situation that triggers them (e.g., "I'm going to say the wrong thing on my date"), core beliefs are "global, overgeneralized and absolute" (J. Beck, 1995, p. 167). For example, the core beliefs of someone with Social Phobia might be, "I am unlikeable" and "I am inadequate." Clearly, core beliefs can also serve to maintain anxiety disorders. If these sorts of beliefs lie at the core of a person's sense of self, there is no doubt that they will avoid situations that make these beliefs even more salient. Chapter 6 provides many techniques for helping patients to recognize and change the thought patterns that maintain anxiety.

Physiological Maintaining Factors

The other factors that maintain anxiety are physiological sensations. When people experience anxiety, they experience anxious thoughts, behave in an anxious way, and also often *feel* anxious. When Felicia saw a pigeon lurking nearby, her whole body became alert. She felt her heart race, her chest pound, and her hands sweat. She felt shaky all over.

As we have already noted, no one likes to feel anxious. While people might like to feel their hearts race and might enjoy working up a sweat when out for a job, experiencing these same sensations in an anxiety-provoking situation is uncomfortable. These uncomfortable feelings feed into anxious thoughts and behaviors. When Felicia experienced these feelings, she thought, "Gee, I must really be in a dangerous situation here." And, when she felt the feelings, she was all the more inclined to escape and get away from the pigeons as soon as possible.

Looking Beyond the Anxiety

When considering the behavioral and cognitive patterns that are likely maintaining a patient's anxiety, it is important to also look beyond fear triggers (e.g., social situations, germs, subways). Clinicians should also inquire about interpersonal relationships, for example. If a patient with Social Phobia is married, it is important to inquire about his spouse. Is his spouse also socially anxious? If so, the marriage might be a relevant maintaining factor–if both members of the couple have problems with social anxiety, one individual's avoidance can serve to maintain the others. The couple gets invited to a party and one person says, "I don't think we should go." The other readily agrees, "You're right! Let's stay in instead."

In some couples, one spouse is highly critical of another. If a wife constantly criticizes the social skills of her socially anxious husband, this too can serve to maintain his anxiety. Similarly, clinicians should inquire about patients' lives at work and/or school. Factors in these environments might also play a role in the maintenance of a patient's social anxiety. If, for example, a patient with social anxiety has a solitary job as a technician in a laboratory with little social interaction and lives alone, the lack of regular social experiences likely contributes to the anxiety when confronted with a social situation.

What About the Positive?

The Power of Motivation

On the flip side of maintaining factors are factors that motivate patients to seek treatment for their anxiety problems in the first place. These motivating factors are also essential to the case conceptualization. Patients who have little motivation are less likely to do well in CBT than patients who have a great deal of desire to change. Is the patient coming to treatment because a parent or spouse has forced them to come? This knowledge has a major impact on the case conceptualization. It helps inform the clinician that motivation might be a problem and that special methods (like motivational interviewing, see Miller & Rollnick, 2002) might be helpful. Conversely, is the patient coming for treatment because she really wants to get rid of her anxiety in order to accomplish a particular career or family goal? A new mom with Social Phobia might be very motivated to become more outgoing so as to facilitate social interactions for her daughter. Clinicians can come back to this powerful motivator again and again when the going gets tough in treatment. If the patient refuses to do an exposure because it is too difficult, the therapist can say, "I agree that this is a really hard exposure. But, let's think about what brought you here for treatment. Why is it important to you to be able to do this?" If the patient does not readily provide a response, the clinician can remind her, "You told me that you don't want your daughter to fear social situations like you do. And, we agreed that getting you past your own social anxiety was the best way to prevent this from happening. Can you keep that in mind as you prepare to do the exposure this week?"

Building on the Patient's Strengths

Clinicians can inquire about how the patient has been able to manage difficult situations in the past, and uncover some of the patient's core strengths and resiliency. It is likely that patients have previous instances of successfully navigating difficult situations. Clinicians can utilize this information to conceptualize the patient's current difficulties with anxiety and the way in which the patient is able to harness the "fighting spirit" to work through problematic situations. Some patients benefit from having significant social support. Others find that they can face challenges when they can clearly see the benefit in a certain area of their life. Others have learned that the only thing to do when times get tough is to "pick yourself up by your bootstraps and keep going." Clinicians can get at key strengths by asking patients, "What are some areas of your life about which you are very proud?" "How have you forged ahead in times of stress, anxiety, or conflict in the past?" and "Where does your strength come from?"

Clinicians can make note of the way patients describe their core capabilities and strengths. If a patient feels highly competent in one area of her life, the clinician can use their courage and capabilities to help the patient stay motivated as times become difficult. This process works best when clinicians can reflect back to some of the patient's own wording about his or her strengths. In presenting the conceptualization and treatment plan, the clinician can highlight the fact that the patient has overcome other obstacles in life and the anxiety treatment will function the same way. This helps to build patients up and motivate them to begin treatment with a courageous and optimistic spirit.

To summarize, clinicians must embark on treatment with an understanding of the factors that likely maintain a patient's anxiety. Table 4.1 offers suggestions of questions that clinicians should be able to answer at the end of an evaluation in order to adequately conceptualize a case.

TABLE 4.1

Questions to Aid Case Conceptualization

- What is the patient overtly avoiding (e.g., what will he or she not do *at all*)?
- What sorts of subtle avoidance strategies is the patient engaging in?
- What automatic thoughts does the patient experience when he or she confronts the feared stimuli?
- Does the patient experience uncomfortable physical sensations when exposed to the feared stimuli? If so, how does this experience relate to anxious thoughts and avoidance behaviors?
- What interpersonal factors might be playing a role in the maintenance of the anxiety?
- What are some possible core beliefs that might underlie the patient's automatic thoughts?
- What led the patient to seek treatment? What is his or her level of motivation to change? What strengths does he or she bring to treatment?

Using the Case Conceptualization to Develop a Treatment Plan

Why is it so important to embark on treatment with a clear hypothesis of the factors that likely maintain a patient's anxiety? Simply put, this hypothesis leads directly into the treatment plan. Knowing what maintains anxiety informs what needs to be changed to "undo" anxiety. This is how the case conceptualization ties into the treatment plan.

There are excellent CBT protocols available to treat each of the anxiety disorders. The commonality of all of them is that the protocols consist of: (1) exposure to feared situations, and (2) discontinuation of avoidance behaviors that maintain anxiety. Many also include exercises aimed at helping patients dispute their anxious thoughts. These are easy concepts for even the newest clinicians to grasp. But, figuring out what exposures to do, identifying all of the subtle avoidance strategies that must be discontinued, and deciding which thoughts to restructure are skills that improve with practice. Clinicians should go into the first session of treatment with a rough idea of what treatment will entail. In addition to the cognitive and behavior exercises just described, clinicians should also be mindful of other areas that might demand focus. For the patient with the critical wife, for example, treatment might include some assertiveness training. The new mom with Social Phobia might benefit from some social skills training focused on how to initiate and maintain conversations with other new moms.

A sample case conceptualization and treatment plan for Felicia is included in Figure 4.1.

Sharing Hypotheses with Patients

It is important to note that the case conceptualization need not be perfect at the initiation of treatment and that the treatment plan need not be adhered to exactly. As clinicians begin working with patients, they will alter their case conceptualizations as their understanding of the case deepens. This changing understanding will then impact the treatment plan.

Clinicians should go into the first treatment sessions with a clear hypothesis about the factors that might be maintaining the patient's anxiety. This hypothesis should then be shared with the patient in their first meeting after the assessment. An important contributor to the case conceptualization is the patient's own understanding of the maintaining factors for their anxiety disorder. It is not necessary to hand them a hard copy of the case conceptualization, but it is important to share it with patients in a way that is meaningful. Remember that the case conceptualization serves as the road map for treatment. If it does not mesh with patients own understanding of their problems, it is less

Patient: Felicia W.

Age: 19

Education/employment status: College junior, psychology major

Diagnosis: Specific phobia, animal type (pigeons)

Background: Onset of phobia occurred six months ago after a pigeon landed on her friend's head, becoming entangled in her hair. Felicia was walking with her friend at the time. Since then, she has had a terrible fear of pigeons. Felicia is very motivated to work on her fear of pigeons. The fear causes significant interference and distress on a daily basis. Also, Felicia is unable to visit her relatives in Italy because of her belief that she could not handle the number of pigeons in popular tourists areas.

Maintaining factors:

- **(Behavioral)** Since the incident, Felicia avoids places with lots of pigeons (e.g., Italy). When she sees pigeons, she crosses to the other side of the street. She always wears hats or a tight ponytail to protect her hair. At times, she has carried an umbrella even if it is not raining. She is very vigilant to pigeons, thinking all birds are pigeons.

- **(Cognitive)** Felicia believes that pigeons are dangerous. She believes that they land on people's heads very frequently. She is 95% certain that one will land on her head. She is 100% sure that if one did, it would get stuck in her hair. She fears that it would be so terrible that she would not be able to manage.

- **(Possible core beliefs)** Felicia described many other events in her life that had "bad outcomes." At numerous times during the assessment, she noted that "Bad things always happen to me" and "I have bad luck."

- **(Physiological symptoms)** Racing heart, pounding chest, sweating, shaking. These sensations heighten Felicia's beliefs about the danger of the situation and likely increase escape and avoidance behavior.

Treatment Plan:

- Spend two sessions **gathering more information** and doing **psychoeducation** on nature and treatment of specific phobias.

- **Design a hierarchy** of feared situations in Session Three.

- Spend two to three sessions on **cognitive restructuring**, helping Felicia to reframe her beliefs about the danger of pigeons.

- Then, begin **exposure** to feared situations as per the hierarchy (approximately 6 sessions, plus homework).

- Via exposure, help Felicia to see that her physical sensations are not dangerous and typically decrease with continued exposure.

- Possible work on **core beliefs** at the end of treatment.

- Spend last two sessions reviewing **treatment gains** and discussing **relapse prevention.**

FIGURE 4.1 *Sample Case Conceptualization*

likely that they will engage fully with treatment. Therefore, clinicians should present the case conceptualization as a working hypothesis, asking patients every step of the way if it maps out to their own understanding and revising it if the patients correct some aspect of it. Figure 4.2 illustrates how Felicia's clinician shared with her the case conceptualization. The most important aspect of this figure is to demonstrate to patients how the cognitive and behavioral aspects of the anxiety set up a vicious cycle. The faulty beliefs perpetuate avoidance and the avoidance prevents the disconfirmation of feared beliefs. It is important to show patients how anxiety has "trapped" them! Clinicians can write this diagram on a dry-erase board, making it easy for patients to follow and to make corrections where necessary.

The diagram can then also be used to illustrate to the patient how treatment will work (see Figure 4.3). The important aspect of this figure is that established techniques are available to help patients chip away at the cognitive and behavioral aspects of anxiety in order to break out of the "anxiety trap."

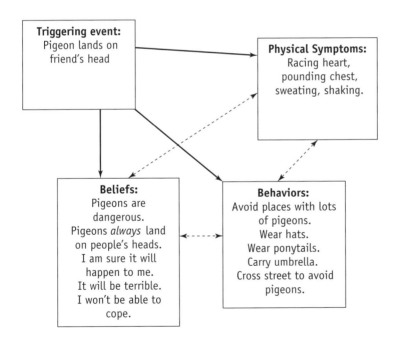

Note: The solid lines show how the triggering event leads to specific beliefs, physical symptoms and behaviors. The dotted lines show the interaction (or "vicious cycle") between thoughts, feelings, and behaviors.

FIGURE 4.2 *Case Conceptualization for Felicia*

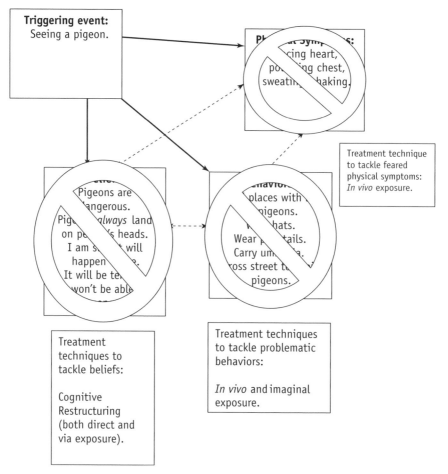

FIGURE 4.3 *Treatment Plan for Felicia*

As Treatment Progresses

The other reason that the case conceptualization and treatment plan is not set in stone at the start of treatment is because it naturally changes as treatment progresses. As clinicians get to know patients better, their understanding of the case might change. As "life happens" for the patient, different problems might become the focus of treatment. Motivation might wax and wane during treatment, again impacting the conceptualization and treatment plan. Even knowing this, however, it is still important to begin treatment with a rough road map so that the clinician and patient do not get lost on their trip together.

References

Beck, J. S. (1995). *Cognitive therapy: Basics and beyond.* New York: Guilford.

Craske, M. G., & Barlow, D. H. (2001). Panic Disorder and Agoraphobia. In D. H. Barlow (Ed.), *Clinical handbook of psychological disorders* (3rd ed.). New York: Guilford.

Miller, W. R., & Rollnick, S. (2002). *Motivational interviewing: Preparing people for change.* New York: Guilford.

Persons, J. B. (1989). *Cognitive therapy in practice: A case formulation approach.* New York: Norton.

Roth Ledley, D., Marx, B., & Heimberg, R. G. (2005). *Making cognitive-behavioral therapy work: Clinical process for new practitioners.* New York: Guilford.

Treatment of Anxiety Disorders

THE WILEY
CONCISE GUIDES
TO MENTAL HEALTH

Anxiety
Disorders

CHAPTER 5

Client Psychoeducation

Education is an integral part of the treatment of anxiety disorders. There are many components to educating patients about anxiety including: how anxiety works, the patient's specific manifestations of anxiety, the treatment approach in general, and the idiosyncratic treatment approach based on the patient's particular presenting issues. Depending on the patient's situation, clinicians may also want to do psychoeducation with the patient's significant others.

What To Say

Conceptualizing Anxiety for Patients

The meat of psychoeducation is presenting to patients why anxiety "sticks around" and what needs to be done to make it go away. Prior to covering this material, it can be helpful to begin with more general material. Patients should learn about the distinction between normal and problematic anxiety and some descriptive features of the anxiety disorder that they have. Since this information is very general and nonthreatening, it serves as a nice way for patients to begin to acclimate to the therapy environment.

Normal versus Problematic Anxiety

Prior to talking to patients about their anxiety *disorder*, clinicians should explain what "normal anxiety" is and help patients to see that anxiety can be adaptive, protective, and helpful.

Anxiety derives from fear, which is a natural, basic emotion that has existed throughout evolution for a reason. In sharing this information with patients, clinicians can say:

> If you were living during the caveman era and you came face to face with a bear while you were walking in the woods, the fear would produce an activation of the sympathetic nervous system. This leads to the adrenaline response that creates the adaptive "fight or flight" reaction.
>
> Then, the next time you stepped out into the woods, you'd be on high alert about the possibility of seeing a bear. This high level of alertness and the accompanying worry are fueled by anxiety. The anxiety is actually advantageous because it may help you to walk in safer areas, not carry food that could attract a bear, walk quietly, or whatever else is helpful in keeping bears at bay.

This illustration shows how anxiety exists to help us. It serves a protective function. Having some level of anxiety actually gives us the energy we need to perform tasks and the vigilance we need to keep ourselves as safe as possible. Back in caveman days, people would run the risk of getting attacked by the bear if they had no anxiety. In present times, anxiety can motivate us to prepare for a test or a talk, be on our best behavior on a first date, or walk safely when alone at night. Without the safeguard of some healthy anxiety, we would be at risk of failing at tasks, making social gaffs, and putting ourselves in dangerous situations.

However, too much anxiety is as problematic as too little anxiety. Like many things, too much of a good thing creates problems. Anxiety exists on a spectrum: Too little anxiety means that you are not sufficiently energized to deal with potential problems. Too much anxiety means that the anxiety that was once helpful has become problematic.

This leads to the question: "When does anxiety become a disorder?" According to the *DSM-IV*, anxiety disorders are characterized by marked distress and/or significant impairment in functioning. A number of other factors included in the following checklist can help clinicians decide if anxiety is pathological:

The anxiety has . . .

____ Interfered with functioning at work, school, or home

____ Caused impairment in the ability to complete tasks of daily living

____ Created significant emotional upset and turmoil

____ Interfered with sleep, eating, or healthcare

____ Become excessive compared with the realistic threat or risk in a situation

____ Led to relationship and communication difficulties

____ Taken up significant amounts of time and caused one to get behind on important tasks

____ Resulted in legal problems

____ Been responsible for a major loss in life, such as a relationship or job

Educating Patients about Their Anxiety Disorder

Patients are often interested to learn some facts about the anxiety disorder that they have. Patients often like to know about the prevalence of the disorder, the age of onset, sex differences, and theories of etiology. While it is not necessary to get into a great deal of detail on this latter topic, therapists can briefly explain that anxiety disorders typically result from a combination of biological predisposition, learned behavioral responses, environmental stressors, and interpersonal factors.

Patients should also learn about the efficacy of CBT for the disorder that they have. Again, it is not necessary to go into a great deal of information about treatment outcome studies. Therapists can distill the information that they read in Chapter 2 of this book into "tidbits" that are interesting and helpful to patients. For example, when treating patients with OCD, therapists can say: "Exposure and ritual prevention therapy for OCD has been studied extensively. Across many studies, over 80% of patients respond to treatment and most of those are able to maintain their gains over the long-term." It can often be helpful to show patients a graph from a treatment outcome study that illustrates improvement rates. Visual presentation of data can really help patients to see how much treatment can help them.

This material can be used later in treatment if motivation wanes or treatment adherence is a problem. Some patients will ask: "What is wrong with *me* that I'm not improving but most other patients in studies did improve?!" The clinician can use this question as a motivator. Good treatment outcome is associated with treatment compliance—patients who truly *do* the treatment, tend to do well. Helping patients to see this might help them overcome their own resistance to doing certain parts of the treatment that seem too hard.

During this early phase of psychoeducation, therapists should also provide patients with some information on their professional experience with anxiety disorders. Establishing credibility and expertise is important because during treatment, therapists will often recommend that patients do things that they really do not want to do. People with anxiety disorders have often spent years avoiding feared stimuli and in treatment, they are suddenly instructed to confront these very things. If patients trust the therapist's judgment and expertise, they will be more likely to push themselves to do the exposure.

In the treatment manual *Mastery of Obsessive Compulsive Disorder: A Cognitive Behavioral Approach-Treatment Guide*, authors Kozak and Foa recommend that clinicians let patients know that the results of treatment are primarily based on what the client invests in the treatment. They offer the analogy of comparing the therapist to a baseball coach and the patient to a baseball player. The coach will use his experience to recommend some new exercises for the player to try. Some of these exercises may sound challenging to the baseball player and some don't seem to be directly related to his playing abilities. If, however, the coach is an expert and knows the right exercises to assign and *if* the baseball player does them, the baseball player will improve. If the coach is not an expert and does not assign the right exercises, if the player rejects the coach's suggestions, or if the player accepts the advice but does not practice, the player will not improve. The process of cognitive behavioral therapy works similarly.

Understanding the Maintenance of Anxiety
Drawing a Model of the Patient's Anxiety

In Chapter 4, we demonstrated how clinicians can draw a model, specific to each patient, that demonstrates why problems with anxiety "stick around," despite the patients' best efforts to change. Models can get a bit more complex than the one shown in Chapter 4, depending on each patient's unique symptoms.

In drawing the model, clinicians must demonstrate to patients how both behaviors (especially avoidance) and thoughts play a role in the maintenance of anxiety.

Explaining Avoidance

Avoidance is the hallmark of the anxiety disorders. Anxiety, even when adaptive (as in our bear example), is an aversive state. It is uncomfortable to feel your heart racing and to think scary thoughts. Understandably, people do whatever they can do to avoid this experience. In the short-term, it can be great to avoid anxiety! Avoidance provides immediate relief. However, over the long-term, avoidance can become very problematic. This can be demonstrated to patients through the following metaphor:

> Imagine that a child is walking down the street one day and she encounters a neighborhood dog, a Collie. She approaches it from behind to pet it and it becomes startled and turns around and snaps at her, lightly biting her. The child screams and runs away to her mother. After this incident, the child becomes very fearful of dogs. She refuses to walk down the block where she got bit by the dog. Then she begins avoiding any place that she thinks a Collie could be. She then refuses to go inside her neighbor's house because they have a pet Poodle. She turns and walks the other way when she sees a big German Shepard coming down the street. Over time, she begins to avoid small dogs too—she won't play at her friend's house because they have a little Cavalier King Charles Spaniel. She won't walk down a particular block because she knows that a Beagle and a Chihuahua live there.
>
> This whole experience is very troubling to her family because their child previously loved dogs and they were thinking about getting a Golden Retriever that spring. Before being bit, their daughter had been very excited about getting a puppy. But now their daughter throws a tantrum at the very thought of it.

With an example like this one, patients will see the role that avoidance plays in maintaining anxiety. Avoidance prohibits essential learning. It prevents people from learning that the feared stimulus is not necessarily dangerous. It also prevents people from learning that even if their feared outcome were to occur, it would rarely be as horrible and catastrophic as they imagine. The light bite that the child in our example got from the Collie had no consequence—it did not break the skin, or even hurt very much. Dog lovers actually relish a little nibble from their pets! By avoiding all dogs, this child will not learn that dogs rarely bite, and when they do bite, it is usually a playful, harmless nibble.

Another problem with avoidance is that it limits functioning and reduces pleasure in different activities. Prior to the child's frightening experience with the Collie (and subsequent avoidance), she was enthusiastic about getting a dog and was counting down the days on her calendar. After several months of avoidance, she did not want a dog and she and her family would miss out on the companionship and enjoyment that the puppy would bring to the household.

In explaining avoidance, clinicians should refer to some of the avoidance patterns that are common with the patient's presenting issues. If the patient has Panic Disorder with Agoraphobia, the discussion can center on how not leaving the house prohibits him from realizing that he could handle the situations (even *if* he did actually have a panic attack). Agoraphobic avoidance disallows the patient the opportunity to see that he will not go crazy, lose control, or die in the situations that he fears. The avoidance also comes with a huge cost—not being able to go out of his home and have an active, rewarding career or social or recreational life.

To summarize, a key principle that must be taught during psychoeducation is: *Avoidance limits both learning and enjoyment.*

The Role of Thoughts

A tenet of cognitive behavioral therapy is that it is not events themselves that cause anxiety, but rather our interpretation of events. People with anxiety disorders have experiences that are common to us all, but it is the way that they process and interpret these experiences that can get them into trouble. For example, research has shown (Rachman & deSilva, 1978) that 90 percent of the population experiences intrusive thoughts. People without anxiety disorders might think, "Gee, what if I shoved that person onto the subway tracks?" or "What if I drove off this bridge?" Nonanxious people who experience these thoughts either barely notice them, or laugh them off—"What a weird thought." In contrast, anxious people react to them with fear and worry that the thought is equivalent to *wanting* to do one of these terrible things. This leads to problems—since anxiety is aversive, patients need to do something to ward off the anxiety. They might reassure themselves ("I am a good person; I wouldn't do that!"), seek reassurance from others, say a prayer to prevent bad outcomes, or avoid fearful situations like riding the subway or driving over a bridge. This all comes about because they interpreted a nonsensical thought in an anxious way.

Here are some common examples of how this process of cognitive distortion can play out in the various anxiety disorders:

- *Obsessive Compulsive Disorder*—After using a public bathroom, a patient might think, "I am going to get AIDS and die."

- *Social Phobia*—After walking into a classroom late, when all of the other students are assembled, a patient might think, "Everyone is looking at me and they think I am a freak."

- *Panic Disorder*—A patient is running late for work and rushes onto the subway as the train is pulling out of the station. He notices his heart racing and his hands shaking. He thinks, "I am having a heart attack and I am going to die."

- *Specific Phobia*—A patient has to go on an elevator and thinks, "I am going to get trapped and I will never get out."

- *Generalized Anxiety Disorder*—A patient is waiting for her husband to come home from work and thinks, "He must have died in a car crash and I will be alone forever."

- *Separation Anxiety Disorder*—A child says goodbye to her mom in the morning when being dropped off at school and thinks, "Mom is never coming back to get me and I will never see her again."

The commonality of all of these examples is that our patients found themselves in totally normal, everyday situations—saying goodbye to a loved one, riding an elevator or subway, using a public restroom. The difference between anxious people and nonanxious people is in the way that people think about these situations. Two cognitive errors are common among anxious patients (see Craske & Barlow, 2001). First, patients catastrophize, thinking that disastrous outcomes are lurking around every corner. And second, they overestimate the likelihood that these bad things will happen. CBT involves helping patients to view their thoughts objectively, question whether they are rational, and reframe them to be more adaptive if they are irrational or erroneous.

To summarize, another key principle that must be taught during psychoeducation is: *It is not events themselves that cause anxiety, but rather our interpretation of events.*

Avoidance of Thoughts

In the previous section, we talked about things that people do in response to anxious thoughts: self-reassurance, seeking reassurance from others, or saying something to "neutralize" a bad thought (like saying a prayer). People might also try to stop thinking about the thought. During psychoeducation, patients must be taught about thought suppression since it is simply another avoidance strategy that can maintain anxiety. Over the course of CBT, patients learn that they should just let thoughts be there—as soon as they stop trying to control thoughts, the thoughts lose some of their power to provoke anxiety.

Here is a good metaphor for explaining thought suppression to patients:

Having an anxious thought is like playing with a beach ball in a swimming pool. When you push the ball down under the surface of the water, it bounces back up. When you try to stop thinking about something, the thought acts just like a beach ball. It pops back up and the more you try to push it down, the more it sticks around. If, however, you were to just leave the ball alone, it would just sit on the surface of the water. It would be there, but it would likely just start to float away, to some other part of the pool. This is what we will learn to do with anxious thoughts in treatment. It is going to be important to learn to just leave anxious thoughts alone. When we stop trying to get rid of them, they typically start to float away and become less and less distressing.

To summarize, another key principle that must be taught during psycho-education is: *The more we try to not think about something, the more we will think about it!*

Understanding the Treatment of Anxiety

At this point, the patient and therapist have drawn out a diagram illustrating the patient's anxiety and what has maintained it over time. They understand that thoughts, behaviors, and the interaction between thoughts and behaviors keep anxiety going over time. At this point in psychoeducation, patients can feel slightly dejected. They see a vicious cycle and no way to break out of it. It is time to educate patients about how CBT will help them to get out of the anxiety cycle and function better. This involves orienting clients to CBT in general, and to what CBT will be like for them, given their specific anxiety disorder.

Educating the Patient About CBT
Collaborative Empiricism

Patients often come into therapy thinking that they will speak freely about their problems and that once in a while, the therapist will pipe in with a profound interpretation. This is how therapy is typically depicted in the movies. Most patients are pleasantly surprised to learn that CBT is a very different approach. One of the hallmarks of CBT is *collaborative empiricism*. This term refers to the fact that the therapist and patient work together in a collaborative way to gather information (for example, through self-monitoring), develop hypotheses, and test them out. It is a scientific, data-driven process. For example, the clinician could describe to a client with generalized anxiety disorder:

> Together we will collect information about how the anxiety comes up and inter-feres with your life. We can think of the anxiety as an entity outside of yourself that kind of bosses you around and gives you a hard time. The anxiety will have some hypotheses about all of the horrible outcomes that could occur. One example that you told me about is the anxiety's prediction that you will do a horrible job on your project at work and embarrass yourself in front of your boss. Together we'll come up with some alternative possibilities to think about different outcomes that can occur and plan ways to confront situations. Then we'll test out the anxiety's theory that a horrible outcome in your job will occur.

One of the most important parts of collaborative empiricism is the impact on the therapeutic relationship. It sets up a mutually-generated treatment plan and helps to reinforce the idea that the patient and clinician will be working together as a team against the anxiety. This is also a useful message to convey to parents, spouses, or other support people in the patients life—that everyone will present as a unified front together against the anxiety that interferes with the patient's life.

The Nuts and Bolts of Treatment

Regarding the length and structure of sessions, let patients know how long your individual sessions will be, either 45-, 50-, or 60-minute sessions. At times, such as during exposure and ritual prevention treatment for OCD, clinicians may decide to conduct double sessions (90–120 minutes) to afford enough time to go out and do exposures. Regarding the length of the treatment, CBT is a relatively short-term treatment and the average number of therapy sessions for a full course of treatment is around 16–20. While it is helpful and important for patients to know that the treatment approach is very active and short-term (particularly compared to other types of therapies), it is also a good idea to communicate that it is flexible. Unless you work in a setting that dictates the total number of sessions (usually in the context of research studies), you probably have some flexibility in the number of sessions you provide. Some patients are more long-term cases based on the severity of their presenting issues, comorbidity of disorders, motivational issues, family dynamics that need to be addressed in treatment, and other factors that complicate the process. The rule of thumb is that as long as the patient is making progress, while their progress may be slower than other patients, the length of treatment can be flexible to meet their needs.

Another aspect of the process of treatment is the fact that it is a present-focused and problem-focused approach. Treatments for anxiety are highly focused on getting rid of the anxiety in the present time, not on exploring why the anxiety exists in the first place. The treatment will be focused on reducing the problematic anxiety in the here and now.

The role of homework is an integral part of the treatment. One of the reasons that CBT for anxiety disorders is so effective as a short-term treatment is that it is very active and the patient does a good deal of work between the sessions. Imagine how slowly changes would occur if the patient relied on one hour per week to make the changes. On the other hand, imagine how much more effective and efficient treatment is when the patient works for an hour every day on overcoming anxiety.

The Treatment Itself

In Chapter 4, two diagrams were presented. One showed the vicious cycle of anxiety and one showed how CBT can be used to chip away at this cycle. This second diagram serves as the framework for introducing the core CBT techniques and how each will help the patient to feel less anxious and function better.

In Chapter 2, the core CBT techniques were introduced. In this chapter, we provide samples of how to introduce each technique to patients during psychoeducation.

Cognitive Restructuring

As you can see from the model we drew, thoughts can maintain anxiety. Every time you see a pigeon, you think:

Pigeons always land on people's heads.

I am sure it will happen to me.

It will be terrible.

I won't be able to cope.

These thoughts cause you to feel anxious and they also impact your behavior. They prevent you from doing things that you want to do—from simple things like eating a snack on the way to class all the way to visiting your family in Italy. The process of cognitive restructuring involves becoming more aware of what you are thinking, examining the thought to see if it is rational or irrational, and—if it is irrational—helping you to consider different ways of viewing the situation. Looking at situations in different ways can affect how you feel (e.g., it can help you feel less anxious) and how you behave (e.g., it can make it easier to do the things that you currently avoid).

Exposure

Your model suggests that two major things are maintaining your anxiety—your thoughts and your behaviors. We just talked about how cognitive restructuring can help you to think in more rational ways. This can then have an effect on your behavior. If you have more rational thoughts about pigeons, it will be easier to be in situations where you might encounter pigeons. Another way to make it easier to be around pigeons is through exposure, another core CBT technique.

Exposure involves confronting the very situations that cause you anxiety and distress. There are two goals of doing exposures. First, with repeated exposure, anxiety habituates. In other words, the more that a person confronts a feared situation, the less anxiety that situation causes. Related to this, as you repeatedly confront your feared situations, you will learn that your feared outcomes are much less likely to occur than you think. Furthermore, if your feared outcome does occur (which is usually very unlikely), you will learn that you can manage that situation.

Together, we can do all sorts of exposures in our sessions. We can visit some pigeons in a lab here at the University. We can go to all the places in the city that you avoid because you fear confronting pigeons. And, we can work on dropping the more subtle avoidance behaviors like covering your head when you are around pigeons. We will see that pigeons aren't as scary as you think and that you don't have to do anything special to prevent your feared outcomes from occurring.

Exposure sounds really scary. But, here are a few things to keep in mind. First, we will do exposures gradually starting with the easiest things first and moving up to the most difficult. As you complete easier exposures, your confidence in being able to manage more difficult exposures often increases. Since you have seen anxiety habituate many times and have shown yourself that your feared outcomes are unlikely to occur, those "scariest" exposures often aren't that scary by the time we get to them in treatment.

Furthermore, in treatment you will be learning skills to deal with anxiety that you don't have right now. You will be learning how to challenge anxious thoughts and think in a more rational way. You will also be learning how to identify avoidance behaviors and get rid of them! Remember, that while avoidance helps in the short-term, it maintains anxiety in the long-term. Patients often find it a huge relief to see that they can confront feared situations without having to resort to avoidance behaviors—and that their feared outcomes still don't occur!

Homework

An important part of CBT is homework. Homework sounds like a drag, but it will probably be much more rewarding than the homework that you had to do when you were in school! Homework might include monitoring thoughts and/or behaviors, doing cognitive restructuring exercises, doing exposures, or practicing other techniques you have learned in session.

There are a lot of reasons why homework is so important to our work together. Homework allows you to practice your new skills in the "real world." This means being able to deal with thoughts when they are "hot" (e.g., right when they are happening) and confronting feared situations as they naturally occur. Engaging in exposures in the "real world" will show you that you have learned valuable skills in therapy and that you can cope with feared stimuli without a clinician. The most important reason for doing homework is that practice makes perfect: the more you practice your new skills, the more ingrained they will become.

Other CBT Techniques

Depending on the patient's specific problems, the clinician might also introduce other CBT techniques and demonstrate how they will be used to chip away at the anxiety cycle. These are covered in Chapter 9 and include assertiveness and communication skills training, problem solving, and relaxation.

Inspiring Hope with Success Stories

While psychoeducation is primarily about teaching, clinicians can also spend some time inspiring motivation during this part of treatment. When patients drop out of therapy, it is often because they are not hopeful and optimistic that it will help them. They see the treatment as a difficult one, which it can be, and do not feel confident that they will be able to reduce their anxiety even if they do the tough treatment.

We recommend helping the patient to become hopeful at the beginning of treatment and to stay motivated throughout the process. There are several ways to do this. The first is by normalizing their experiences. The second is through client success stories. The third is by presenting relevant research data.

When clinicians show the patient that they understand what the patient is going through because they have treated patients with similar issues in the past, the patient is likely to think, "Wow, others have these same types of fears—I'm not alone with this weird thing ..." And when the clinician provides some success stories to show how their patients have triumphed over their fears, the patient is likely to think, "This therapist helped others like me and can help me too!"

It is best if clinicians are able to come up with some success stories based on their own patients because then it will show new patients that *they* are capable of helping patients and it will build their credibility. Of course, it is critical to maintain confidentiality and not give away any identifying information about past patients. But, it is fine to discuss, in a very general way, their anxiety disorder and the course of their treatment.

Discussing success stories is a time when a clinician should not be too modest—it is important to inspire confidence in the patient and help her to think that she is in the right place to work on her anxiety issues. If a clinician does not yet have success stories of his/her own, those of other therapists can be used. Because it is best to have a motivational story to match each patient's presenting issue, any one clinician will not have stories for all patients. This is another reason to rely on stories of colleagues, and it highlights one of the many benefits of supervision groups and collaboration with other clinicians, even for clinicians who are already licensed and in their own practice.

How to Provide Psychoeducation

As with most forms of communication, the process of educating patients rests not only on what is said, but often more importantly, on how it is said. This beginning stage of treatment is crucial in establishing rapport and a working relationship with the patient. The creation of trust in the therapeutic relationship is critical in helping the patient to confront the situations that she is fearful of and in helping her to take the therapist's recommendations and suggestions. There is a myth that cognitive behavioral therapy is not about the therapeutic relationship but more about the clinician telling the patient what to do. This is simply not true. To make CBT for anxiety disorders most effective, a trusting working relationship between the therapist and patient is vital.

Interactive Discussion

Psychoeducation actually serves as a means of establishing strong rapport right from the start of treatment. While clinicians want to establish expertise and experience in treating anxiety disorders and be sure to teach a new patient valuable information, remember that the patient is the expert on her own life. She is the one who truly knows how her anxiety manifests and impacts her.

People learn best when the education is interactive. Nobody wants to be lectured at, especially a new patient who does not know what to expect from the therapist and the treatment. They are better able to process information and draw their own conclusions when they are spoken *with* rather than spoken *to*. When patients feel that their voices and thoughts are heard and don't feel that the clinician lectures them, an optimal rapport and treatment relationship results.

Socratic Questioning

One way to make psychoeducation interactive is by using Socratic questioning. Clinicians who effectively use this skill ask a series of questions to help patients understand concepts, search for answers within themselves, and process information so it is best remembered. For example, say the clinician wants to learn more about how the patient behaves in social situations, like attending parties. After having worked with many patients with the same difficulties, the clinician could say, "You must not talk much when you go to parties." But, the discussion will be much more effective and interactive if the clinician says: "What do you do when you attend parties to help reduce your anxiety?" This will allow the patient to identify her own subtle avoidance strategies like talking minimally, only talking to people she knows well, or having a few drinks.

The Socratic questioning process helps the patient feel that he is in charge of his own treatment and draw his own conclusions. It is never beneficial for the patient to feel as though the treatment is being conducted on them, rather it is best when they feel that they are taking an active part and are in control of the treatment process. We will discuss this idea in more detail when we get into the way to frame exposures, but it is useful to incorporate into the early psychoeducation phase as well.

Empathy, Active Listening, and Positive Regard

Clinicians should remember that the patient will learn a great deal of new information during the psychoeducation part of treatment. A lot of this information is completely contrary to everything the patient has done thus far to manage her anxiety. Clinicians should pay close attention to how patients are processing the discussion by actively listening to what patients say and trying to read between the lines or directly ask to see whether they have concerns or questions about the treatment.

Empathy and positive regard are integral parts of therapy for anxiety disorders. Patients will often show resistance and at times unwillingness to take in the psychoeducational material. Or they may become more anxious as they learn that the treatment requires them to confront the things they have been avoiding. When clinicians are able to have empathy and positive regard for the patient, they see that the "resistance" is not driven by stubbornness or obstinacy; rather it is driven by fear that is the very reason that they presented for treatment. Showing the patient empathic understanding by reflecting back their feelings can go a long way in establishing rapport and laying the groundwork for a strong working alliance.

Pacing

The other consideration is how quickly clinicians should move through psychoeducational material. Some patients will pick up on the ideas and metaphors right away. Other patients may let their clinicians know that they aren't quite getting it by their verbal or nonverbal responses. Clinicians should be aware that patients may act as though they are on the same page as the clinician but in reality they are not fully understanding the material. They may be too shy or nervous to request additional explanation.

When clinicians move too quickly with anxious patients, they are likely to become more anxious and may become scared off from returning for treatment. While CBT is traditionally action-oriented and time-limited (for example, in many treatment protocols there is only one session allotted for education), clinicians must consider the patient's pace and tailor psychoeducation accordingly.

One strategy is to check in with the patient directly. Clinicians can say, "I know we are covering a ton of material and some people feel overwhelmed by getting all this information, so I wanted to check in and see how you're doing."

A Delicate Balance

An issue that often arises in treating patients with anxiety disorders is: Where does psychoeducation end and reassurance begin? Reassurance-seeking is a ritual or safety behavior that frequently arises with anxious patients. The patient feels nervous so he feels compelled to ask for reassurance to feel better. As with any ritual or safety behavior, reassurance-seeking needs to be eliminated in order to break the cycle of anxiety and avoidance.

Most of the feared beliefs that are held by anxious patients are unrealistic or highly unlikely to occur. Because of this, it is often useful to do some psychoeducation about the situation that they are concerned about before going into exposures. If, for example, a patient is afraid of contracting HIV or AIDS, and has been avoiding public restrooms and kissing people who she dates, it is helpful for her to learn about how HIV is truly transmitted. Sometimes this education is enough to alleviate the patient's concerns, but this is not typically the case.

Clinicians often find that patients come into treatment having thoroughly educated themselves as a means of seeking reassurance. Patients have spent hours on Google reading about their fear in hopes of learning that it won't come true. Since these are ritualistic behaviors, it is unlikely that they did anything to alleviate their anxiety and in fact, it is likely that these behaviors are partially responsible for the patient's anxiety increasing.

Clinicians must realize that there is a difference between educating patients about the things they are afraid of (for example, providing a patient with information on the likelihood of getting mad cow disease from eating meat), versus providing undue reassurance. The last thing that clinicians should do is feed into anxiety by providing reassurance. In general, it can be a good idea to begin treatment by gathering accurate information on the topic at hand and then agreeing that the patient now knows the facts and does not need to ask for further reassurance from the therapist or anyone else.

When patients ask for reassurance, clinicians are faced with the decision of how to respond. Here is a brief checklist of questions for clinicians to ask themselves to determine the appropriate response:

1. Does the patient already know the answer to this question?

2. Would providing the answer be giving a reassurance and serving to push down anxiety?

3. Has the patient asked you or others the question before?

4. Is the question one that really cannot be answered (i.e., the patient is looking for a guarantee on something about which there is no guarantee)?

5. Is the patient avoiding something or using the question as a distraction from anxiety?

Clinicians often need to suppress their natural responses to avoid giving reassurance to the patient when he asks a question that is in fact a ritual. Dr. Kase had a patient whose ritual was to apologize. At the beginning of treatment, she would apologize every few minutes. Dr. Kase's natural response to hearing someone say, "I'm sorry" was to say, "It's okay" or "Don't worry about it." She had to train herself to say, "That sounds like a ritual" and not respond to the apology.

In deciding whether to educate a patient or not, clinicians should consider the previous questions and be wary of being pulled into a ritual by the patient's anxiety. Ideally, clinicians help patients to be their own therapists and realize when they need to know something or when it is an anxiety-fueled ritual. Then the clinician can say, "Do you think I should answer that?" and the patient will respond, "No, probably not."

References

Craske, M. G., & Barlow, D. H. (2001). Panic Disorder and Agoraphobia. In D. H. Barlow (Ed.), *Clinical handbook of psychological disorders, third edition*. New York: Guilford.

Kozak, M. H., & Foa, E. B. (1997). *Mastery of obsessive compulsive disorder: A cognitive behavioral approach-treatment guide*. San Antonio: The Psychological Corporation.

Rachman, S., & deSilva, P. (1978). Abnormal and normal obsessions. *Behavioural Research and Therapy, 16*, 233–248.

CHAPTER 6

Cognitive Tools

Cognitive Therapy and Anxiety Disorders

As discussed in the previous chapter, fear itself is an adaptive response to a threatening situation. It helps people prepare themselves for the worst and best manage a difficult or dangerous scenario. If someone were afraid, for example, because a hurricane warning was issued for her town, her fear would be helpful because it would motivate her to quickly pack up and evacuate. With no fear or anxiety, she would dismiss the warning and evacuation plan as "no big deal" and would take her time getting out, or she would just stay put, thereby potentially putting herself in real danger.

The problem with pathological anxiety is that patients misinterpret threat. They see threat that is not really there. Patients overestimate the likelihood of a catastrophic outcome and, if that outcome were to in fact occur, they overestimate the potential cost of it and underestimate their ability to cope with it. These are some of the ways that thought patterns become distorted by clinical anxiety.

Cognitive therapy helps patients to recognize distorted thoughts and understand how they contribute to the maintenance of their anxiety disorder. Cognitive therapy also helps patients to evaluate situations differently and draw more accurate, less anxiety-driven conclusions.

When to Use Cognitive Tools

There are a number of contexts in which cognitive tools are beneficial. These are described below:

When Patients Distort Reality

Dr. Aaron Beck describes cognitive interventions as effective for patients whose thought processes show distortions in reality (Beck, 1976). A patient with social anxiety, for example, may think, "*Everyone* thinks I'm awkward," or "*Nobody* wants to speak with me." These thought processes are not realistic reflections of reality. It is virtually impossible that everyone in the world thinks that the patient is awkward and has no interest in speaking with him. Cognitive interventions can help a patient create a more realistic appraisal of their current reality.

When Patients Have Illogical Thinking

Cognitive therapy also works well to address illogical thought patterns that many anxious patients possess. Beck states that faulty logic may lie in the incorrect premises by which patients draw conclusions about situations (Beck, 1976). Remember that we noted in Chapter 5 that it is not *situations* that cause anxiety, but rather our *interpretations* of them.

Someone with a phobia of dogs, may think, "If I go near dogs, they will bite me." In this case, the premise may be an inaccurate one, such as "all dogs are dangerous." On the other hand, perhaps this patient has accurate premises, such as "some dogs are dangerous," and a "dog bit me in the past," but draws a faulty conclusion: "Dogs are sure to bite *me* now so I should avoid them."

When Patients Have Low Self Efficacy

The use of cognitive tools at the beginning of treatment can help the patient build confidence. Cognitive interventions can help the patient to look differently at his anxiety and gain a sense of understanding and control over it. At times, patients start to view anxiety in such a different way that they do not need to do exposures.

For example, a patient with Panic Disorder had the mistaken belief that the symptoms of panic were dangerous—she believed that they would make her go crazy or have a heart attack. When the patient had panic attacks, she misinterpreted the physical sensations she noticed; she then became nervous and noticed more physical sensations; she then focused on the symptoms, and had a catastrophic thought ("I'm having a heart attack!") which led to more physical sensations. This was a vicious cycle fueled by the patient's interpretations. If, through cognitive therapy, she realized that the symptoms are just regular bodily sensations that are harmless and temporary, she would be unlikely to continue having panic attacks. With a new set of interpretations, the cycle would no longer be fueled. The patient would be able to interpret the panic attack as harmless and would not fear having another one, thus no longer qualifying as having Panic Disorder.

Cognitive interventions are usually most effective when combined with in vivo and/or imaginal exposures. Because they can help to build self-efficacy and a sense of mastery and control over the anxiety, they work well to prepare the patient for exposures. For some patients it is difficult or even inconceivable to launch right into exposures. Cognitive tools can help them to see that they can in fact manage their anxiety when they begin to approach it differently. They are then more motivated to pursue the exposures.

This approach can work very well with children. Clinicians working with young patients often like to begin treatment with cognitive interventions to help them understand and feel in charge of their worries. As we describe in more detail in Chapter 12, patients can learn how to externalize their worry or anxiety and give it a name, like "worry bug," "OCD man," "anxiety monster," or "worry brain." This treatment can focus on helping the child to realize how the anxiety is often wrong. The child can then feel empowered and ready to really prove the "worry bug" wrong by doing exposures.

When Processing Exposures

Cognitive interventions can also be used during and after an exposure as a way of processing the exposure and drawing new conclusions from it. As we will discuss in Chapter 7, simply doing an exposure does not necessarily result in learning. Exposures work best when patients make predictions about what will happen during the exposure, and then evaluate these predictions once the exposure is completed. By framing exposures with cognitive tools at the front and the back end, clinicians can ensure that exposures facilitate the disconfirmation of faulty beliefs.

A Caution About Reassurance

Cognitive tools are useful for most patients with anxiety disorders. One caveat is that for some patients, the conclusions reached from cognitive restructuring can come to serve as reassurance. Some patients are more prone to this than others. People with obsessive-compulsive disorder, for example, frequently use cognitive restructuring or calming self-talk as a reassurance. They tell themselves, "that won't happen," or "my fear is unlikely to come true." In effect, these thoughts become mental rituals, enabling the patient to endure exposures. However, the mental rituals block the effectiveness of the exposure.

In Chapter 1, we introduced the case of Phillip, a very compliant patient. After a few sessions of psychoeducation, he willingly did all sorts of exposures from touching old books in the library, to walking by street people, to cleaning the kitchen floor with bleach. He was not engaging in any overt rituals, like hand washing, holding his breath, or spitting out germs. As part of a clinical study that he participated in, he underwent an assessment partway through treatment. To the great surprise of his clinician, his symptoms had barely budged. At the next treatment session, his clinician (who had not done the midtreatment assessment) tried to uncover this mystery. It turned out that Phillip was doing a mental ritual during *every* exposure. He was saying to himself: "Well Dr. Ledley is doing the exposure, so it must be safe." This little cognitive trick was preventing Phillip from getting well. From thereon in, Phillip was asked to do all of the exposures by himself (without modeling from his therapist) while his therapist constantly reminded him to discontinue any mental rituals he might be engaging in. It was only at this point that Phillip's OCD symptoms began to remit.

To summarize, cognitive tools must be used with caution with OCD because they can quickly feed into the OCD and function as mental rituals. This same process can occur with the other anxiety disorders as well. One of the main problems is that the patient learns to subtly avoid her fear and does not allow herself to completely activate the fear structure and experience habituation (Foa & Kozak, 1986). As with any other safety behaviors, the patient could attribute her ability to handle the situation to the mental reassurances rather than to the fact that she could handle it regardless.

Cognitive Tools

Many effective cognitive tools and techniques can be used with anxious patients. The way in which the clinician decides to integrate them into treatment will depend on the factors discussed previously and the clinician's judgment regarding when to use cognitive tools versus a behavioral intervention. Recall that behavioral interventions utilize cognitive tools since they are designed to challenge assumptions and unhelpful thought processes. The results and goals, therefore, are frequently similar: to replace the patient's maladaptive predictions and fears with more realistic and likely appraisals of the situation.

Thought Records

The first step in conducting cognitive therapy with a patient is to gather information about the thoughts that are currently present and contributing to the patient's anxiety. Self-monitoring is used to help patients become aware of their thoughts and notice when they are most likely to occur. Many anxiety-fueled cognitions are automatic thoughts of which patients are not aware. Self-monitoring helps clinicians to see the functional role of cognitions in the maintenance of the patient's anxiety disorder. Self-monitoring also helps track changes in thought processes over time.

The most frequently used self-monitoring tool is the Daily Thought Record (DTR). The DTR includes the date, the situation, the automatic thought that went through the patient's mind, the physiological sensations, and the consequences of the situation. Each of these variables can be listed as a heading for columns, and in the rows, the patient can record the time of day and the information to complete each column. The consequences category addresses what the patient did to handle the situation or anxiety. It is the patient's response to any of the other categories (situation at hand, thoughts, and physical sensations).

Clinicians assign completion of a DTR to patients for homework and then review the data collected in the next session. Ideally, patients will complete a DTR each day and record all of the thoughts related to their anxiety. For instance, if you meet with patients once weekly, they would come into the next session with seven thought records, each containing somewhere between two and ten thoughts per day.

It is important to review the DTR with the patient in session. It will show that the clinician places a high degree of importance on self-monitoring and on homework completion in general. Clinicians will also be able to glean additional information from the self-monitoring when it is discussed with their patients.

Cognitive Restructuring

Once the patient and clinician have some examples of how anxiety-fueled thoughts arise and the nature of those thoughts, the clinician can begin the process of cognitive restructuring (CR) with the patient. As we discussed in Chapter 2, cognitive restructuring is a four-part process: (1) identifying the anxious thought, (2) labeling the thought, (3) questioning the thought and considering whether there is a different way to view the situation, and (4) coming up with a more rational and adaptive way of viewing the situation.

CR is carried out collaboratively between the clinician and the patient. The patient reports a thought that he is having and the thought is then looked at as a hypothesis to test out. The job of the CB therapist is *not* to convince patients that their thoughts are "wrong." Rather, CBT therapists take a very neutral stance toward thoughts and help the patient to explore their veracity. Patients learn that their cognitions may or may not be accurate reflections of reality. They discover how to look for objective criteria by which to evaluate thoughts. Thus, patients learn how to recognize their initial thought, and then gather alternative explanations. The outcome of this process is to create a more realistic appraisal of the situation and to come up with some strategies to deal with the feared situation if it were to occur.

At the point in treatment when patients begin actively restructuring their thoughts, a new form for self-monitoring homework should be used. The patient is now ready to begin actively challenging the thought processes and looking for ways to counter their negative thoughts, rather than simply monitoring what occurs. The new form might include as columns (Barlow, 1993):

- Trigger or situation
- Automatic thought
- Anxiety rating (for example, from 0–8)
- Probability that the thought is accurate (0–100%)
- Countering examples–Evidence against the thought and alternative explanations
- Realistic probability after considering the alternative evidence

Patients and clinicians can design some variant on this form depending on the patient's unique presentation and concerns.

As we noted above, CR is a four-step process. The first step is identifying thoughts. Some patients have easy access to their anxious thoughts. They are readily able to report what they are thinking in anticipation of, or during, anxiety-provoking situations. Other patients find this more difficult. Therapists can help patients to identify anxious thoughts by asking, "What were you thinking when that happened?" "What was racing through your head?" or "What did you think would happen?" For patients who have a very hard time reporting what they were thinking in a given situation, self-monitoring homework can be given so that patients can "grab" the thought and write it down as it is happening.

After thoughts are identified, they should be labeled. In effect, labeling thoughts describes what is "wrong" with the thought. There are many different kinds of cognitive distortions or misattributions that occur with anxiety disorders; these are described below.

Counter Probability Overestimation
Probability Overestimation

Probability overestimation is a type of cognitive distortion that frequently occurs in patients with anxiety disorders. It means that patients overestimate the likelihood that a negative outcome will occur. A person without anxiety would agree that the feared outcome would be a difficult thing if it were to occur, but would recognize that it is highly unlikely to occur. A patient with an anxiety disorder, on the other hand, would not realize that the feared outcome is highly unlikely to occur.

The problem with probability overestimation is that it impacts functioning. When patients are *so* convinced that something bad is going to happen, they begin to avoid all sorts of things. In the case example of Susan, the 30-year old mother with Panic Disorder and Agoraphobia, Susan predicted an 80 percent likelihood that she would "go crazy" and end up schizophrenic like her brother if she had a panic attack. As a result, she went to such lengths to avoid panic attacks that she became virtually housebound.

Once patients have labeled a thought, they need to begin to challenge it. This is step three of the cognitive restructuring process. The clinician working with Susan helped her come up with some countering examples to her fear that she would go crazy and become psychotic if she had a panic attack. The clinician introduced this exercise by saying to Susan, "That is one possibility. What are some other possibilities?" Together, the clinician and Susan came up with some alternative explanations:

1. I might not have a panic attack at all.

2. I might have a panic attack but not go crazy.

3. I might have a panic attack and temporarily feel unreal and out of it, but these feelings won't last forever.

These potential alternatives can be further challenged. Patients can ask themselves, "What's the evidence?" or "What has happened in this same situation before?" In further examining the evidence for Susan's concern that panic would lead her to be psychotic, she and her clinician calculated how many panic attacks she had experienced in her life. They calculated that she had experienced an average of one attack per day over the past six months, but two per day over the past month. This equaled around 210 panic attacks—a lot of panic attacks!

Using this information, the followed dialog ensued:

Clinician: How many times has it actually happened that you went crazy and needed to be hospitalized for becoming psychotic?

Susan: None.

Clinician: So that is a zero percent probability that your fear has come true based on your past experience, right?

Susan: Yes.

Clinician: Earlier you said that it is about 80 percent likely that your fear would occur if you had a panic attack. What do you think it is now?

Susan: Well, now I'd say that it's around 20 percent likely.

Clinician: How does that fit with what happened in the past?

Susan: I know.... I have never gone crazy and psychotic from panic. But, I still *feel* like it could happen.

At this point, the clinician could use continuing cognitive techniques to challenge the patient's beliefs. She could point out the discrepancy between reality (that Susan has never become psychotic) and Susan's prediction (that there is still a 20 percent chance that she could become psychotic). Or, the clinician could end the cognitive work right there and use Susan's prediction for exposures. Cognitive restructuring allowed Susan to concede that the chance of her becoming psychotic was much less than she originally thought. This allowed her to be able to do some exposures she was previously unwilling to do. She then embarked on exposures with the prediction that there was a 20 percent chance she would become psychotic—a very easy prediction to evaluate (and disprove!) through exposure.

Step four of CR involves coming up with a more rational and adaptive way of viewing the situation. At the end of their discussion, Susan's therapist asked her, "What did you learn?" Susan replied, "Panic doesn't equal psychosis." This brief "mantra" was a fabulous tool for Susan to carry with her. She reminded herself of this when she felt panic symptoms coming on. Often, just thinking this thought made the symptoms recede before a full-blown attack occurred. Susan also used the thought to motivate her to do tricky exposures.

Reduce the Catastrophic Expectations and Perceived Costs
In addition to probability overestimation, another common cognitive misconception with anxiety disorders is *magnified perceived cost*. Patients overestimate the catastrophic nature of their feared outcome and underestimate their ability to cope. They believe that the cost (or horrible response) is much worse than it probably would be.

Jeff, the 27-year-old law student with Social Phobia, feared saying the wrong thing or making mistakes when called on in class. He thought that if he were to say something incorrect or embarrassing, the outcome would be absolutely disastrous. He believed it would be a horrible reflection on his credibility that would follow him around for life—something he could never live down. In reality, people would probably quickly forget his verbal blunder and it would not tarnish his reputation or career.

One way to address Jeff's catastrophic views is with imaginal exposures, which are covered in detail in Chapter 8. Another method is through in vivo exposures, discussed in detail in the next chapter. A third method is through cognitive restructuring to help Jeff to see that the cost of his feared consequence is probably much less than he predicts.

Probability overestimation and *catastrophizing* often go hand in hand. Catastrophizing typically results from probability overestimation combined with an underestimation of the patient's ability to cope with the feared outcome. The clinician who treated Jeff used cognitive restructuring to tackle his probability overestimation by asking him how likely it truly was that he would say something ridiculous in class. Jeff was asked how many times this had actually happened to him. He may have felt that he said something outrageous, but cognitive restructuring was used to help him see that he had no evidence of this happening at all.

Once Jeff realized how unlikely it was that he would say something ridiculous, the clinician asked two further questions: "If it did happen, would the consequence be as terrible as you imagine?" and "If it did happen, would you be able to handle it?" By answering these questions, Jeff was able to see that there were a number of possible outcomes to making a blunder. One possibility was that Jeff's original hypothesis was true and that he would never live down the negative reputation created by his verbal blunder. Another possibility was that many people would not even notice and the conversation would continue despite his comment. Or maybe people would notice and think it a bit odd, but forget about it within a few minutes. It was also possible that Jeff would say something very interesting and thought provoking after his initial comment and people would remember the interesting comment more than the silly comment. Maybe Jeff's comment was considered stupid only by him and others found it useful. Or perhaps people were busy thinking of what they were going to do that evening and were not even paying attention. At the end of this process, Jeff came up with a summary coping statement: "Blunders are rarely made and rarely horrible." As was the case for Susan, this statement helped Jeff to take more risks in his classes.

The goal of cognitive restructuring is for the patient to see that there are many alternative possibilities, most of which are not nearly as catastrophic as the patient initially believes. Remember that this process works best if the patient comes up with alternative explanations and reaches a new conclusion for himself. The clinician can assist with the process by posing Socratic questions and providing some ideas to get patients thinking.

Combat All-or-None Thinking

Probability overestimation and catastrophizing occur in most patients with anxiety disorders (see Bourne & Garano, 2003). Underlying these cognitive errors are all sorts of automatic thoughts. One of the most prevalent is *all-or-none thinking*. This kind of thinking error is easy for patients to recognize. When patients engage in all-or-none thinking they see the black or the white, but miss the shades of grey in the middle. This type of thinking can relate to the two types of cognitive distortions discussed previously. For example, a patient could overestimate the likelihood of a bad outcome occurring and think that it is either one hundred percent likely to occur or one hundred percent likely not to occur. The patient neglects to consider all of the possibilities in the middle—the negative outcome may in fact be only 10 or 20 percent likely to occur.

All-or-none thinking also arises with catastrophizing. A patient who worries about her ability to lead other people in her job thinks that either she will be completely calm and in control or she will be an incompetent mess. Combine this catastrophizing thought with probability overestimation and she feels that it is highly likely that she will be an incompetent mess and not be able to function as a leader whatsoever. She does not think about the fact that she may be slightly out of control or nervous momentarily but she could quickly regain composure and handle the work situation very well. The patient does not consider that it can even be a good thing to appear slightly flustered or concerned at work. Sometimes leaders actually gain respect when they show some trepidation and do not seem superficial. People often like those who appear real and show some emotion. But the patient does not think of all of these potential outcomes—because of probability overestimation, catastrophizing, and all-or-none thinking, the patient thinks it is highly likely that she will lose composure, that the results will be horrendous, and that only bad can come from the situation.

Clinicians can help patients overcome all-or-none thinking by helping them to see the grey areas. When patients realize that they are neglecting to consider all of the information on the range of possibilities, they can start to consider those in between pieces of information.

It can be helpful to draw a vertical line and place the all-or-none thoughts on the line. On one end of the line is the thought that the patient feels is zero percent likely to occur. At the other end is the thought the patient fears is one hundred percent likely to occur. The patient can then fill in points on the line to show some additional possibilities. This helps patients to see the shades of grey and that life rarely turns out to be as black or white as they predict.

A question to ask patients who show all-or-none thinking is, "What is the middle ground?" This helps them to see that there are additional possibilities and that often the middle ground is the most likely possibility. Ask the patient to try to put some percentages into the equation. If she says, "I feel like a failure," say, "What percent of you feels like a failure?" She responds, "Thirty percent." This means that seventy percent of her is not a failure.

Mind Reading and Fortune Telling

Another type of automatic thought common in patients with anxiety disorders is *mind reading*. Patients assume that they know what others are thinking and feeling. For example, Jeff, the socially anxious patient, was sitting in a small group in one of his classes one day. He was thinking about a comment he made that he felt was stupid. In his group was one of the brightest and most ambitious students in his class. "I know that she is disappointed that she got stuck in a group with me," he thought to himself. "She thinks that I'm going to bring our whole group down." A couple of great countering questions to this type of cognitive error are: "Do I know for sure that this is true?" or "What is the evidence?"

Fortune telling occurs when patients predict the future. Patients think that they have a crystal ball—and what they see inside is overwhelmingly negative. When she had panic attacks, Susan saw a grim future for herself. She saw herself in a tiny white room, with padded walls, in the local psychiatric hospital. She saw an image of herself as "out of it" and "crazy" and could easily conjure up the terrible pain of being separated from her family. Some great countering questions to this type of cognitive error are: "Do I have a crystal ball?" "Can I see into the future?" or "How do I know that this is going to happen?"

Sometimes, patients say that they *know* something is going to happen because they *feel* like it is true. In these situations, the clinician can discuss *emotional reasoning* with the patient. Emotional reasoning involves drawing conclusions based on one's feelings rather than the facts. Clinicians can help patients to look at the objective data and draw appropriate conclusions. Jeff might have *felt* like the woman in his group was disappointed to have to work with him, but through cognitive restructuring, he realized that he had no concrete evidence to support this feeling.

Overgeneralizing

A final type of automatic thought common to many patients with anxiety disorders is *overgeneralization*. Patients draw a conclusion based on one piece of evidence. A patient remembers one negative experience and generalizes it to all similar situations. For example, if a patient lost her train of thought and could not articulate an idea in a meeting, she feels she should never speak up in meetings again. A patient who vomited on a bus thinks that buses will always make him vomit. The future is clouded by one negative event from the past. A great countering question to this type of cognitive error is: "What is the evidence?" This question cues patients to remember all of the times that they spoke up in a meeting and got their point across, or took a bus and did not vomit.

Another intervention is to help patients simply accept that they do not know what will happen in the future. They might have vomited on the bus once and it is unlikely that it will happen again based on the fact that they rode the bus for years previously without vomiting. It is, however, impossible to be sure that it will never happen again. Clinicians can help patients get away from all-or-nothing words like "never," "definitely," or "always" and accept the range of possibilities that can occur.

Being One's Own Therapist

One of the possible reasons for why CBT is associated with good long-term outcomes once treatment is over is that patients learn to be their own therapists. They learn how to challenge their anxious thoughts, just as a therapist would. At the end of treatment, patients should be very comfortable with the cognitive restructuring process. Once patients identify and label a cognitive error, they should get into the habit of asking themselves a few questions.

First, they should ask themselves, "*What is the evidence?*" Jeff believed that his classmate was unhappy to have him in her group because she had a dissatisfied expression on her face. Patients can then ask themselves, "*Is there another way to view this situation?*" Jeff could certainly just accept that his classmate was unhappy to have been paired with him, but he also created a list of other possibilities, including:

- She did not like the project that was assigned.
- It was after lunch and she may have eaten something that disagreed with her.
- Her general facial expression is unhappy because her mouth slopes downward.
- She was unhappy that her ex-boyfriend was also in the group.
- She was tired and unmotivated to work on another project.
- She is anxious before all projects because she puts pressure on herself to be at the top of the class.

By generating a number of alternatives, Jeff saw that there were different interpretations to a single situation and he started to think that his original interpretation was less likely than he first believed.

Patients should then ask themselves, "*What would happen if X really occurred?*" Jeff asked himself what would happen if his classmate really was unhappy to have him in her group. He realized that she would still work hard, since she cared about her grades and that the project would likely turn out quite well. He recognized that the consequences were not nearly as dire as he originally thought.

Finally, patients should ask themselves, "*What did I learn?*" Based on the entire process of cognitive restructuring, they should come up with a mantra that summarizes everything they have learned and the conclusions they have drawn. Jeff came up with the summary: "I am not a mind reader." Jeff reminded himself of this prior to group meetings and felt calmer and more engaged while working on the assignment.

Cheerleading and Reinforcement

As patients learn to be their own cognitive therapists and change their self-talk, they can utilize reinforcement to further help themselves. Patients can learn to use reinforcement for cognitive restructuring and their constructive self-talk. They can do so by cheerleading for themselves and recognizing a job well done.

Patients can also take note of how their changes in cognitions lead to changes in their lives and goal attainment. During treatment, Jeff kept a journal in which he noted how changes in his self-talk led to positive changes in his behavior. When he realized that the woman in his group project was unlikely to be upset that he was in her group, he gained confidence and decided to participate more actively in the group. As a result, he made some valuable contributions. One day, his classmate told him that she really valued working with him and thought his ideas were great.

Noticing the positive changes that occur as a result of modifying thought patterns reinforces the use of beneficial cognitive strategies. It also builds the patient's self esteem and self-efficacy. These changes will further motivate patients to confront their anxieties and complete in vivo exposures. The next chapter will describe how to create an in vivo exposure hierarchy and conduct exposures.

References

Barlow, D. H. (1993). *Clinical handbook of psychological disorders* (2nd ed.). New York: Guilford.

Beck, A. T. (1976). *Cognitive therapy and the emotional disorders.* New York: Penguin Books.

Bourne, E., & Garano, L. (2003). *Coping with anxiety: 10 simple ways to relieve anxiety, fear, and worry.* Oakland, CA: New Harbinger Publications.

Foa, E. B., & Kozak, M. J. (1986). Emotional processing of fear: Exposure to corrective information. *Psychological Bulletin, 99*(1), 20–35.

CHAPTER 7

In Vivo Exposure

Exposure is a component of virtually every cognitive behavioral treatment (CBT) protocol for anxiety disorders. In fact, some studies have suggested that exposure is the most important component of treatment (e.g., Hope, Heimberg, & Bruch, 1995). In vivo exposure refers to exposure that is done to real or live stimuli, in contrast to exposures that are done in imagination. In this chapter, the "how-to's" of in vivo exposure will be described.

Clinicians Must Be Ready

When Dr. Ledley was training to be a psychologist, she was assigned to a study examining treatment of spider phobias. In the study, patients were exposed to as many steps on a hierarchy of feared situations relevant to spider phobias that they could handle. Each step was first demonstrated by the therapist. While Dr. Ledley could easily hold a jar with a spider in it, and even touch a spider with the tip of a pencil (gently, of course!), she had to admit that having a spider crawl in her hand was not her idea of fun. However, in the interest of making a good impression on her boss, she knew that she had to get over her slight fear of spiders prior to confronting them with patients.

Dr. Ledley set herself up in a room with all of the materials for the study and she worked up the hierarchy gradually until she could do the top step, holding a spider in her hand, with no anxiety. It was important that she model good coping skills to the study participants. If she were frightened, no doubt they would be too. Her own fear would confirm their beliefs that spiders were dangerous and disgusting, making it very difficult to disconfirm these beliefs and help them get past their anxiety disorder.

Simply put, clinicians who do CBT must be able to do anything that they ask their patients to do. Furthermore, they must be able to do the exposures without outwardly showing fear or engaging in subtle avoidance strategies. This results in CBT clinicians having all sorts of bizarre therapy experiences. Our own favorites include eating snacks off dollar bills (for an OCD patient who needed to wash her hands extremely carefully after handling money); touching all sorts of chemical-laden products in a hardware store prior to feeding a patient's baby (the patient feared that her baby would get autism from chemical contamination); and visiting pigeons in a lab (yes, there really was a "Felicia"). We do not know a single colleague who has not stuck their hand in a toilet for the benefit of an OCD patient. One of our colleagues visited a snake cave with a patient who was terribly afraid of snakes. In addition, most of us have spent a lot of time in glass elevators, on subways, with dogs, and with other stimuli that provoke anxiety.

It is very normal that from time to time, a therapist must do something in the service of therapy that is difficult for them. There is no alternative but to get over the fear on one's own prior to treatment. It can sometimes be very helpful to share these experiences with patients. Dr. Ledley often shares the story about the spider study—not necessarily with patients who fear spiders, but with any other anxious patients to show that: (1) she can relate to their experiences, and (2) she knows firsthand that exposure works. Patients appreciate this honesty and vote of confidence for the treatment approach.

Explaining the Rationale for Exposure

Patients will not do exposures, particularly difficult ones, if they do not understand why they are being asked to do them. They must understand the rationale that underlies the treatment technique. Chapter 4 described how to share a case conceptualization and treatment plan with patients. To review, patients must understand two key points:

First, avoidance maintains fear. Avoidance prevents people from learning that their anxiety is manageable and that their feared outcomes are unlikely to occur.

Second, in order to stop feeling anxious about a given stimuli, patients must expose themselves to it. They must do exposures without relying on any subtle avoidance strategies. Rather, they must "lean into the anxiety" and fully experience it. Only in this way will patients learn that their anxiety will decrease on its own over time, that they can manage feeling anxious for as long as it lasts, and that their feared outcomes are unlikely to occur. Through exposure, patients will experience a shift in their beliefs. As they see that their fears are ungrounded in reality, their beliefs about the feared stimuli will change. This does not mean that a patient who fears snakes has to develop a love for snakes. He just needs to feel neutral toward them, rather than fearful.

The Hierarchy of Feared Situations

As we discussed in Chapter 4, treatment cannot proceed without a road map. Embedded within the larger treatment plan is a plan for exposures. Specifically, exposures should be completed according to a hierarchy. The hierarchy lists all of the situations that patients will work on during treatment, arranged in rank order from least to most fearful.

Prior to constructing a hierarchy, patients need to be taught a metric for assigning fear ratings to their anxiety triggers. This metric is called the Subjective Units of Discomfort Scale, or SUDS. The range of the scale can be from 0–10 or from 0–100 depending on the preference of the therapist. A scale of 0–10 is typically used with children. The scale is useful for a number of reasons. Mainly, it allows anxiety triggers to be rank ordered. If a patient assigns a rating of 60 to "speaking with a new person at a party," the clinician can then ask for the next item, "Is making a speech at a wedding easier or harder than speaking to a new person at a party?" When patients come to treatment, they feel scared of many situations and too overwhelmed to start working on any fears. Assigning each situation a rating shows patients that some situations are indeed easier than others and gives them a reasonable place to start.

The other advantage of the SUDS ratings is that they serve as an excellent metric for change. It can be very helpful midway through treatment and at the end of treatment to go through the hierarchy and reassign SUDS ratings to each item (without first looking at the original ratings). Patients will see that their SUDS have decreased for the items that they have done many exposures to, reinforcing their confidence in the treatment approach.

What Makes a Good Hierarchy?

There are many ingredients for a good hierarchy. There are no set rules on how many items a hierarchy has, but somewhere between 10 and 20 items is probably ideal. These items should represent a nice range of SUDS ratings. The lowest items on the hierarchy should be those in the middle range (e.g., a 5 on a 0–10 scale or a 50 on a 0–100 scale). Items lower than these are likely items that patients can already do exposure to without great distress. Middle-of-the-road items are great for first exposures because they provoke anxiety, but not so much anxiety that a patient has to escape the situation. There should then be a nice range of higher items (some 60s, 70s, 80s, 90s and a couple of 100s). If patients have only items in the 50s, it is possible that they are avoiding putting their most feared situations on the hierarchy. Patients must be encouraged to put all items on their hierarchies, regardless of how difficult the items seem. Clinicians can say, "I know that speaking in front of a group of 50 experts in your field *seems* impossible now, but I think we should put it on the hierarchy anyway. By the time you get to that item, you will have learned new ways of dealing with anxiety. You also would have tackled all of the items lower on the hierarchy. How might these experiences affect this most frightening exposure?" The idea is to have patients articulate that as they tackle each exposure they will gradually come to see that anxiety is manageable and that their most feared outcomes are unlikely to occur.

Conversely, some patients rank every item on their hierarchy as a 100 SUDS. These patients have difficulty seeing variability from item to item—every one just seems terrible! Therapists must take the time to help patients see that there likely is variability. They can ask patients, "Of all of these items, which do you think you could do first?" and "Of all of these items, which do you think would be the absolute hardest?" This might give a starting point for the lowest and highest items, opening a discussion of where the other items fit between these two poles.

A good hierarchy must also have sufficient detail. The item, "Having a conversation" is terribly broad. Is it harder to have conversations with strangers or people the patient knows well? With men or women? One-on-one or in groups? These questions are essential to constructing a good hierarchy since they likely have very different SUDS ratings. Articulating these subtle differences ensures that the treatment will progress gradually from least to most feared situations.

SUDS ratings should be made if the patient will do exposures *without using subtle avoidance strategies*. For example, when a patient with OCD assigns SUDS ratings to items involving contamination, they should assume that they will not wash their hands when they are done with the exposure. This is important since anxious patients will do all sorts of things if they know they can rely on their avoidance behaviors, safety behaviors, or rituals. A patient with OCD might touch the door handles in a hospital so long as she can use her sleeve to cover her hands and then thoroughly wash her hands when she gets home. SUDS ratings must be based on the assumption that the patient will touch the door handles with her bare hands and not wash afterwards.

Finally, hierarchy items must be relevant to the patient. Many patients with Social Phobia fear public speaking, but it is not an essential hierarchy item for everyone. For some patients, this fear is completely irrelevant, never coming up in their daily lives. For others, it is crucially important to their work or for an upcoming social event (like making a toast at a wedding). CBT is time-limited and it is important to spend time wisely on situations that truly affect the patient's current and future functioning. Furthermore, patients will be more engaged with the treatment if they feel that the treatment plan is relevant to them. Quick tips for designing hierarchies are included in Table 7.1.

TABLE 7.1

Tips for Designing Hierarchies

- Include 10–20 items.
- Include items with a range of SUDS ratings from 50–100 (or 5–10 on a 10-point scale).
- Make sure items are sufficiently detailed to take into account subtle variations in situations (e.g., for a person with a phobia of dogs, include big dogs, small dogs, dogs on leashes, dogs running free, etc.).
- Ratings should be based on the assumption that subtle avoidance strategies/safety behaviors/rituals will not be used to decrease anxiety.
- Make sure all hierarchy items are important and relevant to the patient.

In Chapter 1, the case of Susan was introduced. Susan was a young mother with severe Panic Disorder and Agoraphobia. As you might recall, Susan had her first panic attack "out of the blue" when she was at home. She then had a panic attack at the supermarket. Over the next few months, Susan had panic attacks in more and more places, even at home. By the time she presented for treatment, she was totally housebound and unable to be at home alone. Figure 7.1 shows a sample hierarchy for Susan.

It can be very helpful to construct the hierarchy on a computer with the patient present. A table can be set up with one column for the exposure item and one for the SUDS rating. The advantage of this method is that the table can then be sorted according to SUDS ratings, so that a final hierarchy in correct order is available. Later in treatment, additional columns can be added when hierarchy items are rerated so that patients can clearly see the shift in their anxiety as they tackled hierarchy items.

Choosing the First Exposure

As already noted, middle-of-the-road items (e.g., 5s on a 0–10 scale and 50s on a 0–100 scale) are great for first exposures because they provoke anxiety, but not so much anxiety that a patient has to escape the situation. It is very important that patients have a successful experience during their first exposure. How does one define a successful exposure? First, patients should not be fleeing in horror during the first exposure! They should be able to stay in the situation long enough to learn two essential lessons. Specifically, we want patients to see that: (1) their anxiety will come down on its own without having to resort to avoidance strategies/safety behaviors/rituals and (2) feared outcomes did not happen.

It is also important for a first exposure to be done in session. The clinician should lead patients through the whole process of doing an exposure before they do one on their own at home. Consider a patient that fears he will cause harm

Item	SUDS
Being upstairs with the baby when mom/husband is downstairs	50
Walking around the block	60
Driving close to home	60
Taking baby to pediatrician appointment in the hospital	70
Taking baby to a playgroup	75
Going to the grocery store	80
Taking baby to the park	80
Riding on public transportation (e.g., train into the city)	85
Staying home alone with the baby	90
Driving into the city	90

FIGURE 7.1 *Sample Hierarchy*

to others because of his carelessness. Even if "leaving home without checking the locks" is the only 50 on his hierarchy, this would not be a good first exposure since it cannot be done in session. Rather, it might be more appropriate to step up the hierarchy to a slightly higher exposure that can be done in session. For example, he might use the bathroom at the clinic and not check the faucets and toilet to make sure they had stopped running. This would provoke his fear that he would be responsible for bad things happening (e.g., flooding the clinic). Success with this exposure would certainly motivate him to try leaving home without checking the locks since both exposures target the same feared outcome.

How to Make Sure That Exposures Result In Learning

The point of exposures is for patients to learn something new about their feared stimuli. As we mentioned in Chapter 6, cognitive techniques can be used on the front and back end of exposures to ensure that this crucial learning takes place. When they come for treatment, they associate the feared stimuli with anxiety and with negative outcomes. Exposure (and concomitant cognitive work) allows them to develop new feelings and beliefs about those stimuli. Setting up exposures correctly ensures that this will happen.

The first step is to design the exposure. Let's use the item, "Driving close to home" from Susan's hierarchy as an example. After discussion with her therapist, it was decided that Susan would drive from home to her local supermarket and back. Since exposures must be done without safety behaviors, they further decided that Susan would go alone (other people served as safety signals for her) and would not take her cell phone or bottle of water with her (both could be used in the event of a panic attack to prevent bad outcomes).

Next, Susan was asked to make some predictions about the exposure. Specifically, she was asked what she was most afraid might happen and how certain she was that this outcome would occur. She stated, "I am scared that I will have a panic attack and cause a car accident." Her therapist helped her to break these two predictions down. She believed with 100 percent certainty that she would have a panic attack and with 80 percent certainty that the panic attack would cause her to have an accident. With most anxiety exposures, it is also helpful to ask patients how anxious they expect to feel during the exposure. Susan expected that her SUDS would be 90 on a 0–100 scale.

Finally, it is helpful for patients to set a goal for the exposure. This goal should be easily measured once the exposure is over. Susan set the goal: "I want to get to the supermarket and back without using safety behaviors" (see Table 7.2).

This exposure exercise happened when Susan's therapist came to her home for a visit (see "Going Where the Anxiety Is" later in this chapter). Susan went out to do the exposure while her therapist waited on the front porch of the house. When she came back, they went inside to process the exposure.

TABLE 7.2

Sample Exposure Worksheet

Before the Exposure

Exposure: Drive to the supermarket and back home by myself.

Safety Behaviors to Drop: Bringing cell phone and water bottle.

Predictions: I will have a panic attack (100% certain). I will have a car accident because of my panic attack (80% certain).

Predicted Anxiety: 80

Goal: Get to the supermarket and back without using safety behaviors.

After the Exposure

What actually happened: My anxiety was 60. I did not have a panic attack. I did not have a car accident.

Did I meet my goal? Yes

What I learned: I was less anxious during the exposure than I thought I would be. I was able to drive to the supermarket without my feared outcomes occurring. Even though I *felt* anxious, it did not lead me to have a car accident.

Take-home message: ANXIETY DOESN'T ALWAYS MEAN CATASTROPHE.

When Susan returned home, she said, "That was a total failure." Her therapist was surprised and asked why Susan said this. She replied, "Because I was anxious." This is a trap most anxious patients will fall into from time to time. Anxious patients often evaluate the outcome of exposures (and naturally occurring events in life) based on how they *felt*, not on what they *did*. This error can serve as another maintaining factor for anxiety disorders. The next time they confront the same situation, they will expect to "fail" and will be attuned to their anxiety. As soon as people are looking for anxiety, they can easily find it and again assume that the situation was a failure.

When a clear goal is set for the exposure, the therapist can remind the patient that "not feeling anxious" was not the goal. They can then redirect the patient to evaluate whether or not they met the goal that they had in fact set. Susan conceded that she had gone to the store and back, without engaging in safety behaviors.

It is also important to evaluate predictions. Susan noted that she felt anxious during the exposure (about a 60 SUDS), but did not have a full-blown panic attack. Furthermore, she did not have a car accident.

At this point, the most important part of the exposure occurs. The therapist must cue the patient to summarize what they learned. Susan said that she learned three things: (1) She was less anxious during the exposure than she thought she would be, (2) she was able to drive to the supermarket without her feared outcomes occurring, and (3) even though she *felt* anxious, it did not lead her to have a car accident. She summarized, "Anxiety doesn't always mean catastrophe." Her therapist encouraged her to keep this mantra in mind when she repeated this exposure for homework during the week. It can also be helpful for the patient to maintain a running list of "take-home messages" that he or she can refer to as encouragement for doing exposures between sessions.

What If "Bad" Things Happen?

Sometimes, feared outcomes really do occur during exposures. It is always our hope that they don't occur during the first few exposures since our desire for these is complete success. We want patients to have the thought, "Wow, that wasn't nearly as bad as I thought." This then serves as a motivator for future exposures.

However, when bad things do happen during exposures, therapists must "make lemonade out of lemons." These experiences can be very powerful and have a significant impact on a patient's progress. A patient with OCD contamination concerns was staying at a private home during treatment since she lived far away from the treatment center. She had arranged to stay with a family who hosts families who come to the city for medical treatment. A few days into her treatment (she was doing treatment everyday for three weeks), her toilet at the host's home overflowed. Suddenly, there were urine and feces all over the bathroom floor. These were her most feared substances. Typically, she wore rubber gloves to go the bathroom in order to not come in contact with her own bodily fluids but she knew she had to clean up this terrible mess. She did not have her gloves on because her homework for the evening was to go to the bathroom without them. She considered putting them back on, but knew this was the wrong thing to do. Therefore, she started cleaning up the mess. An hour later, when everything was sparkling clean and she had informed her host family about the trouble, she called her therapist to tell her of this "horrible" event. The therapist felt terribly! However, she made lemonade out of lemons. She helped the patient to see how she had managed this most feared situation. She had always worried that the contamination would feel so bad that the bad feeling would *never* go away. Meanwhile, the event had only happened one hour ago and she felt a little shaken, but mostly fine. She had worn gloves for so long that she did not realize that the contaminated feeling came and went quite quickly, even in this extreme situation. After this fortuitous event, the patient proceeded very quickly with treatment and did very well.

Obviously, all exposures must occur with patients' consent. We should never purposefully set up "over the top" exposures, simply because we think they might propel the patient to faster success. However, when feared outcomes do occur in the context of exposures, therapists need to think on their feet and come up with a way to help the patient see the positive. Most often, the message is that even in extreme situations, patients have much more ability to cope than they think.

Interoceptive Exposure

There is a special kind of exposure, called interoceptive exposure that is used specifically with patients who fear the physical symptoms of anxiety. Rather than do exposure to a particular situation or object, interoceptive exposure involves exposure to a particular physical sensation like a racing heart, sweating, or shaking. Interoceptive exposure is used most often in the treatment of Panic Disorder. As you might recall from Chapter 1, Panic Disorder is characterized by a fear of physical symptoms. Patients worry, for example, that if their heart is racing, they might be having a heart attack. Interoceptive exposure is used to show people that even if their heart is beating very quickly, it will not result in a heart attack. For a list of interoceptive exposure exercises helpful for patients with Panic Disorder see Table 7.3. Table 7.4 lists the panic symptoms that are most strongly elicited by each interoceptive exposure exercise (see Antony, Ledley, Liss, & Swinson, 2006). This is particularly useful for selecting exercises that

TABLE 7.3

Interoceptive Exposure Exercises

- Shaking one's head rapidly from side to side for 30 seconds
- Placing one's head between the knees for 30 seconds and then lifting the head quickly to a normal position
- Spinning around (while standing) at a medium pace for one minute
- Holding one's breath for 30 seconds
- Hyperventilation (i.e., breathing in and out rapidly, as if panting) for one minute
- Breathing through a narrow straw for two minutes, while making sure not to breathe through the nose
- Staring continuously at a fluorescent light on the ceiling for one minute, and then trying to read
- Staring continuously at oneself in a mirror for two minutes
- Staring continuously at a spot on the wall for three minutes
- Tensing all the muscles of the body for one minute
- Running in place for one minute
- Sitting facing a heater for two minutes
- Placing a tongue depressor at the back of the tongue for 30 seconds

Source: See Antony, Ledley, Liss, & Swinson, 2006.

would help a particular patient based on the panic symptoms they most frequently experience and most fear.

Interoceptive exposure can also be used in the treatment of other anxiety disorders when patients fear physical symptoms. Many patients with Social Phobia worry about others noticing their symptoms of anxiety and drawing negative judgments about them based on these symptoms. Interoceptive can be combined with in vivo exposure to challenge these beliefs. For a patient who fears appearing out of breath, an exposure could involve running up and down some stairs (interoceptive exposure) prior to having a conversation with someone (in vivo exposure). This exposure would help the patient to challenge two beliefs: (1) that other people will notice her physical symptoms and (2) that others will draw negative conclusions about her based on these symptoms.

TABLE 7.4

Symptoms Most Strongly Elicited by Interoceptive Exposure Exercises

Exercise	Symptoms Most Strongly Elicited
Shaking head from side to side	1. Dizziness or feeling faint 2. Pounding/racing heart 3. Breathlessness/smothering sensations
Putting head between knees and lifting quickly	1. Dizziness or feeling faint 2. Breathlessness/smothering sensations 3. Numbness/tingling in face or extremities
Spinning around	1. Dizziness or feeling faint 2. Pounding/racing heart 3. Breathlessness/smothering sensations
Holding one's breath	1. Breathlessness/smothering sensations 2. Pounding/racing heart 3. Dizziness or feeling faint
Hyperventilating	1. Breathlessness/smothering sensations 2. Dizziness or feeling faint 3. Pounding/racing heart

TABLE 7.4 *(continued)*

Exercise	Symptoms Most Strongly Elicited
Breathing through a straw	1. Breathlessness/smothering sensations 2. Pounding/racing heart 3. Choking
Staring at a light and reading	1. Dizziness or feeling faint 2. Feeling unreal or in a dream
Staring at a mirror	1. Feeling unreal or in a dream 2. Dizziness or feeling faint
Staring at a spot on the wall	1. Feeling unreal or in a dream 2. Dizziness or feeling faint
Tensing muscles	1. Trembling/shaking 2. Breathlessness/smothering sensations 3. Pounding/racing heart
Running in place	1. Pounding/racing heart 2. Breathlessness/smothering sensations 3. Chest pain/tightness
Sitting facing a heater	1. Breathlessness/smothering sensations 2. Sweating 3. Hot flushes/chills
Using a tongue depressor	1. Choking 2. Breathlessness/smothering sensations 3. Nausea/abdominal distress

Source: See Antony, Ledley, Liss, & Swinson, 2006.

Video Feedback

Video feedback is another interesting variant on exposures. In Chapter 6, we introduced the concept of emotional reasoning. Patients take as truths what they *feel* to be true, rather than basing judgments on reality. Video feedback helps to counter this and is particularly useful with patients with Social Phobia. They worry that because they *feel* anxious in social interactions, they must look anxious and come across badly to others. Video feedback is a special exposure technique used to challenge these faulty assumptions (see Clark, 2005).

When video feedback is used, exposures are videotaped and patients predict how they will come across to others. Patients view the video as a means of objectively evaluating these predictions. The way in which patients are instructed to view the video is crucial to the success of video feedback. First, patients must clearly articulate to the therapist what they expect to see. These predictions must be very clear. Clark (2005) suggests, for instance, that if a patient believes that her face was very red during the exposure, she should select a book from the bookshelf that is "as red" as she thinks her face was. The book can then be placed against the television screen to objectively evaluate whether her face was as red as she *felt* it was.

Once these predictions are made, patients are instructed to view the video as if they are an objective observer. When patients watch the video without this instruction, they tend to be very critical, picking out every little negative thing that they said and did. When they are told to watch themselves as if they are just another person across the room at a cocktail party or an actor in a movie, they are able to see themselves as they are seen by others. This distancing allows patients to see that their felt sense in social situations is incongruent with the image they are projecting to others.

Therapists often worry about doing video feedback because some patients really do look anxious during exposures. They might stumble over their words or blush or leave uncomfortable silences in the conversation. The important thing to remember is that video feedback sets up a contrast between the patient's felt sense and reality—not between the therapist's observations and reality. In most cases, patients' self-images are extremely negative and distorted. Even if they really did look anxious during the exposure, it is almost always the case that they look much better than they expected. This contrast leads to the powerful learning experiences that can come about through video feedback.

Being Creative

Designing Exposures

Being a cognitive behavior therapist requires a great deal of creativity. The trick to doing good exposure work is to figure out how to activate the client's unique fears. Consider two patients who fear using public restrooms. One might fear getting sick from using them. Typically, he uses a public restroom, does a long and thorough hand wash, leaves the bathroom by using his sleeve to open the door, and then uses antibacterial lotion in his office prior to eating lunch or touching any of his possessions. Exposures for him would include using the restroom and touching various surfaces in the restroom (e.g., the toilet, countertop, door handles, etc.). Of course, concurrent with this, he would have to refrain from washing his hands, open the door directly with his hand, come back into his office, touch his possessions, and have his lunch.

Another patient also fears public restrooms, but for her, the fear is spreading contamination to her family. She doesn't feel a great deal of anxiety while she is out in public, but is flooded by anxiety when she gets home and has to prepare dinner. She strips off her clothes and shoes in the garage (which thankfully has a door that leads into the house!), takes a shower, changes into clean clothes, and then prepares dinner. When her husband arrives home, he gathers up her clothes and does the laundry so that her clothes are ready for her to wear again. Touching the contaminated clothes once she is "clean" would simply be too difficult. For her, exposures would entail touching surfaces in the bathroom just like our other patient. The exposure would then need to continue at home where the patient would have to walk in and prepare dinner in her "outside" clothes, without showering or washing her hands.

These examples are meant to show how important it is for therapists to understand the patients' feared consequences were they to confront feared stimuli *and not engage in any safety behaviors.* This knowledge informs the design of the exposure. A cookie-cutter approach will not yield the best treatment outcomes for patients. Rather, treatment must be tailored to each individual's unique fears, thereby allowing for disconfirmation of their beliefs.

Going Where the Anxiety Is

In addition to tailoring exposures for each patient, cognitive behavioral therapists should be willing to do exposures "where the anxiety lives." This means leaving the office setting. Sometimes it is as simple as going down the hall to the bathroom, or down a few floors to a cafeteria. Other times, it means leaving the building completely!

Some patients can benefit from home visits. Home visits allow the therapist to see how anxiety affects a patient's day-to-day life. A patient with contamination concerns might have an impeccably clean house. On the other hand, he might actually have an unbelievably dirty house. This sounds unlikely, but it happens. Some patients are so concerned about touching dirty things that they can't clean the things they perceive to be dirty! Similarly, some patients with OCD are frightened of being contaminated from household cleansers, so while they would like to be able to clean, they cannot. One look is worth a thousand words.

Home visits also allow clinicians to lead patients through exposures in their own environments. Some patients can do exposures in the clinician's office, but then cannot repeat them at home. Often, the stakes are higher at home. A patient with OCD might be able to chop vegetables with a huge knife in the therapist's office without much problem. However, doing this at home with their baby nearby might provoke intense concern about accidentally stabbing the baby. This kind of exposure might be so frightening that the patient could not do it for the first time without the support and encouragement of the therapist.

Home visits are perhaps most important in the treatment of patients with OCD who hoard. It is very difficult for patients to bring hoarded material to the clinician's office to throw away. Some patients have collected every *New York Times* since the 1970s. While the patient could bring a pile to session to throw away, it makes more sense for clinicians to go to the homes of patients who hoard and help them throw things away and learn to categorize things that are necessary to keep (e.g., tax returns and other important paperwork).

In addition to home visits, therapists should feel comfortable going to other places with their patients. In the chapter on working with children, we will discuss the utility of making school visits. With adults, anything goes. For a patient with Social Phobia who fears ordering food in a restaurant, an exposure could involve going to a local coffee shop and ordering coffee and a snack. For a patient with Panic Disorder who fears subways, a session could involve the therapist and patient taking the subway. For a patient with a specific phobia of having blood drawn, a session could be used for the therapist to accompany the patient to the lab to have her blood drawn.

The idea is not for the therapist to provide reassurance, but rather to model for the patient how exposures should be done. As we noted previously, exposures are all about learning. Exposures must be correctly set up and processed for learning to occur. Often, patients come away from exposures believing that they failed because they felt anxious. Therapists want to ensure that patients see that simply staying in a situation without resorting to rituals means that the exposure was a success. Therapists also want to make sure that patients see that their feared outcomes did not occur. Doing as many exposures as possible during sessions ensures that these important learning opportunities are seized.

Over the Top

Readers might have read the above examples and thought, "I would never do that!" Often in the treatment of anxiety disorders, we ask patients to do things that we ourselves would not typically do. Most of us do wash our hands after using public restrooms and before eating. Most of us would not purposefully have a spider walk across our hands. Knowing this, patients often ask, "Would you do that?" Whether the answer is yes or no is irrelevant. Rather, clinicians must explain to patients why these somewhat "over the top" exposures are so important to their treatment. Basically, if patients can engage in their most feared behaviors and see that there are no negative consequences, then they can certainly engage in every day, "normal" behaviors. The woman described previously could come in from doing errands (and using the bathroom at the mall) and simply start making dinner. After directly touching the toilet at the mall and making dinner without hand washing first, and seeing that nothing bad happened to her family, doing "everyday" activities would be simple.

Treatment for OCD is most often associated with "over the top" exposures. However, pushing the limits in this way can be useful in other anxiety disorders. David Clark of the University of London refers to this in his cognitive therapy for Social Phobia as "interrogating the environment" (see Clark, 2005). He asks patients to really play up a symptom that they fear experiencing during social interactions. For example, consider a patient who feared that her hands would shake when she was drinking or eating in front of others. This patient was so afraid that her hands would shake and she would spill her food or beverage that she either avoided eating in front of others or grasped her glass and silverware so tightly that she looked rather odd! This patient did numerous exposures eating and drinking in front of others, all the while dropping her safety behavior of holding so tightly to her glass and silverware. She began to believe that her shaking was less noticeable than she had previously thought. However, she continued to be terrified of spilling something, assuming that everyone would think she was a "freak" and would no longer want to associate with her. So, the patient was asked to purposefully spill her drink at the work cafeteria. She refused, but agreed to try spilling a drink at a nearby coffee shop with the therapist present. They used a session to go and do this exposure and the patient was shocked to see that no one noticed the spill. She then did the same exposure at work the next day. She made her hands as shaky as possible as she carried her tray and then dropped the entire thing. She was amazed by the reaction of her co-workers. Everyone rushed to help her clean up, they all asked if she felt okay, and one friend even went back through the line to get her another lunch. Only by playing out this most feared consequence was the patient able to dispute the beliefs that had been maintaining her social anxiety for years.

In Session Versus Homework Exposures

As we have noted, it is best to do the first exposure in session. Therapists can use their skill to ensure that patients leave the exposure seeing it as a successful experience. They also must teach the patient how to do exposures correctly. Exposures are not simply about putting oneself in a feared situation. Rather, they are about learning something new in that situation. Setting up exposures in the way we suggested earlier in the chapter facilitates this learning experience.

Once patients have done an exposure in session, they can be assigned a homework exposure. Usually, the first homework exposure should be a repeat of the first in session exposure. Patients have already had a successful experience with this exposure and this can then be solidified outside of session. When patients carry out an exposure on their own, the learning experience can be even more powerful than what occurred in session. They cannot attribute their success to the support or safety of the therapist. Rather, they see that they can manage anxiety on their own.

Early on in treatment, it can be helpful to continue assigning exposures for homework that have already been done in session. As patients are acclimated to doing exposures on their own, homework exposures can be dedicated to those that cannot be done in session. Therapists should spend time at the end of each session assigning exposure homework and helping patients to set up their exposure worksheet. The exposure can be defined, predictions made, and goals set. Patients then do the exposure on their own and complete the remainder of the worksheet. The next session should begin with a review of homework. Patients should describe how the homework went and review the sheet with the therapist. This ensures that patients recognize the importance of homework (i.e., the therapist didn't just assign it and forget about it!) and allows the therapist to make sure that important learning experiences are taking place.

References

Antony, M. M., Ledley, D. A., Liss, A., & Swinson, R. P. (2006). Responses to symptom induction exercises in Panic Disorder. *Behavior Research and Therapy, 44,* 85–98.

Clark, D. M. (2005). A cognitive perspective on Social Phobia. In W. R. Crozier & L. E. Alden (Eds.), *The essential handbook of social anxiety for clinicians* (pp. 193–218). Hoboken, NJ: Wiley.

Hope D. A., Heimberg R. G., Bruch M. A. (1995). Dismantling cognitive behavioral group therapy for Social Phobia. *Behaviour Research and Therapy, 33,* 637–650.

CHAPTER 8

Imaginal Exposure

Imaginal Exposure and Thought Suppression

When people are anxious, it is clear that they avoid many things. In addition to avoiding different people, places, objects, and situations, a less obvious avoidance often exists: their own thoughts. Patients with anxiety are often so nervous about their fearful thoughts that they try to avoid or suppress them. People with OCD, for example, fear intrusive, disturbing thoughts or images. Those with Social Phobia try to not picture the disastrous consequences that they fear would occur if they speak or interact with others in public. Patients with Panic Disorder are horrified at the thought that they could have a heart attack or go crazy. People with Generalized Anxiety Disorder try to push away all sorts of worries that come up for them. Patients with specific phobias go to great lengths to not picture what could happen if they were exposed to their feared stimulus.

The Ineffectiveness of Thought Suppression

As Abramowitz, Franklin, and Cahill point out in an article in *Cognitive Behavioral Practice* (2003), thought suppression is paradoxical. Often, thought suppression actually leads to an increase in the frequency of the thoughts that the patient is trying not to have. While pushing thoughts away might feel very practical to the patient, it unfortunately does not work.

In a classic set of experiments (see Wegner, 1989 for a summary), Dan Wegner asked college students to not think of white bears or pink elephants. After receiving this instruction, it was all that they could think of! Therapists who specialize in treating anxiety disorders often use the "pink elephant" example to help their patients understand the concept of thought suppression. If you have never done this, experience it for yourself:

Try as hard as you can to not picture a pink elephant in your mind. Imagine or think about anything that you want as long as it isn't a pink elephant. Try to not picture a pink elephant for as long as you can ... what happened?

Most likely, like the students in Wegner's experiments, you pictured a pink elephant. This experience shows you that trying to push down or suppress your thoughts does not work—and often makes the thoughts that you try to avoid come back with greater frequency or intensity.

Obsessive thoughts and worries are not dangerous or harmful. In fact, they are normal. It is estimated that 90 percent of the normal population experience intrusive thoughts (Rachman & deSilva, 1978). When patients allow themselves to have the thoughts by purposefully bringing them on, they see that the thoughts are not dangerous. In turn, they are able to stop resisting the thought and feel less anxious. Over time, patients experience a decrease in the frequency of their fears and worries as they stop suppressing them.

Many people, including psychologists and other clinicians treating patients with anxiety, make the mistake of feeding into this problematic attempt at controlling thoughts. They tell an anxious person, "just try not to think about it," or "if you start worrying, distract yourself so you don't get too nervous." While this response is certainly natural and normal, it does not provide an effective solution to the patient's concerns.

When clinicians help patients to end thought suppression and simply allow thoughts to be there, patients may experience a reduction in anxiety. Therapists can explain to patients:

> Now we see that pushing thoughts down or trying hard to suppress them often results in them popping back up. One solution to this vicious cycle is to simply allow the thoughts to be there. Picture yourself placing the thought on a big, puffy cloud. Then allow the thought on the cloud to drift away on its own.

Some patients are very successful when they try to just let a thought "be there." Others find it more difficult, simply because the thought is so anxiety provoking. Patients need help in knowing *how* to just let a thought be there. An effective strategy is to tell patients to let the thought be there, but get busy with something else rather than focusing exclusively on it. This does not mean that they should stop the thought. Rather, they should just let it be there, like leaving the radio on at low volume when reading a book or cooking a meal. Patients often need help coming up with ideas of other things that they can do when they are experiencing troubling thoughts. Clinicians can help them come up with a list that they can refer to when they find themselves in such a situation. For example, they might call a friend, go for a walk, or have a nice, hot bath. The basic idea is to show patients that they can continue to function, *even with the aversive thought*, and that if they do not try to stop it, it will gradually ease away on its own.

Imaginal Exposure as a Treatment Strategy

Sometimes, however, thoughts are resistant to going away on their own. A useful analogy to think of is: these persistent thoughts are like a helium balloon. Imagine that there is a helium balloon in your living room and you want it to come down. You could climb up a ladder and push it down. Then it pops back up in the way that fearful thoughts pop back up when you try to resist them. You could allow it to be there and not resist it. Eventually it will lose its helium and come down. Alternatively, if you wanted a more efficient and effective result, you could climb up the ladder and pierce a hole in it. Imaginal exposure is like piercing a hole in the helium balloon. It exposes the weakness in the anxious thought patterns and helps the patient to overcome the anxiety. The effect of imaginal exposures can take place quickly, as if one pierced a giant hole in the helium balloon. We have had patients experience significant anxiety reductions after just one imaginal exposure because they realize how ludicrous their fear truly is. At other times, patients need to repeat the imaginal exposure dozens of times to experience habituation.

When to Use Imaginal Exposure

Imaginal exposure involves having patients vividly imagine themselves in situations that they fear—the situations they typically avoid and the situations that evoke their urges to perform rituals or engage in safety behaviors. Imaginal exposure is most often associated with the treatment of OCD and PTSD, but it can be used in the treatment of patients with all of the anxiety disorders. A commonality to all of the anxiety disorders is that patients expect a horrible outcome should they be exposed to a particular event or stimuli (e.g., getting sick from a contaminant, forgetting what to say during a speech, getting bit by a dog, etc.). The key to the kinds of fears experienced by anxious patients is that they are typically unlikely to occur. As we have discussed throughout this book, even when feared outcomes *could* occur, patients typically overexaggerate the probability of their occurrence and the cost should they occur. For example, if a patient fears being bit by a dog, she might expect that every dog she sees will bite her (exaggerated probability) and she might imagine that if the dog did bite her, the cost would be catastrophic (e.g., a life-threatening injury). The main point of imaginal exposure is to show patients that their feared consequence is unlikely to occur and that even if it did occur, the costs that they associate with it are greatly overblown.

When In Vivo Exposure Is Not Possible

Imaginal exposure is preferred over in vivo exposure when it is impossible to do an in vivo exposure. There are times when the clinician realizes that an in vivo exposure would be the best treatment for the patient, but it is difficult or impossible for the patient and clinician to set up an in vivo that truly addresses the patient's fears.

In the example of Felicia, the 19-year-old college student with a terrible fear of pigeons, recall that her fear was that a pigeon would land on her head. She and her therapist did some in vivo exposure to pigeons, including visiting a science lab that housed pigeons and walking down city streets where pigeons were plentiful. Felicia did begin to feel a bit better, but even with these repeated exposures, still feared pigeons. The first goal of the clinician in conducting exposures is to understand the patient's greatest fear. Felicia's clinician reexamined this after the in vivo exposures had not led to a great reduction in fear. It turned out that Felicia had gotten used to being near pigeons, but continued to fear that a pigeon would land in her hair, be stuck there, and stay there for a long time. While the in vivo exposures showed her that this fear was unlikely, she still feared the cost should it happen. She believed that she would never get over this discomfort and would never want to leave her house again if this happened. In vivo exposures could never truly get at this feared consequence. However, imaginal exposure would serve as an easy and effective way to target these feared consequences.

When In Vivo Exposure Is Not the Best Option

There are times when an in vivo is contraindicated for a particular patient. Take, for example, the fear of vomiting. A complete in vivo exposure to vomit phobia would require the patient to vomit to learn that throwing up is not as catastrophic or horrible as they expect, that it only lasts for a brief period of time, and that they are likely to feel better afterwards. Some clinicians who specialize in anxiety treatments do complete this in vivo exposure with patients with vomit phobia and it can be an important and necessary part of treatment. Often, however, clinicians are not comfortable recommending patients to throw up. We have had, for instance, several teenage girls with vomit phobias or the fear of vomiting as part of OCD symptomatology. For obvious reasons, we did not feel comfortable teaching teenage girls with some body image issues how to vomit, so an in vivo to vomiting was not appropriate.

With a Future Feared Consequence

When the feared consequence is expected to occur sometime far in the future, it is impossible to test it out with an in vivo exposure. With in vivo exposure, clinicians set up the exposure so the patient experiences habituation between sessions and/or within sessions. When a feared consequence extends out into the future, the patient is unlikely to experience habituation because they are not able to disconfirm their fear. Imaginal exposure works nicely to address this challenge because you can easily fast-forward hours, days, weeks, months, or years in your mind.

One of our patients was afraid that she would get cancer from using artificial sweeteners containing aspartame. This is an example of a case where it is impossible to do an in vivo exposure because the patient feared that she would get cancer in about ten years. While some in vivos (involving drinking diet soda with extra artificial sweetener) were helpful, an imaginal exposure to getting cancer because of the diet sodas she drank was extremely helpful.

To Prepare Patients for In Vivo Exposures

Another important function that imaginal exposure serves is the preparation of patients to engage in an in vivo exposure. Frequently imaginal exposures are not quite as anxiety producing as in vivo exposures because patients feel a little safer confronting the feared stimulus in their minds than they do in person.

While clinicians typically do not include imaginal exposures directly on the in vivo exposure hierarchy, they can be included in the treatment as a stepping-stone to certain in vivo exposures. Some patients balk at the exposures with the higher SUDS ratings. When this occurs or if clinicians anticipate this reaction in advance, an imaginal exposure can be conducted to help the patient habituate to the feared consequence.

Consider the case of Jeff, the patient with Social Phobia who dreaded being called on in law school classes. Imaginal exposure was used in Jeff's treatment for two reasons. First, early in treatment, he was too anxious to do in vivo exposure to answering questions in class. Furthermore, most of Jeff's feared outcomes were completely unlikely to occur. Together, the clinician and Jeff devised an imaginal story in which Jeff was trying to hide in class by avoiding eye contact so that he would not be called on. Despite his efforts, the professor bellowed out his name and asked him a difficult question. Jeff, in response, froze and could not think of an answer. When he finally did answer, he gave a ridiculously incorrect answer. The room erupted with laughter. The professor said that Jeff's response was by far the stupidest answer he had heard in his 30 years of teaching. The professor told Jeff that he might as well drop out of law school right then and save himself the time and money. His classmates refused to associate with him and people sat in the aisles of class to avoid having to sit next to Jeff in the future.

After Jeff did this imaginal exposure several times, he realized that his worst fears were highly unlikely to come true. In fact, after a number of repetitions of the story, Jeff started to laugh at the absurdity of it (although he had practically been in tears during the first few repetitions because it felt so real). This realization gave him the confidence to attempt the in vivo exposure and purposefully answer questions in class. When he did, he received further information that his feared outcomes would not occur. In fact, he learned that answering questions was advantageous for him and he commited to answering questions on a regular basis.

When to Not Use Imaginal Exposure

Imaginal exposure is a very effective and useful treatment strategy for anxious patients; however, this type of exposure is not appropriate for all patients. It will be ineffective with some patients and it is occasionally contraindicated.

When Patients Cannot State Their Feared Consequence

If patients cannot articulate feared consequences of exposure to their feared stimuli, it will be difficult to create an imaginal exposure and the exposure may not be very effective since it won't be specific to their feared consequence. For example, some patients with OCD simply fear feeling badly when exposed to their feared stimuli. They might worry that if they touch something that they perceive as contaminated, they will just feel uncomfortable. With probing, some patients explain that they fear the feeling will *never* go away and they will no longer be able to function. This would make for a perfect imaginal exposure. However, if the patient truly is only concerned with feeling uncomfortable for a short period, with no consequences, imaginal exposure is unlikely to be useful.

Other common situations where a patient does not have or is not able to articulate a feared consequence include:

- The primary concern is disgust and not anxiety.
- The patient is a child and cannot say what specifically they are afraid of and only says, "I'm scared."
- The patients have not allowed themselves to think about what they are afraid of.

When Patients Are Not Able to Imagine

Imaginals work best when the patient engages in the exposure and creates a powerful image of the feared consequence. Some people are not able to picture situations in their minds. If the patient has difficulty being able to bring a vivid image of the intended situation or stimulus to mind, imaginal exposure will not be helpful.

Patients may or may not know whether they are good at imagining. When you begin the imaginal exposure and the patient does not become anxious, it is possible that he is not able to create a mental image of the situation. When a patient vividly pictures the feared situation, she is likely to become nervous; therefore, a lack in anxiety during the exposure can be attributed to an inability to imagine.

There are some ways to help a patient with bringing images to mind. First, keeping the eyes closed tends to help so that outside distractions do not get in the way. Similarly, eliminating other distractions is important. Patients should not listen to imaginal exposure tapes on their way home from their session or when they are making dinner. Rather, they should set aside some dedicated time when they can really concentrate. Finally, some patients do well with some rehearsal to imagining nonfearful situations. For example, the clinician can have the patient vividly imagine being on the beach. Getting used to using all of one's senses to create the image can then facilitate imaginal exposure to the feared situation.

When it Is Better to Use In Vivo

Often, in vivo exposures are the most effective because they are as vivid as possible since they are in real life. If the patient's feared situations can be confronted in real life it may not be necessary to conduct imaginal exposure. Imaginal exposure should not be used as a substitute for in vivo exposures because that can feed into the patient's avoidance. As mentioned, however, imaginal can be used as a stepping-stone to a challenging in vivo exposure.

In the Presence of Significant Depression or Thought Disorder

It is unclear whether certain imaginal exposure topics should be avoided with depressed patients. Imaginal exposure to feared stimuli that are specific to the anxiety disorder are likely to be fine. For example, with a patient who has comorbid depression and a spider phobia, imaginal exposure to spiders is unlikely to cause great distress.

For some patients, however, their anxious cognitions and depressive cognitions can be closely related. Take for example a patient with depression and Social Phobia who worries that her social fears will lead her to be alone forever. Doing an imaginal to this most feared consequence (e.g., repeatedly failing in efforts to establish relationships, ending up alone and destitute) is probably not a good idea. Since patients with severe depression are often hopeless, there is the risk that they can become caught up in the negative thoughts about the future and not see how the fears in their imaginal exposure are unlikely to occur.

While we do caution against doing imaginals to depressed patients' depression-related cognitions, there might be some benefit to helping patients stop suppressing or avoiding their thoughts and feelings about the depression. In one study (Hayes et al., 2005), patients with depression wrote about their depression each week, thereby reducing avoidance and increasing processing of thoughts related to the depression. Patients who completed this writing task showed reduced levels of depression as compared to patients who did not complete the task. This study suggests that *avoidance* of depression-related cognitions is not indicated. However, the question remains of whether clinicians should expose patients to outcomes that they most fear as a result of their depression or associated anxiety disorder.

There are a number of reasons why patients with thought disorder should not engage in imaginal exposure. First, they might not be able to create a coherent story that addresses feared consequences. Furthermore, imaginal exposure is most effective when patients are able to distance themselves from the fear and realize how unlikely the fear is. Therefore, it is necessary that the patient be able to engage in reality testing. Without this ability, patients might be "sucked in" to the imaginal and believe that it is really happening.

As was discussed in Chapter 1, some clients with OCD have overvalued ideation (OVI). This means that they truly believe that their fears are accurate. Most patients with OCD realize that their fear is irrational, yet have difficulty refraining from rituals. Those with OVI, on the other hand, do not realize that their fears are irrational and do not have the reality-testing abilities to see that their rituals do not prevent their feared outcomes from occurring. An OCD patient with OVI truly believes that he will be responsible for someone dying if he doesn't do his ritual. Patients with OVI really think that they will get a fatal illness if they don't shower several times a day and wash their hands before eating. While imaginal exposure can (and should) be used with patients with OVI, it can be much more difficult for patients to habituate to the story. It might take more repetitions of the imaginal exposure for the patient to feel less anxious, and even after this, the patient might still harbor some fears that the negative outcome will occur. These patients might do well with additional interventions, such as cognitive restructuring. For example, the clinician can ask the patient how likely it is that their feared outcomes would happen to someone else and why there is a difference between how they see their own risk versus the risk for others.

Introducing Patients to Imaginal Exposure

As the idea of imaginal exposure is introduced to patients, clinicians should keep in mind that the patients are being asked to do something which is likely to sound very odd and unreasonable to them. It is the opposite of what they have been doing (e.g., avoiding such thoughts!). The way in which clinicians present imaginal exposure is critical to its effectiveness. When a clinician conveys a sense of confidence that imaginal exposure will help, patients become motivated and ready to do their exposures.

The Rationale

Clinicians should begin by explaining to patients that the purpose of imaginal exposure is to confront their feared consequence that can't be addressed with the exposures on their hierarchy or that they fear will occur at a time in the future. Patients with anxiety disorders carry around with them many scary thoughts. The idea of imaginal exposure is to externalize these thoughts and see whether the patient might think differently about them once they hear them "outside" of their minds and truly confront them, rather than avoiding them.

Depending on the reason for using imaginals, the clinician may also want to explain that they can be used for patients who are not willing to do the in vivo exposures right away. If this is the case, clinicians should be clear that the goal is to move onto in vivo exposures as soon as possible.

Metaphors

As with many aspects of anxiety disorder treatment, metaphors can help patients to understand the purpose of imaginal exposure. A good metaphor to use is that of a horror movie. The clinician can say:

> Have you ever watched a horror movie? If it was a REALLY frightening movie and you watched it one time, would you be afraid? What do you think would happen if you watched it five times? How about twenty times? What about fifty times? Would you be as afraid of the movie the fiftieth time as you were the first time? How else would you feel about the movie?

Patients will often say that after fifty times watching a horror movie, it would no longer be scary. Instead, it would be predictable, amusing, silly, or boring. A similar outcome occurs and is desirable with imaginal exposure. Clinicians can further process the horror movie example with patients to help them see how repeated exposure reduces fear and anxiety. The goal is to help patients see that the imaginal exposure allows them to experience habituation without completing an in vivo when an in vivo is difficult or impossible to do.

The Patient's Own Examples

Once the patient understands the concept of imaginal exposure, the clinician and patient can begin to consider which aspect of the patient's anxiety to focus on. One thing to consider is whether there is an underlying fear that, until resolved, could prevent habituation to other exposures.

As we discussed previously, Felicia's greatest fear was of having a pigeon land on her head and stay there for a long time. Obviously, this is a difficult exposure to set up *in vivo*. Even after doing other in vivo exposures, Felicia continued to worry about her biggest fear. While she habituated somewhat to being around pigeons, she continued to think, "But what if one lands on my head and stays there?" Because of this fear, she had difficulty habituating to her other in vivo exposures. A plan was thus made for her to complete the imaginal exposure before proceeding with her in vivo exposures.

Creating the Script

Once the topic of the imaginal is agreed upon, a script is created. The script should paint a vivid imaginal picture for the patient of his or her most feared situation and its consequences. It is useful to create a script before telling the imaginal story because it will ensure that the patient understands the way to create an imaginal, includes all of the necessary aspects, and becomes properly engaged and anxious.

Making It Over the Top

As the clinician helps the patient write the script, it is important to be sure that it is "over the top." For example, our patient with Panic Disorder, Susan, was afraid that she would go crazy and end up in a mental hospital because of her panic attacks. Her imaginal script involved her literally losing control and losing her mind and ending up in a mental asylum for the rest of her life. The imaginal went on to say that no one even visited her because they were too embarrassed to have a crazy person in their lives. The staff members all said that she was the craziest person they had ever seen come into the hospital, and so on. While this might sound cruel to clinicians who do not usually do imaginal exposure, it is important to realize that this content comes directly from what is buzzing around in the patient's mind. Patients' fears are often driven by very catastrophic thoughts that are unlikely to ever actually happen. The clinician is simply helping them to externalize it so that they can begin to gather some new perspective. When the story is extreme, patients are able to realize that their fears are irrational.

Getting All the Fears Even if They Sound Ridiculous

The imaginal script should read like a story that has a beginning, a middle, and an end. The imaginal exposure should include an ending that encompasses the most feared scenario and its consequences, which are unlikely to happen in real life. In the example of Susan, it is highly unlikely that a panic attack would result in going crazy and being involuntarily committed for life. The end of Susan's imaginal exposure described her dying in the mental institution, after spending her final years completely alone, abandoned by her family.

In creating the unlikely catastrophic ending, be sure that the fear truly depicts the patient's core fear. Other patients with severe Panic Disorder like Susan might have other feared consequences associated with going crazy, such as:

- Missing out on seeing their children grow up
- Not living up to their true potential
- Being out of touch with reality
- Being hospitalized against their will and unable to make their own decisions
- Dying alone in the hospital
- Being resistant to any treatments and remaining "crazy" forever

Clinicians must spend time exploring the patient's most significant underlying fears as they create the imaginal exposure script together. There may be one major underlying fear or several equally disturbing fears. The script can be prepared by the therapist and patient during the therapy session. Another option is to have the patient draft a script for homework and then modify it together during the next treatment session.

Imaginal exposures should be done hierarchically, with more severe concerns and feared consequences being included in later images. Scripts should be written in the second person, present tense as if the patients are telling the story to themselves or as if the therapist is telling it to them. Scripts should include a lot of detail, including information gathered by the five senses, such as the sights, sounds, smells, feelings to the touch, and tastes. They should also include how patients are feeling and thinking throughout the imaginal story. The length of the story is not as important as the quality of the story, but should generally be around ten minutes or longer. With shorter stories, you will probably need to do more repetition or add more details. Be sure that the story is vivid and long enough for the patient to become engaged and sufficiently activated. For example, the imaginal script could read:

> You are feeling lightheaded and shaky and out of it. You realize a panic attack is coming on. "Oh no!" you think. "This is going to be the one that sets me over the edge. I'll really lose it and I will go crazy this time for sure!" Your heart begins pounding and you start sweating. Your head is spinning and your thoughts are racing. Now you feel very unreal and out of it. You look in the mirror and don't even recognize yourself. The room is spinning and you hear a ringing sound. Your hands are shaking and clammy. You feel nauseated. "Okay, I'm definitely going crazy now!" you think to yourself.

> It turns out that you're right this time, you are going crazy! You lose all connection with reality and don't know your name, where you are, or what to do with yourself to feel normal again. You are terrified! Your thoughts are racing, but you're aware of only one thought: "It's all because I had that panic attack–I knew I should never have allowed myself to have a panic attack–It's making me go crazy!"

> Your husband comes home and realizes that you have totally lost it. "Oh my gosh! My wife had one too many panic attacks and is now a mental case!" he exclaims. He calls an ambulance. You are completely out of it but hear the sirens coming and feel the medical professionals taking you away. You hear your husband cry out, "Your kids will miss you! They won't have their mom anymore–too bad that panic attack made you go crazy."

> You wake up in a little bland room in the mental hospital. There's nothing on the walls or floor. You're groggy in the bed and unable to move. You hear some psych techs talking out in the hall, "Did you see how out of it Marie was when she came in last night? I've never seen anyone that crazy before. They say it's all because of a panic attack that lasted hours and that she couldn't recover from."

> You live your days in the hospital, out of touch with reality and with all the people who were once important in your life. Over time, people stop visiting you in the mental hospital. Your husband doesn't want his kids seeing a crazy mom and being scared that they could end up like that too. Your parents are embarrassed and mortified by what has transpired. You pass your days all alone. When you're actually aware of your own thoughts, you think about how you've let everyone down and how your kids won't have a mom. Even the staff and other patients in the mental institution want nothing to do with you because you're so bizarre. They are all frustrated that you haven't responded to any of the treatments and they're stuck with you for life. You're lonely and sad and out of it. You die alone in the mental hospital.

From this example, it is clear that imaginal exposures need to incorporate all the patient's fears and have the most catastrophic ending possible. Now that the patient has a good script, it is time to conduct the exposure.

Conducting the Exposure

Once the script is created, a recording should be made of the actual exposure. The technology to use for the recording is up to the clinician and the patient. Be sure to use something that the patient can regularly listen to. For example, making an audiotape may not be the best idea because many patients no longer have access to a tape player. The best bet is probably to hook up a microphone to your computer and create a digital file. You can put the file on a removable storage device (such as a CD) or email it to them with their permission and understanding that electronic transmission is *not* a secure method that ensures privacy.

The therapist typically tells the story using the script created by the therapist and patient together. During the imaginal exposure, the clinician will ask the patient for SUDS ratings approximately once every five minutes. The imaginal exposure is repeated several times during the therapy session with the clinician recording the patient's SUDS ratings to track the anxiety levels. The patient typically completes the imaginal exposure with his eyes closed to get a vivid image of the scene he is describing.

At the end of the session, the recording is given to the patients with instructions to listen to the tape daily for homework. The patient should listen to the story several times for about 30–45 minutes of exposure homework per day. Clinicians ask patients to record their SUDS levels prior to beginning the story, at the end of the story, and at the point in the story when their SUDS peaked. They should also record what was happening in the story at this peak moment. It can also be helpful to ask patients to write a brief narrative after each homework session, explaining how they are thinking and feeling about the story. After only a few repetitions of the story, patients might write, "This feels so real. I am sure this is going to happen." After repeated exposures, their beliefs should shift quite significantly. For example, they might write, "This is getting ridiculous. This is never going to happen to me or anyone else. People don't go crazy from panic attacks."

Imaginal exposures are repeated until the narrative does not elicit much discomfort or anxiety. This is indicated by both a drop in SUDS ratings and a shift in beliefs about the likelihood that the feared outcome will occur. It is important to check to see if the patient has other disturbing disastrous consequences that come to mind. If so, another recording is created in the same manner. If the patient habituates to most aspects of the story with the exception of one, a new recording can be created which flushes out the one fear-producing aspect in detail.

Challenges that Can Occur

In this section, we will go through some of the common challenges and objections that can occur before and during imaginal exposure as part of the treatment for anxiety disorders.

Patient Objections

Some patients will not like the idea of doing imaginal exposure. They may think that it is silly or they may feel embarrassed to create the script with their therapist. Some patients also doubt whether it can help them. Finally, some patients are too scared to do imaginal exposures at all.

If a patient feels that imaginal exposure is silly, the clinician can empathize with their concerns and acknowledge that it does feel like an odd thing to do. It is certainly not what patients would do on their own and it can sound strange to come up with the extreme ideas that go into the imaginal script. The clinician can then return to the rationale and explain the process of exposure to fears and habituation. The therapist can also provide examples of how previous patients benefited by doing the imaginal exposure despite feeling initially skeptical about the process. It can be helpful to encourage the patient to suspend their judgment on the process since they have not yet tried it and to evaluate the effectiveness as they go along.

As with in vivo exposure, the effectiveness of the treatment will be determined in large part by how much the patient invests in it. If the patient is too skeptical or refuses to do it, the treatment is less likely to be effective. It is never a good idea to sacrifice the therapeutic relationship or make the patient feel that she is being forced into something against her will.

It is uncommon to have patients refuse to do an imaginal all together. More frequently, they will express concerns that it will not work for them. These concerns should be treated in a manner consistent with the empirical stance of cognitive behavioral therapy. The belief that it will not work for them is one hypothesis, but the answer remains to be seen (because they have not tried it). Therefore, the belief needs to be tested to see how true it actually is. Clinicians should encourage patients to have an open mind about imaginal exposure and at least try it to see if it will be of any help.

For patients who are too scared to try imaginal exposures, clinicians can try to figure out something less anxiety provoking to start with. There might be an imaginal exposure that the patient is willing to do with less fearful content. Sometimes though, clinicians have to get creative. A patient who fears going to hell if she does not pray correctly, may be too frightened at first to do an imaginal about being in hell. She reports that she is scared of even saying the words, "Devil," or "Hell," let alone picturing herself there! Rather, it might be necessary to spend a few sessions doing exposure to just these words. In a very gradual manner, the patient can write the words, then listen to the clinician say the words, and finally say the words. This may seem slightly silly, but for a patient with such strong fears of going to hell, baby steps might be necessary to prepare the patient for exposure.

Habituation Does Not Occur

If the clinician notices that habituation is not occurring after several repetitions of the imaginal exposure, it is possible that more repetitions are necessary. Habituation frequently occurs between the exposures rather than within the exposure session. If, however, after many imaginal repetitions, the patient continues to be highly anxious without experiencing habituation, it is probable that rituals and avoidance are occurring. The patient may hide them from you or the rituals may be so habitual that the patient is not aware of them himself.

Avoidance may be very subtle. The patient might think of something else instead of completely paying attention and listening to the imaginal. Patients may engage in mental reassurance, telling themselves not to worry because those horrible feared outcomes are unlikely to occur. When habituation does not occur, it is important to directly ask the patient if they are engaging in these behaviors. Clinicians must remind patients that rituals and avoidances may initially decrease anxiety but that the anxiety will always "bounce" back up until they fully experience the imaginal exposure and give their anxiety a chance to habituate.

Over- and Underengagement

Failure to achieve habituation can also occur when the patient is not properly engaged. Typically, the more emotionally engaged patients are in imaginal exposures, the more effective the exposures are in producing the desired result. To become optimally emotionally engaged, patients should listen to imaginal exposure tapes with their eyes closed when they are not doing something else. There are times, however, when you need to modify the method of the imaginal exposures to increase or decrease the patient's engagement level.

Overengagement

Overengagement refers to times when the patient is incredibly distressed or anxious during the exposure. While the clinician certainly wants the patient to activate his anxiety with the exposure, if the patient becomes overwhelmed with anxiety, the exposure will not be effective. Some signs that the patient may be overengaged include:

- The patient is extremely emotional as evidenced by crying, protesting, or shaking.
- The patient gets up out of her chair or tries to leave the room.
- The patient seems to have lost touch with reality.

If the patient appears overly engaged, the clinician should process the experience with the patient to see whether she was aware of her reactions and to see how she does with reality testing. Recall that imaginal exposures are less likely to be effective with those with difficulty reality testing and in fact can be detrimental if the patients are not able to realize how extreme the story is.

With overengaged patients, clinicians can suggest that the patients do not close their eyes while listening to the therapist tell the story. The clinician can also ask the patient to begin by telling the story as if it is happening to someone else rather than herself. It is also possible that the patient would become less engaged by telling the story herself rather than listening as the therapist tells it.

Underengagement

Another challenge that can occur is underengagement. When patients are under-engaged they do not get into the story and do not become anxious as they tell it. An underengaged patient may never report SUDS exceeding a 60 or so.

One potential reason for underengagement is that the script did not get at the patient's true feared consequence. It may have only touched the surface but did not delve into what the patient is really afraid of. The fear structure was not sufficiently activated (see Foa & Kozak, 1986). In these cases, time must be spent in session fleshing out a new script that better taps the patient's most feared outcomes.

Another explanation for underengagement is that the patient is not able to imagine the scene as they hear it. Some people simply cannot get visual images in their minds. You can understand how much the patient is imaging and processing by asking some questions like, "What is happening now? What is going through your mind?" If patients have difficulty engaging with the image, the clinician can explore whether they would be more engaged if they narrated the story themselves. If patients are unable to get a mental image or engage with the imaginal, the clinician should move on to another treatment method.

Finally, patients often listen to their imaginal exposure tapes at less than optimal times. They might listen driving home from session or in the kitchen while making dinner. This is a surefire way to be underengaged. Imaginal exposures require full concentration to have their desired effect. Patients should be advised to set aside specific time during their day when they can focus solely on their imaginal exposure homework.

Patient Doesn't Practice

Another difficulty with imaginal exposures is that while patients need to practice regularly, they sometimes do not. It is typically not enough to practice the imaginal only once per week in the therapy session. There are many reasons that a patient chooses not to listen to the imaginal outside of session. It is important the clinician be patient, understanding, flexible, and empathic to the patient's reasons for not listening to the imaginal.

If, for example, the patient says that he did not listen to it because he did not have time, you can help him problem solve and improve time management skills so he can listen to it the following week. If the patient says that it was too upsetting and she could not sleep at night when she listened to it, you could help her plan to listen to it earlier in the day.

Remember that the process of imaginal exposure can be difficult for patients. They need to feel support from their therapists and feel as though it is a collaborative process. When a patient has objections to the imaginal exposures, work on negotiating and resolving the objections to make the exposures as effective as possible.

References

Abramowitz, J. S., Franklin, M. E., & Cahill, S. P. (2003). Approaches to common obstacles in the exposure-based treatment of Obsessive Compulsive Disorder. *Cognitive Behavioral Practice, 10,* 14–22.

Hayes, A. M., Beevers, C. G., Feldman, G. C., Laurenceau, J. P., & Perlman, C. (2005). Avoidance and processing as predictors of symptom change and positive growth in an integrative therapy for depression. *International Journal of Behavioral Medicine, 12*(2), 111–122.

Rachman, S., & deSilva, P. (1978). Abnormal and normal obsessions. *Behaviour Research and Therapy, 16,* 233–248.

CHAPTER 9

Other CBT Techniques

While the primary treatment strategies of cognitive behavioral therapy (CBT) for anxiety disorders are exposures and cognitive restructuring, many additional techniques can serve as useful adjuncts to treatment. In fact, many different treatment strategies fall under the umbrella of CBT, or are closely related to CBT. Some of these techniques are particularly helpful with anxious patients. In this chapter, we will describe the additional CBT treatment strategies for anxiety disorders. A discussion of the conditions under which to use these techniques, and how to use them effectively will also be included.

Assertiveness and Communication Skills Training

When to Use Assertiveness and Skills Training

Communication and assertiveness training can be useful when patients' anxiety is centered on their relationships with others. These skills are also helpful when a lack of knowledge regarding communication skills exists. For example, many patients with Social Phobia have spent years avoiding social situations and they have not had the experiences to utilize effective communication skills. Thus, their difficulty may be due to their anxiety *and* a lack of knowledge regarding how to interact since they have not had sufficient experience.

Clinicians should recognize that skills training works best when tailored to the individual patient. Patients need to be made aware that skills training provides some ideas and guidelines, but not standards or rules. It will give them a launching pad or set of behaviors to try out. Patients can later adapt the skills to their own personality and style as well as the situations they encounter. The communication skills necessary for a given situation will vary greatly based on the type of situation, individuals involved, purpose of the meeting, cultural variables, and many other factors. The necessary communication skills in a fast-paced meeting between high-powered executives are different from those needed when someone is trying to cut back on their workload and stop saying yes to every-thing; which is different from skills necessary to navigate a job interview or meet someone new at a party. Therefore, clinicians can present communication skills training as some basic strategies that the patient can learn to modify to suit his or her work and social situations. This section provides an overview of some potential areas for development in communication skills.

Assertive Communication

People tend to communicate in one of three ways: passively, aggressively, or assertively. Passive communicators want to please. They concede to other peo-ple's needs and wants, but do not have their own needs and wants met. Aggres-sive communicators lie at the other extreme. They are concerned with getting their own needs and wants met, even if it means bullying other people to accom-plish their goals. Assertive communication involves getting one's own needs and wants met, while also taking into account the other person's needs and wants. It is the ideal form of communication, since all involved parties leave the interac-tion feeling satisfied.

Many anxious people are passive communicators. Passive communicators worry that if they ask for what they need and want, they will be judged badly by others. Therefore, they are often taken advantage of in work and in relationships.

Passive communication is not always indicative of a skills deficit. For many anxious patients, passive communication serves as an avoidance or safety behav-ior. They avoid communicating assertively because they fear negative outcomes from doing so. With this in mind, it is always best to focus on treating the anx-iety disorder first before moving on to communication skills training. Often, as patients learn to eliminate avoidance behaviors, communication ceases to be a problem.

Patients with Social Phobia, for example, often go to great lengths not to draw attention to themselves. Their verbal and nonverbal behaviors are designed to help them blend in and not call attention to their perceived deficits. Common safety behaviors include standing far away from people, slouching or avoiding eye contact, speaking quietly, saying very little, wearing bland clothing to avoid standing out, and pausing before speaking. All of these behaviors are character-istic of passive communication. Over the course of treatment, as safety behav-iors are limited, many patients will naturally become more assertive. As they make better eye contact, stand up straighter, and take the risk of asking for what they want, they often get good results. These successful interactions then lead to further attempts at assertive communication.

There are times, however, when communication continues to be a problem even once treatment is complete. This can occur with socially anxious patients, as well as patients with other anxiety disorders. They might have been so immersed in their anxiety disorder for so many years that they really do not know how to communicate effectively or how to form meaningful relationships. This is when assertiveness training can be helpful.

Assertiveness training encompasses many areas including: saying no, making requests, asserting an opinion, and giving and receiving feedback. Unapologetically saying no is a common problem for anxious patients. Patients with anxiety worry about offending or disappointing others, appearing rude or selfish, and getting rejected. Clinicians can help patients to see that these fears are unlikely to be true and in fact patients may gain esteem and respect in the eyes of others when they stand up for themselves. In *The Assertiveness Workbook*, author Randy Paterson offers several excellent suggestions that patients can use to assertively say no, such as:

- Never volunteer to do something that you are not interested in doing if you have not been asked.

- Use assertive body posture (including eye contact, relaxed posture) and voice (loud volume, clear wording).

- Do not apologize or make excuses. Apologies suggest that you are in debt to the other person and owe them something because you said no. Excuses can be argued with and enable the person to ask you again another time.

- If people do not accept your answer, strengthen your position or use the broken record technique and repeat your position.

- Do not try to convince others about your point or wait for their approval. They do not need to like your answer.

The ability to make a request is another important assertive communication skill. Paterson (2000) makes an excellent point that assertively making requests is not equivalent to trying to control someone else's behavior. Rather, it is about a person stating his or her own needs and desires. The other person can then decide how to act.

Paterson recommends utilizing the DESO process put forth by Bower and Bower (1991). DESO stands for Describe, Express, Specify, and Outcome. The first step is to concisely describe the specific situation or behavior. Patients can then express their emotions by using "I" statements, remaining positive, and staying calm and nonaggressive. The third step is to specify a request with a specific behavior, such as "I'd like you to take the trash out." The final step in assertively making a request is the outcome or consequence. This step can include the patient's feelings, the expected results of the request being completed, or a reward in return ("Now I'll have time to make you a nice dinner.").

Another challenge for many anxious patients is giving or receiving feedback. Patients, especially those with social anxiety, frequently have difficulty asserting their opinions. They can practice by first providing neutral opinions and feedback. Once they become comfortable with relatively neutral or positive opinions, they can work on expressing somewhat controversial views, and giving less positive feedback to others. Next, patients can practice actively disagreeing with others and expressing controversial views. When giving opinions and feedback, clinicians can help patients to be assertive and unapologetic. This involves taking into account others' beliefs, but also voicing one's own (e.g., "I appreciate that you support abortion, but I would like to explain to you why I feel differently."). Patients should not be aggressive, passive-aggressive, or intimidating to others when they give feedback or express opinions.

Receiving feedback may also be challenging for some patients. Accepting compliments can be difficult and a good subject for exposure practice. Patients can work on simply responding by saying, "thank you," or "yes, I feel good about it too." Receiving criticism or negative feedback can be especially troubling for some patients with anxiety. Patients and clinicians can discuss the many options that are available to deal with negative feedback. For example, patients can validate the other person's point of view, thank the person for their feedback, respectfully disagree and state their case, agree with part but not all of what was said, or ask for more detailed feedback.

Listening Effectively

Listening is one of the most important aspects of communication. Anxious patients sometimes have difficulty listening because they are worrying about something off into the future so they are not paying attention in the present. Patients with OCD may be distracted by their broken-record obsessions. Those with GAD sometimes get caught up in their worries and do not hear what others are saying. Patients with Social Phobia may be planning what they will say next rather than listening to what the other person is saying. Exposure based treatments will typically help with these challenges and improve listening skills. Some patients, however, will still need some additional assistance with listening skills.

Authors McKay, Davis, and Fanning (1995) suggest that active listening involves useful techniques, such as maintaining appropriate eye contact, paraphrasing what the other person is saying, and asking questions to understand what the person has said. Another strategy is to provide immediate feedback, which shows that one has clearly heard what was said. They also recommend the use of empathy when listening to someone. The use of empathy involves putting yourself in the other person's shoes and trying to understand his or her perspective.

Patients can practice active listening in session and gain feedback from clinicians or confederates (who they speak with during an exposure) on how they expressed that they are listening and interested. Video feedback can be very helpful in achieving this goal. With video feedback, clinicians can help patients to observe the video as an objective viewer and see if they would feel "heard" if they were the other person in the conversation.

Initiating, Maintaining, and Ending Conversations

Some anxious patients, especially those with Social Phobia or those who have been isolated for many years due to anxiety, genuinely do not know how to have conversations. Even when they have dropped safety behaviors (e.g., mental rehearsing, mental reviewing), they still struggle with what to say in social situations. Therapists can help patients become more comfortable with casual conversation.

An area of greatest concern for patients is initiating conversation. Some patients do not know how to break into a group that is already chatting and they do not know what to say. Cognitive restructuring can be used to help with the first problem. Patients often think that they will be judged negatively for starting to talk to people who are already speaking. They can be asked to consider how they would feel if someone broke into a conversation that they were having. For example, a patient could be asked to imagine that she is having a conversation with a friend at a wedding. Another woman comes over to her and her friend and says, "Hi. I'm Jane. How do you know the bride and groom?" It is very unlikely that the patient would view this negatively. She would understand that Jane is eager to meet some other people at the wedding and have a nice time. This can then be used to reframe the patient's own beliefs about breaking into conversations.

Therapists can also coach patients in appropriate topics for conversation. A key lesson is to look at the shared context. Following the previous example, the perfect way to start a conversation at a wedding is to ask the other person how he knows the bride or groom. A college student can ask the person sitting next to her in class what year she is in, what other classes she is taking, or what dorm she lives in. At a new job, a person could ask a fellow employee how long he has been at the company, where he likes to eat lunch near the office, or what project he has recently been working on. The idea is to coach the patient to look at the context that is shared by himself and the person with whom he would like to converse. This will provide him with all sorts of ideas of things to chat about.

Patients sometimes worry about how to keep a conversation going once it is started. They can become so worried about what to say next that they miss cues that would help them know what is appropriate. The key here is to help patients stay focused on the "back and forth volley" of the conversation, almost as if they are watching a tennis match. Often, the cue for what to say next comes from what the other person in the dyad has just said.

Therapists can also help patients to see that conversation is a two-way street. They are not 100 percent responsible for keeping the conversation going. If it does fizzle, it might be because the other person did not keep up their end of the conversation. As soon as patients stop thinking about how important it is for them to keep the conversation going, conversation often flows much better!

Finally, conversations do need to end at some point. Conversations naturally fizzle out, or people need to leave the situation, or might want to move on in order to talk to someone else. Patients sometimes need some coaching on how to gracefully end a conversation. Therapists can teach them some appropriate phrases like, "It was great talking. Maybe we can catch up again later," or "I just saw Bob walk in. I haven't seen him in ages so I am going to go and say hi." The skills of initiating, maintaining, and ending conversations can be practiced in the context of sessions, with therapists giving coaching tips afterward.

Problem Solving

When to Use Problem Solving

Problem solving skills are beneficial when patients feel overwhelmed by a problem or feel as if a problem is insurmountable, thus driving anxiety. Problem solving can be useful when patients have deficits in making decisions, and beginning or completing tasks. The goal of problem-solving skills training is to help patients generate multiple possible solutions (rather than jumping to one solution very quickly); tackling the problem in an organized way; and re-evaluating the usefulness of their problem-solving plan after it is implemented. Problem solving is an iterative process—the appeal of generating multiple possible solutions is that if the first solution does not work out, other solutions can be implemented. This means that problems will usually be solved effectively—even if they are not solved on the first attempt.

When Not to Use Problem Solving

The main reason not to use problem solving is if the problem can be better addressed by conducting an exposure. At times, it may seem that the patient lacks problem-solving skills, but in reality, he or she does not want to confront a situation because of anxiety. In these instances, breaking the situation down into a series of graduated exposures is the best way to handle it. Breaking a problem down into manageable steps is essentially a problem-solving skill. When clinicians help patients to do this, the patient is able to learn both how to create graduated exposures *and* how to solve problems.

For example, a patient with OCD was nervous about contracting illnesses from riding on the subway. He came into an early therapy session, proudly announcing that he had been able to ride the subway to and from work all week! When his therapist asked him how he did this, he said that he had read about problem solving in a self-help book and has made a plan for dealing with his anxiety. He wore long pants, a long shirt, and gloves (even though it was summer). He wore all white because it allowed him to see if he had gotten dirty, and he carried a bottle of bleach and a change of clothes to work. Once he got there, he took off his gloves and washed his hands and face with bleach and if his clothes appeared dirty, he changed them. Rather than feeling overwhelmed by anxiety and having to miss work, he had generated a plan for getting there successfully and according to him, the plan worked. His therapist quickly explained to him the problem with avoidance and they devised a gradual exposure plan for helping him to get to work without rituals.

Generate Alternatives

In many cases, however, anxious patients can benefit a great deal from learning problem-solving skills. Patients sometimes face a problem and cannot come up with any methods for dealing with it. The situation may be so anxiety-provoking that they cannot generate potential responses. Alternatively, the situation may present a novel scenario that the patient cannot begin to consider how to handle.

At other times, patients become stuck on one potential solution. They do not like alternative solutions so they become fixated on something that is not a viable option or something that is unlikely to lead to the most favorable outcome. Patients may find it stressful to think about the problem and easier to just settle on the first problem-solving method that comes to mind. This method might be ineffective or less effective than other options.

Patients with problem-solving difficulties often put the situation off all together and procrastinate. They lack practice with facing difficult situations and revert to their habitual response of avoidance.

Problem solving involves six steps: (1) define the problem and set a goal; (2) generate alternative solutions; (3) weigh the pros and cons of each solution; (4) pick an action and make a plan; (5) carry out the plan; (6) review progress toward accomplishing the goal and revise the plan if necessary.

Define the Problem and Set a Goal

Patients are often so overwhelmed by the problem that they do not even know what the problem is! Therapists can help patients to articulate the problem that they would like to solve and clearly state a goal. The latter is important so that patients can evaluate at the end of the process whether they have indeed solved their problem or whether they need to select another solution and try again.

Let's return to the case example of Rose, the patient with GAD who was introduced in Chapter 1. She always worried about being on time and getting all the things done that she needed to accomplish, but she was highly unproductive because she worried, procrastinated, and became overwhelmed. One task that Rose avoided was opening the mail. She would end up with stacks of mail and her bills and other important documents would be neglected.

Rose stated that her problem was never opening her mail and she stated two goals: to process the mail she currently had and to come up with a plan for keeping on top of new incoming mail. Her therapist encouraged her to begin with the first goal and put the second goal on the agenda for an upcoming session.

Generate Alternative Solutions

Generating alternative solutions is often one of the hardest tasks for anxious patients. They are typically used to just avoiding problems, or jumping to one quick solution without considering other options. Then, if that solution does not work out, they feel stuck and ineffective. During problem solving, patients can be asked to write a list of ten things that they could do in the situation to achieve a desirable outcome. This is quite similar to coming up with alternative interpretations for situations during cognitive restructuring–it gets back to the core concept that there are multiple ways to view a single situation.

During this process, the clinician should provide encouragement and help the patient not to censor him or herself when coming up with alternatives. In fact, a useful exercise to reduce censoring is to first come up with a list of wacky responses–the wackier, the better. Patients can then be helped to generate a list of realistic alternatives and decide which option is the best one in the given scenario.

Rose's therapist helped her to come up with several options for taking care of the mail. Rose's typically strategy was to ignore the mail; this was included in her list of potential solutions. Rose's list included the following alternatives:

- Continue to let the mail accumulate in a huge pile.
- Throw everything away.
- Sort everything out into two piles–keep or throw away.
- Sort everything out by type of mail (magazines, bills, etc).
- Ask her husband to take his mail out of the pile first.
- Sort mail out by priority.
- Begin opening the mail that appears easier to deal with (i.e., not bills or other potentially disturbing things).
- Open each piece of mail one by one beginning with what's on the top of the pile.
- Open the biggest pieces of mail first to shrink down the pile.

When Rose engaged in this process, she saw that there were many alternatives. The sheer number of alternatives overwhelmed her, so her clinician helped her to quickly narrow the list down to the top couple of actions.

Weigh the Pros and Cons of Each Solution

Anxious people often try to solve a problem with the first solution that comes into their minds. There is no thought involved. The next step in problem solving is to evaluate each potential solution, *prior* to making a decision of how to act. Rose and her clinician spent quite a bit of time then discussed the pros and cons of each potential action.

Pick an Action, Make a Plan, and Carry Out the Plan

Patients who have difficulty with problem solving often engage in all-or-none thinking. They see the problem as a giant, overwhelming entity. They are unable to consider how to break the problem down into smaller parts and then proceed forward. It is easy for them to get stuck.

After carefully weighing the pros and cons of each solution, Rose decided to sort her mail out by priority and take care of the high-priority items first. Her therapist knew though that if she sent Rose away to just "do" this, Rose would likely fail. The problem simply seemed too overwhelming and it was likely that Rose would opt to do nothing. Therefore, at the end of her problem solving session, her therapist helped her to come up with a concrete plan. She decided to spend one hour each night on her project starting that night and she planned to enlist the help of her husband. She decided to spend the first night gathering all the bills, the second night paying the bills, and then a few more nights going through the rest of the mail.

Creating a systematic list of the different actions to take in addressing any particular problem can be useful for clients. This helps them tackle all-or-none thinking. It also helps patients to beat procrastination and avoidance and to keep the ball moving once they set it in motion.

Review and Revise

The final important aspect of problem solving is to evaluate the effectiveness of the solution and the steps that he takes. Selecting the "wrong" solution is not a big deal when other potential solutions are available to try next. The important thing is that the patient learns something from the process. The clinician can discuss the various steps in the cycle and help the patient to see where bottlenecks or break downs in problem solving occurred. The patient will be aware of these processes and can respond differently the next time a similar problem-solving opportunity presents itself.

In evaluating the patient's problem-solving abilities, clinicians should be on the lookout for anxiety that got in the way of the process. Opportunities for exposures may present themselves during the patient's decision-making process. For example, a patient with social anxiety had several things to do one day. He became overwhelmed with trying to figure out how to fit everything in, and only did some of the activities. The clinician can help him to see if anxiety stood in the way of the activities that were not completed. Ask the patient which things needed to be accomplished but were not done. If the patient says that he did many of his errands but did not make a return at a clothing store that he needs to do before the 30-day limit for returns expires, then a great opportunity for exposure exists.

Relaxation

When to Use Relaxation

Patients who have a high baseline level of anxiety can benefit from relaxation training. These are the patients who wake up in the morning feeling anxious before they even know what they are feeling anxious about. These patients often report somatic difficulties such as muscle tension, headaches, gastrointestinal problems, and other physical discomforts.

The best way to use relaxation practice is to help the patient cope with general day-to-day stress and bring down their overall level of anxiety. Relaxation can a help patient to feel more calm and in control. This feeling of composure helps the patient to confront challenging situations and commit not to avoid.

When Not to Use Relaxation

Relaxation should not be used in response to a specific anxiety trigger. This may sound counterintuitive at first because it may appear that patients should try to utilize relaxation strategies when they are feeling nervous. Recall that one of the crucial tenets of anxiety disorder treatment is that patients choose not to avoid their anxiety and purposefully expose themselves to anxiety-inducing situations. If patients try to use relaxation during an exposure, it will detract from the impact of the exposure. Relaxation during exposures can also function as a safety behavior. It becomes a strategy to avoid the anxiety and often backfires—making the patient feel more anxious. Therefore, patients should not utilize relaxation to save themselves from situations. Rather they should integrate relaxation into their days at a set time as a preventive measure.

The next sections will describe some specific relaxation procedures from which patients can benefit. The clinician and patient can experiment to see which type of relaxation exercise works best for the patient. Relaxation exercises can also be combined for added benefit.

Deep Breathing

Clinicians can teach patients diaphragmatic breathing during a therapy session in their office. It works well to demonstrate the breathing first and then try it along with the patient.

As the clinician conducts the relaxation training with the patient, he or she can demonstrate and give the following directions to the patient.

> Begin by placing one hand on your chest and one hand on your stomach. Breathe normally for a minute and observe how your hands rise and fall. Then begin to breathe more deeply from the diaphragm. Inhale slowly through your nose for about four slow counts. As you inhale, your stomach should rise. You will see your hand on your stomach rise and the hand on your chest stay in place. Exhale slowly, also around four counts and observe your stomach deflate. It can be useful to include a relaxation cue during the exhale breath. This can be a word such as "relax" or "calm."

One of the keys to experiencing benefit from relaxation is practice. Patients can be instructed to practice every day for around 15 minutes. They should find a peaceful place and close their eyes to maximize relaxation. For deep relaxation, patients should slow their rate of breathing down to about 10 breaths per minute.

Progressive Muscle Relaxation

Many patients with anxiety disorders experience significant muscle tension, stiffness, aches and pains, and a feeling of being restless and "on edge." Progressive muscle relaxation (PMR) works well to combat muscle tension and promote a sense of relaxation. PMR works by first tensing muscle groups and then relaxing them. This process is effective because the relaxation is more pronounced after tension. Patients can really notice the difference between tension and relaxation. This will help them to spot tension in their body and know when it is a good time to use PMR.

The procedure described below is adopted from Bernstein, Borkovec, and Hazlett-Stevens (2000). Clinicians again can demonstrate the PMR in session along with the patients. Provide patients instructions such as:

> Begin by sitting comfortably in your chair and removing any glasses or jewelry that may be restricting. Tense each group of muscles for seven seconds and then relax the muscles immediately after the seven seconds is up. When your muscles are relaxed, notice the difference in sensations between the tension and relaxation. Enjoy the relaxed feelings for about thirty seconds before moving on.

> Begin by tensing facial muscles. For the sake of efficiency, all the facial muscles can be tensed simultaneously. Furrow your brow, wrinkle your nose, close your eyes tightly, and tighten your jaw. Hold for seven seconds. Now, release the tension and notice the relaxed feeling.

> The next muscle group to focus on is your arms, neck, and shoulders. Many people hold their muscle tension in these areas. Tense them by bending your arms, tightening your hands into fists, and holding your arms out in front of you. Create tension by pushing your elbows to the ground and raising your shoulders up to your ears. Push your chin back into your neck to tighten your neck. Tense all of these muscles at once as much as you can and then release.

> Now, focus on tightening your chest muscles and sucking in your stomach. Tense your stomach as if your stomach is a sponge you are trying to squeeze water out of. Hold seven seconds and release. Enjoy the relaxed feeling once you release the tension.

> Tense the thighs by lifting your legs off the ground and at the same time pushing them down. Notice the tension on the top of your legs and clench your muscles as tightly as possible. Relax and feel the difference.

> Finally, tense your calves and feet by stretching your legs out in front of you, curling your toes and then flexing your feet so they bend back towards your body. Tense this group for just five seconds to avoid cramping. Then relax and enjoy the relaxed feeling for thirty seconds.

Clinicians sometimes record the PMR experience so a patient can listen to the recording as they practice, to walk them through the muscle groups. Patients should practice PMR for about 15–20 minutes per day.

Guided Imagery

For patients who are able to get mental images in their minds, guided imagery exercises can be very useful in creating a sense of calm, peace, and relaxation. In the book *Women Who Worry Too Much*, Dr. Hazlett-Stevens states that images are closely linked to emotions. Just as an image or visual memory of something traumatic or painful can evoke intense fear, anger, or sadness, an image of something enjoyable can evoke a state of relaxation.

Clinicians can teach patients how to engage in guided imagery exercises and practice with them in session. Patients can then practice guided imagery at home for about five minutes, once or twice a day. Once they become skilled in drawing forth the image and relaxing, they can use imagery in brief intervals throughout their day. They may wish to combine it with the deep breathing exercise described previously. Hazlett-Stevens recommends the following guided imagery exercise.

> Find a comfortable, quiet place to complete the guided imagery. Select a scene that brings positive feelings, like happiness, calm, and relaxation. It can be a place you have been, a place you would love to go, or something you create in your mind. Now close your eyes and imagine the scene as vividly as possible. Put yourself in the scene and notice all the sights, smells, sensations, and sounds around you. Stay with the scene for about five minutes and observe how you feel when you are very relaxed. Use this exercise once a day and as needed to produce positive feelings and relaxation.

Other Strategies

There are innumerable strategies that patients can use for relaxation. Clinicians should let patients know that there are no right or wrong techniques when it comes to relaxation. Clinicians can help patients find what is relaxing for them. Here are a few more ideas to suggest to patients if they need some help coming up with ideas for relaxation strategies.

Exercise

Exercise serves many benefits in relaxation and stress reduction. Regular exercise provides dozens of physiological benefits that help to bring down overall levels of anxiety and combat anticipatory anxiety. Exercise releases endorphins that naturally promote a sense of well-being, and increases brain levels of the neurotransmitter serotonin, which can offset depression and anxiety. Regular exercise can also improve sleep, sense of well-being, concentration, and self-esteem (Bourne & Garano, 2003).

Clinicians can help patients to decide what types of exercise works best for them. Patients may receive optimal benefit from different forms of exercise depending on their mood, the situation, and their goal. For example, if a patient feels drained from anxiety, a high-impact type of exercise such as jogging or aerobics could be beneficial to help increase energy. If a patient feels wound up and tense, a relaxing form of exercise such as yoga or Pilates could be optimal.

Music

Music has a powerful effect on human emotions. Most people have some favorite types of music or songs that reliably improve their mood or energy level. Clinicians can assist patients with deciding which forms of music are most effective, and how patients can integrate music into their daily lives. Similar to exercise, music can be chosen strategically to affect the patient's mood. Fun, uplifting music can energize patients and get them "pumped up" to do their exposures. Soft, peaceful music can help patients unwind and de-stress after a long day.

Mindfulness

When patients learn to focus on the present moment and pay attention to what is going on around them, they are often able to lower their baseline level of anxiety. When patients completely experience the present moment, it becomes difficult to worry about the past or the future. Mindfulness training helps patients to intentionally and fully experience the present moment (Hazlett-Stevens, 2005).

Clinicians can encourage patients to find some daily activities and experience them with their complete attention. For example, patients can practice mindfulness while doing the dishes by noticing every small step involved with the activity and using all five senses. The patient would notice the feel of the water, the appearance of the bubbles from the dishwashing soap, and the sound of the running water. Patients can be instructed to bring their attention back to the present as soon as they feel it drifting off.

Reading

For many people, reading is a very relaxing activity. Whether it is a book, a favorite magazine, the newspaper, or articles online, patients can find relaxation in reading. Reading can help patients to unwind at the end of the day and fall asleep more easily at night. Some patients enjoy having a favorite article, poem, or mantra handy that they can glance at throughout the day.

In addition to these activities, patients will have their own set of relaxation exercises and habits. It is important for clinicians to remember that what may be relaxing for them, their friends, or other patients is often not relaxing for a particular patient. For example, many people think of going to a movie as a relaxing activity. For a patient with Panic Disorder, a movie could be highly intimidating because they could feel trapped in the middle of the row with no escape. For a patient with social anxiety, the close proximity of many strangers in movie theaters can be difficult. Of course this does not mean that clinicians should encourage avoidance of these activities. It means that some activities should not be thought of as relaxation strategies—instead they should be included on the patient's hierarchy for in vivo exposures.

References

Antony, M. A., & Swinson, R. P. (2000). *The shyness and social anxiety workbook: Proven techniques for overcoming your fears.* Oakland, CA: New Harbinger Publications.

Bernstein, D., Borkovec, T., & Hazlett-Stevens, H. (2000). *New directions in progressive relaxation training: A guidebook for helping professionals.* Westport, CT.: Praeger Publishers.

Bourne, E. B., & Garano, L. (2003). *Coping with anxiety: 10 simple ways to relieve anxiety, fear & worry.* Oakland, CA: New Harbinger Publications.

Hazlatt-Stevens, H. (2005). *Women who worry too much: How to stop worry and anxiety from ruining relationships, work, and fun.* Oakland, CA: New Harbinger Publications.

Peterson, R. J. (2000). *The assertiveness workbook: How to express your ideas and stand up for yourself at work and in relationships.* Oakland, CA: New Harbinger Publications.

CHAPTER 10

Termination and Relapse Prevention

A Time Limited Treatment Approach

Cognitive behavioral treatments for anxiety disorders are typically short-term, so the ending of therapy is known from the beginning. There is no rule that therapy must be 12, 16, or 20 sessions. It is often, however, helpful that patients know that they are involved in a time-limited approach. This knowledge helps them to habituate to the prospect of termination. In addition, knowing that there are a limited number of sessions helps patient to push themselves to make changes (Ledley, Marx, & Heimberg. 2005). When patients feel some external pressure to push them along, they are more motivated to move up their hierarchies. If patients move quickly through their hierarchies, they gain momentum and encouragement from seeing the changes occur. If, on the other hand, patients feel that they have all the time in the world to progress with their treatment, they may be less likely to move quickly and more likely to experience anticipatory anxiety regarding the approaching exposures.

A Useful Analogy

To frame the time-limited approach and the benefits to short-term treatment for anxiety, at the beginning of treatment, clinicians can give patients the following analogy:

> Overcoming an anxiety disorder can be like getting into a cold pool. Let's say that you were sitting at the pool on a day that was a little chilly outside, contemplating getting in to go for a swim. You wanted to get in and get some exercise and enjoyment in the pool, but were hesitant. You go over to the pool and bend over to touch the water and your sunglasses fall in! These are your brand new sunglasses— the first very nice pair you have ever invested in. There is nothing around to fish them out with so you know that you are going in.

Two scenarios can occur. In the first, you're aware of the time and the need to get your sunglasses soon. It's around 4 in the afternoon, so you know that you are losing the nice daytime warmth from the sun and that you should get in quickly. So you give yourself a running start, jump in and get your sunglasses. Once you're in, it is cold at first, but you get used to it quickly. Now that you're in the pool, you decide to take a swim. Twenty minutes later, you get out, happy that you got your sunglasses and got a nice swim.

In the second scenario, you become fixated on how cold the pool is and how much you don't want to get in. You do not pay attention that it is getting late in the afternoon and it's only going to get more difficult as the warm sun fades away. You walk over to the pool and touch the water. It's cold! Then you stick your toes in. You decide to wait for a while to get used to it and then put your legs in. At this point, you are very cold and not at all interested in getting in. "Maybe I don't really need those sunglasses," you try to convince yourself. After an hour, you are only part way in, and you're very cold. You have lost your motivation to get into the pool and are contemplating giving up. You decide to come back the next day and see if it is any different, but it is still cold, so you do not get your sunglasses.

External Pressure Can Be Helpful

In this analogy, the person benefited from realizing that time was limited. She used the knowledge of the loss of daylight to push herself to get into the pool as quickly as possible. By moving quickly, she experienced less anticipatory anxiety, and increased motivation. She was able to experience the positive benefits of being in the pool once she got in—she got her sunglasses and felt good after a swim. The person in the second example did not have sufficient internal or external pressure. She did not pay attention to the time and instead took her time. By taking her time, she found it more difficult to get into the water and her anticipatory anxiety grew. She missed out on some important benefits—getting her sunglasses and having a swim—due to her trepidation and lack of motivation.

External Pressure Can Be Detrimental

It is important that clinicians do not make anxious patients more anxious by overemphasizing the time limits and pending termination. If the clinician is not working within a research setting or providing treatment following a specific manual, then some flexibility can be used. There is really no reason that the patient cannot receive 18 sessions instead of 16, especially if she has been making good progress.

Clinicians should remember that patients will lose motivation and comfort within the therapeutic relationship if they feel that their therapist is pushing them. Patients need to learn how to be in the driver's seat of their treatment. When they assume control, treatment will be much more effective and long lasting.

Multiple Anxiety Disorder Diagnoses and Extended Treatment

If a patient has multiple diagnoses, he may need a significantly longer treatment approach. In treating a patient with several anxiety disorders, the clinician should first ascertain which disorder is primary and then provide the full course of treatment for that disorder. Upon completion of treatment for the primary anxiety disorder, it is likely that the patient's other anxiety issues will be reduced as well, but the patient may require additional treatment.

For example, consider a patient with a principal diagnosis of Social Phobia (meaning that the social phobia causes the most distress and impairment to the patient) and an additional diagnosis of Panic Disorder. This patient's therapist embarked on treatment by providing the patient with 16 sessions of treatment dedicated to the Social Phobia. During these 16 sessions, the patient learned about the importance of allowing oneself to experience anxiety and about how to do cognitive restructuring and exposures. At the end of the 16 sessions, he no longer met criteria for social phobia. As a result of treatment for Social Phobia, his Panic Disorder had also subsided because he was able to apply some of what he learned to this other problem. However, he did continue to experience some distress regarding the physical symptoms of panic so his therapist decided to spend five sessions conducting interoceptive exposures and creating a separate in vivo exposure hierarchy for the patient to complete outside of session. The patient completed 21 treatment sessions and no longer has Social Phobia or Panic Disorder symptoms. Since the same core techniques are used in the treatment of all of the anxiety disorders, the Panic Disorder treatment proceeded very quickly.

Transferring the Role of the Therapist

One of the goals of CBT for anxiety disorders is for patients to learn how to be their own therapists. Clinicians must be careful that patients do not become dependent on them or the process of therapy. Instead, patients must learn how to independently apply the tools learned in therapy so that they continue to be their own therapist once treatment is over.

In the book *Making Cognitive-Behavior Therapy Work*, Ledley et al. recommend helping patients to be their own clinicians throughout the process of treatment. One way that clinicians can help patients to achieve this goal is by providing them with positive reinforcement whenever they find exposure practice on their own. A patient with OCD and contamination concerns came into a session and said, "Over the weekend one of my friends wanted to go to a party. I did not want to go because I did not want to use the bathroom that everyone else used or eat food that other people could have touched without washing their hands. I also knew that the hosts have a pet dog which probably brought tons of germs into their house from the backyard and the street." The clinician asked, "What did you choose to do?" The patient answered, "I knew that it would be a great exposure to really show OCD who's the boss and refrain from doing my rituals since I could not jump in the shower at the friend's house! So I went and it was actually a lot of fun." Here is a perfect opportunity for the clinician to praise the patient for the decision and to ask the patient what he or she learned from the experience.

Another way to help patients become their own clinicians is to gradually shift decision making to them throughout the course of therapy. Over time, patients should assume greater responsibility for planning future sessions, assigning themselves homework, and designing exposures. When patients ask clinicians for their advice, clinicians can use Socratic questioning to help patients solve the problem for themselves.

Termination Anxiety

Many anxious patients are comforted by being in therapy. They feel better knowing that if they have difficulties, they have a therapist with whom to talk and strategize.

Build Self-Efficacy

Patients may mistakenly believe that they are better because of the clinician and the therapy. While this is true to a degree, clinicians can help patients to see that their role is as a facilitator or coach while the patient is responsible for the major changes that occur. Clinicians can recommend actions, but it is up to the patient to put them into practice. If patients have sufficiently reduced anxiety such that termination is approaching, they can be encouraged to give themselves credit for their progress. When they recognize their progress and allow it to help them build self-efficacy, they feel more capable of maintaining changes on their own.

A developmental explanation or metaphor about learning a new skill can help the patient to see how the guidance and responsibilities have shifted to the patient over time. At the beginning of treatment, patients did not know what they needed to do to get better. This is why they presented for treatment. During the course of treatment, they discovered many new ideas and approaches that helped them overcome anxiety. At the point of termination, patients knew what it is that they needed to do to maintain their treatment gains.

The process of anxiety disorders treatment is like learning a new language. If someone embarks on learning a new language, he or she may begin by taking a class. At this point, the instructor knows the language but the student does not. During the course of the student's studies, he begins to learn some of the building blocks of the language. The responsibility for learning the language shifts from his teacher to him. He is now responsible for practicing. If the student immerses himself in the language and practices a great deal, he will improve. At the end of the course, the student knows what he needs to do to further improve his facility with the new language (i.e., practice, visit a country where the language is spoken) and he no longer needs the teacher to tell him how to practice.

A Positive Change

As with any type of therapy, patients completing therapy for an anxiety disorder will have various feelings about termination. The ending of therapy can cause patients to experience anticipatory anxiety about what is ahead. They know that their lives are now changed. Without a reason to hold themselves back from pursuing various goals, they feel that they are ready to do so—but this is frightening.

People prone to anxiety have a tendency to resist change and fear the unknown. Ending treatment and facing an anxiety-free (or anxiety reduced) life is a major change. It is exciting but certainly intimidating for patients as well. Patients may go back into the workforce, make new friendships, engage in challenging new recreational activities, accept a promotion in their job, or many other novel things that they have not done before or have not done in some time. It is normal for patients to doubt their abilities to handle new challenges and to fear that they could relapse.

Many of the changes that patients face started to evolve while the patient was in treatment. This allows the patient to discuss changes with the clinician at the most difficult point—actually deciding to make a change and put the new plan into action (e.g., interviewing for a new job, accepting the offer, and starting the job). Clinicians can purposefully incorporate some of the new changes into the treatment and be sure that the patient becomes comfortable with them while in the active or maintenance stage of therapy. If the new activities have not begun at the time of termination, clinicians can help patients to plan how to best handle them.

Clinicians can also use the termination of therapy to show patients that change is not necessarily bad and in fact, many changes are very positive. Coming to an end of therapy is a highly positive change because it signifies the patient's courage, determination, and progress with overcoming anxiety. Therefore, clinicians can help patients to reframe their beliefs about ending therapy, helping them to recognize this event as a positive one.

Building Positive Activities and Meaning

Termination anxiety may be not so much due to fears about facing something new and intimidating as it is about fears about facing nothing. Patients may have little in their lives that they enjoy or look forward to and coming in for their therapy sessions could be a major source of fulfillment and meaning for them. Patients will often increase their social support systems and involvement in pleasurable activities during the course of treatment. Building up these networks, however, can take a long time and the patient may not have extensive systems in place by the time treatment concludes.

Clinicians can do two things to help patients who face these issues. The first is to spend some time brainstorming and coming up with potential new, enjoyable activities. If a patient lacks social support, the perfect activities may be those that expose the patient to new social networks. Activities based around common interests tend to work very well. For example, if a patient is into outdoor sports, he and his clinician can research some hiking clubs, biking groups, or city walking tours. This way he can meet people and participate in an enjoyable activity.

The second task that the clinician can help the patient with is finding meaning and purpose. This area is frequently addressed in existential and humanistic forms of psychotherapy and is appropriate and useful in the treatment of anxiety disorders as well. Patients who experienced clinical anxiety for years or even decades likely missed out on many crucial life activities. They may have found themselves going through the motions of life, trying to get by despite their anxiety, but without a sense of purpose. Patients may have vague goals or an unsure sense of what is to come next and what is truly important to them. If patients appear to require work in these areas and clinicians do not feel comfortable or well versed, they can make a referral to another therapist or a qualified life coach to help the patient.

Another Helpful Exposure

By the time patients reach the end of treatment, they will be very well versed with the idea of exposure. They will know that it is a good idea to confront whatever they are nervous about. Thus, the ending of therapy can serve as an additional exposure.

The therapist can help the patient to create a set of predictions about the negative outcomes that could occur upon termination of therapy and then test out those predictions. For example, a patient may say, "I could fall right back into my old habits and not be able to get back on track." The clinician can then suggest that the patient sees whether this will happen upon termination. It is unlikely that the patient would revert to old habits *and* be unable to get back on track. In case the patient does in fact revert to old habits, the clinician and patient can together come up with a plan to get back on track. The plan would be very specific and may include a maintenance session or phone call with the therapist. Therefore, even if the patient does begin to relapse, she will see that it is not true that she cannot get back on track. It will be powerful disconfirmation of the patient's anxious prediction and powerful confirmation that the patient can in fact keep her anxiety under control.

Ongoing Treatment

Maintenance Therapy

The end of the primary stage of treatment is not necessarily the end of the treatment process. Many clinicians offer ongoing maintenance therapy for patients who may benefit from it.

There are two ways to structure maintenance therapy. The first is an extension of the primary phase of therapy. The differences are twofold: First, the aim of the treatment is different. The initial treatment aim was, for example, to reduce social phobia. At the cessation of 16 sessions, this goal has been accomplished, so the goal for maintenance will be different. There may be several goals, such as:

- Reduce the likelihood of a relapse
- Manage any relapses that begin
- Increase social activities
- Add new relationships into the patient's life
- Improve existing relationships

In this first approach, maintenance is built into the treatment plan, and the patient and clinician may agree from the beginning about goals for treatment and maintenance. Maintenance therapy sessions typically occur less frequently. If treatment was once or twice weekly, maintenance may occur every three or four weeks. Clinicians may decide to begin with a few months of maintenance with visits scheduled once per month and then switch to conducting sessions once every six or eight weeks.

The second approach to maintenance is to terminate therapy and keep the option of maintenance available. In this scenario, the treatment would be over after the set number of sessions or when the patient was markedly improved and no longer meets criteria for an anxiety disorder diagnosis. Termination would occur and patients would be given information about returning for maintenance therapy if they desired.

The second approach is suitable when a patient is clearly recovered from the initial anxiety diagnosis and when there are no foreseeable triggers for relapse. For example, if Phillip, the patient with OCD regarding contamination, finished treatment with no symptoms of OCD, he may not need a maintenance phase of treatment. If he tackled all of the items on his hierarchy during treatment and feels very minimal anxiety on a day-to-day basis, it is appropriate to simply end treatment with a few sessions about relapse prevention. These sessions (as will be described in more detail below) should include a discussion of how to maintain treatment gains, how to recognize signs of relapse, and knowing what to do if a return of symptoms does occur.

Medication Cessation

Many patients begin to think about tapering down or getting off of their medications as they see improvements from CBT. The decision to stop medications is a personal one and it is up to the patient and prescribing physician to discuss. The clinician can certainly help the patient sort out the different options and reference some of the literature on medication and psychotherapy termination, but should not give any specific instruction on medication discontinuation.

Medications have varying degrees of effectiveness when combined with CBT for different anxiety disorders. With some anxiety disorders, there is evidence that CBT plus medication may actually increase the likelihood of relapse following treatment. In Chapter 2, we discussed the study by Barlow and colleagues (2000) that suggested that the use of medication plus CBT for treatment of Panic Disorder did not produce greater effects than CBT alone and that the risk of relapse may increase upon discontinuation of medications. One explanation for findings like this one is that patients may attribute their treatment gains to the medication rather than the CBT. Some studies suggest that medication cessation works best when it occurs before the ending of the CBT and when CBT is used to help patients process this experience (Spiegel, 1999).

Relapse Prevention

Relapse prevention is one of the most important aspects of treatment. With one or two sessions dedicated to relapse prevention, patients can significantly reduce the probability that a relapse will occur. They can also learn what to do if a relapse begins, thereby preventing a mountain from forming out of a molehill.

Help Patients Remember What They Learned

Helping patients to remember key points from treatment is something that can occur during the relapse prevention sessions or as an ongoing part of treatment. One of the best ways to help patients remember lessons from treatment is to write things down. Clinicians can help patients write down key points from treatment at the end of every session or towards the end of treatment as part of relapse prevention.

The primary reason to write things down at the end of each session or to have patients write down lessons between sessions is ongoing reinforcement. Ongoing documentation of important messages learned in treatment will help patients remember them and stay motivated to complete their exposures. Clinicians can take a few minutes towards the end of each therapy session to ask what the patient got out of the session. The points can be kept as a document that is added onto each session. Alternatively, clinicians can ask patients to write these notes down between sessions for homework.

The therapist and patient can also spend a session reviewing what was learned during treatment as part of relapse prevention. This will help the patient remember the primary lessons for treatment and utilize them on an ongoing basis. Even if clinicians take the first approach and have their patients keep track of lessons learned from each session, it is a good idea to compile the data and review it during one of the last treatment sessions as a way to consolidate memories about the important parts of treatment.

Acknowledge Progress and Identify Potential Problem Areas

The final session can be spent reviewing the progress and successes the patient made in treatment. This process draws patients' attention to their improvements and empowers them to work on continually improving and managing their symptoms.

It can be powerful to show patients objective criteria for their progress to show what has changed. Clinicians can walk patients through their self-monitoring to see the differences from the beginning compared with the end of treatment. Patients can observe the trends and changes recorded in the self-monitoring and see how their behaviors led to those changes.

Patients can be asked to re-rate the items on their exposure hierarchy. They will likely find that items that were once an 80 are now a 10 or lower. Patients are sometimes surprised to see how difficult a particular exposure seemed to them at the beginning of treatment. Particularly once patients complete the exposures at the top of the hierarchy, all of the other items typically seem much easier.

The most objective way to track patients' progress in treatment is to have an assessment administered by a third party. Clinicians may have a bias in their ratings because they have worked with their patients all along. Another clinician could, therefore, provide a more objective assessment of the patient's symptoms at the end of treatment. Preferably, the clinician would use the same assessment measure that was used at pretreatment (see Chapter 3 for information regarding selection of assessment measures). If clinicians do not work in a university, counseling center, or clinic setting, it can be more difficult to find another clinician to conduct the evaluations. If in a group practice, clinicians can volunteer to conduct evaluations for one another.

Once the clinician has the data from the evaluation, it can be used as an objective measure of progress. Clinicians can compare individual items from pre- and post-treatment to see what has changed. Clinicians can also identify the items that remain elevated and discuss them with patients. For example, if it is found that a patient with OCD still shows some rituals (albeit minor ones and much reduced) at termination, the clinician can let the patient know that there is a possibility that the rituals could become more distressing and time-consuming if they are not kept in check. The clinician and patient could then devise a plan to further eliminate or contain the rituals to greatly reduce the likelihood that they would become increasingly problematic.

If the clinician does not have an assessment measure to pinpoint potential problems, then information can be gathered during an interview with the patient. The patient can be asked in what areas they feel pleased about their progress. They can be asked where they feel there is still room for improvement or potential for a backslide. The clinician would then help the patient to proactively make a plan to address those areas.

Sometimes a patient is unable to do the top exposure on his hierarchy because it is simply not feasible in his life during the course of treatment. He may have completely habituated to all the items on his hierarchy and feel recovered from the anxiety disorder. However, having this undone exposure looming over his head could become a problem. Therefore, the clinician could work with the patient to plan the exposure as quickly as possible and may plan one or two additional sessions regarding the last exposure.

Using Tools from Therapy in Different Situations

As discussed at various points in this book, one of the most important aspects of anxiety disorder treatment is to help patients become their own clinicians and learn how to utilize the tools they learned in therapy in a variety of different situations. The wonderful thing about anxiety disorder treatment is that the primary treatment strategies apply across anxiety disorders and anxiety-producing situations.

Susan, the 30-year old mother with Panic Disorder was able to eliminate panic attacks and Agoraphobia during her treatment. Near the end of treatment, Susan was asked to give a speech to a civic organization of which she had recently become a member. She was nervous about getting up in front of the people and afraid that she would not be taken seriously. Her clinician helped her to see how she could take what she learned in panic treatment and use it in this new situation.

The clinician helped Susan to see that the talk created a SUDS level of around 80, suggesting that Susan might want to embark on some lower-level exposures prior to doing her speech in order to gain practice, reduce anxiety and build confidence. On her own, Susan came up with an excellent game plan. She enrolled in Toastmasters so she could speak in front of an audience every week. She planned to give a talk at the next PTA meeting. Susan went to some meetings of her organization and made a point to speak up to give her some mini-exposures before her big presentation. When Susan spoke, she noticed several physical symptoms including racing heart, dry mouth, and sweaty palms. She later did some interoceptive exposures to these symptoms and cognitively reminded herself that they are simply physical sensations that do not need to be reacted to or overly attended to. Susan took all of the concepts that she learned (and came to trust) during treatment for her Panic Disorder and used them to help her successfully make her speech.

Interpreting Lapses

One of the most critical aspects of relapse prevention is the way in which patients interpret lapses. A lapse is a minor reoccurrence of symptoms. A relapse is a major increase in symptoms, perhaps to the level experienced before treatment began. Educating patients about the difference between a lapse and a relapse is critical. Lapses usually occur prior to relapses. The good thing about this is that patients can identify the lapse and deal with it before the problem increases and becomes more difficult to deal with.

The best way for a patient to deal with a lapse is with a calm attitude. Clinicians can educate patients regarding the approach to take when confronted with a lapse. First, patients should expect that lapses will occur. This way, they will not be overly surprised or discouraged when a lapse occurs, and they will be ready for it. It is very likely that patients will experience a resurgence of symptoms at some point—it may be minor, but it is likely that it will occur.

When signs or symptoms of anxiety do reemerge, patients are at risk for all-or-none thinking. They may think, "Oh no! I worked so hard to overcome my anxiety and here I am completely anxious! I must be back to square one." The reality is that a lapse is a minor bump in the road and it does not bring the patient back to the starting point. In fact, lapses can strengthen a patient's ability to handle anxiety. When a lapse occurs and the patient is able to get through it without it leading to a relapse, they learn that they can manage their anxiety and that they are in control of it, rather than it controlling them.

The key is that patients do not over react to lapses when they do occur. The best approach is to look at a lapse as an opportunity to practice what they have learned in treatment. It is as if the anxiety is giving them a small test. They have the ability to pass should they decide to put what they know into action.

Clinicians should also let patients know that they may opt to get in touch with the clinician when signs of a lapse are present. Because there is generally time in between a lapse and a full-blown relapse, patients should call their therapists before the relapse occurs. Clinicians can acknowledge that patients may feel uncomfortable about calling the therapist over something that seems relatively minor, but they need not be. Sometimes a brief phone call or a booster treatment session is critical in preventing a lapse from turning into a relapse (Ledley, Marx, & Heimberg. 2005).

Using Support Systems

In addition to patients becoming their own therapists, they can also learn how to effectively gain support from others. Family and friends can offer support in several ways. First, friends and family can serve as coaches to assist the patient in treatment and relapse prevention. They can help patients to identify signs of a lapse. Sometimes patients are not even aware that they are engaging in a particular behavior that may enable the anxiety. For example, some patients with OCD ask for reassurance from others as a ritual. A family member may notice that the patient is beginning to do this again before the patient notices it herself. The family members can coach the patients and remind them of the different steps that they can take to best manage the lapse and prevent a relapse. This process works best when patients request the support of friends and family and do not feel that they are being told what to do against their will. Patients can describe the way they would like to be reminded to get back on track. It is important that the patient feels support and positive encouragement and does not feel ganged up on. Chapter 14 describes in detail how to involve support systems as treatment supporters.

The second way that support systems can be effective is by providing positive reinforcement. The role of the support systems is that of cheerleader—they can provide continuous reinforcement for the things that the patient does well. For example, the father of a twelve-year-old girl with a phobia of bees can compliment his daughter whenever she goes for a walk in the garden, plays sports outside, or chooses to do something outside rather than inside. He can say, "You've worked so hard to overcome your bee phobia, and you're doing great! Look how you can bring your homework outside and do it on the picnic table. You never used to be able to do that–I'm so impressed with what you have done to deal with your anxiety."

Support people can be excellent cheerleaders. This cheerleading and encouragement continues to send the message to the anxiety that there is a whole team of people on board and it does not stand a chance of coming back. These positive people in the patient's life will also serve the role of social support. They will be available to do enjoyable activities with the patient and help keep the patient active and in a positive frame of mind. Many of the activities that can be done with patients are both exposures and potentially enjoyable and rewarding activities. For example, friends or family of people with social anxiety can go to parties with them. Family members of those with Panic Disorder and Agoraphobia can set up a trip to the beach with patients that involves driving over a bridge. Friends of someone with a specific phobia of heights could suggest hiking up a beautiful mountain. These are all activities that are ongoing exposures but also rewarding and enriching to the patients' lives.

The critical part of the use of support systems is that the patient continues to be in charge of his or her own treatment. Patients should not feel that everyone is their therapist and that everyone looks at them as a patient. The clinician can say something like, "I often recommend that patients identify a few people in their life who can act as supports to help you keep up your excellent treatment gains. Are you open to this idea?" If the patient agrees, the clinician can say, "Great, who would you identify as the people you would like to ask? How comfortable are you with them pointing out rituals or safety behaviors in case you aren't aware that you're doing them? I've often seen it occur that patients don't realize they're doing something and when someone points it out, they're able to stop right away. What do you think about this?" Without the patients' agreement, they will not effectively utilize and may resist support form others.

When to Get Back Into Treatment

Another important task for termination is to help patients understand when they may want or need to return for additional treatment. Without a clear understanding of the reasons to resume treatment, patients may not return or may feel that they need treatment when they do not.

If patients do not understand the factors that necessitate maintenance treatment, they may not call their therapists when they should. Patients may be embarrassed to call about something that they perceive to be inconsequential. They may think that because the treatment is over that they can return. A patient with social phobia thought he could not return to his cognitive behavioral therapist. He thought that the treatment was short-term and finished upon termination so when a need for ongoing therapy came up, he looked for another therapist. The clinician he located was significantly less versed in the treatment of anxiety disorders and in his case follow-up treatment with this clinician was not nearly as effective or efficient as it would have been had he returned to his original therapist. It turned out that he thought he did not have the option to return and that if his concerns were different from social phobia that he would need to go elsewhere. It is often necessary to make these contingencies explicit so patients know when to return and feel comfortable with returning for maintenance treatment.

Another risk is that patients become dependent on the therapist and think that they need to return to therapy when they would be better served by showing themselves that they can handle the problem on their own. If a situation is similar to one that a patient has successfully dealt with several times in the past, it may be in the patient's best interest to address it and see how it goes before coming in for a session. Remember that many patients with anxiety disorders can benefit from building up confidence, courage, and self-efficacy. Thus, it can be useful for them to prove to themselves that they can handle situations independently.

The clinician and patient can together devise a list of situations that indicate that a return to therapy may be a good idea. It may be a good time to get back into treatment when:

1. I have tried many activities to end a lapse or relapse and they have not worked.

2. I notice myself becoming increasingly anxious or depressed.

3. Others notice me becoming increasingly anxious or depressed.

4. I have a major hurdle, obstacle, or stressor coming up, and I'm not sure how to deal with it.

5. There is a significant change in my situation, such as discontinuing medication, that I am apprehensive about.

6. Several rituals, safety behaviors, or avoidances have crept back in.

7. I have a new worry or fear and I'm not very sure how to deal with it.

The list can be customized to the individual patient using examples of her own experiences. Clinicians can educate patients that anxiety disorders can be like chronic medical conditions that are well controlled but can flare up under times of stress. If a clinician will not be available to patients for maintenance treatment, due to a move, change in employment, or other reason, it is important to have other clinicians available who can assist the patient if one or more of the scenarios on the list occur.

References

Barlow, D. H., Gorman, J. M., Shear, M. K., & Woods, S. W. (2000). Cognitive-behavioral treatment, imipramine, or their combination for Panic Disorder: A randomized controlled study. *Journal of American Medical Association, 283,* 2529–2536.

Ledley, D. H., Marx, B. P., & Heimberg, R. G. (2005). *Making cognitive-behavioral therapy work: Clinical process for new practitioners.* New York: Guilford.

Spiegel, D. A. (1999). Psychological strategies for discontinuing benzodiazepine treatment. *Journal of Clinical Psychopharmacology, 19,* 17S–22S.

Additional Issues and Treatment Considerations

THE WILEY
CONCISE GUIDES
TO MENTAL HEALTH

Anxiety
Disorders

CHAPTER 11

Additional Treatment Approaches

In this section of the book, we will introduce additional issues and treatment considerations that will assist you in providing optimal treatment for patients with anxiety disorders. By this point, we have discussed diagnosis, assessment, conceptualization, and treatment planning for anxiety disorders. We have described the primary building blocks of effective cognitive behavioral treatments for anxiety disorders, including psychoeducation, in vivo exposure, imaginal exposure, cognitive interventions, relaxation and other CBT strategies, and relapse prevention. There will be times, however, when clinicians will want to integrate aspects from various forms of psychotherapy orientation and practice.

It is beyond the scope of this book to cover *all* of the treatment approaches that can be useful with patients with anxiety disorders. We will, however, cover a few specific approaches that can be particularly helpful with the treatment of anxiety. In this chapter, we will describe two forms of cognitive behavioral therapy: Dialectical Behavior Therapy (DBT) and Acceptance and Commitment Therapy (ACT). A brief discussion of the application of humanistic and existential approaches will be included as well. Chapter 14 will include information on the application of systems theory and when to augment treatment or transfer treatment to family or couples therapy.

Dialectical Behavior Therapy (DBT)

Cognitive behavioral therapists might be familiar DBT as one of the treatments of choice for borderline personality disorder. An important component of DBT is psychosocial skills training. The skills taught in DBT can be beneficial for patients with various presenting problems, including anxiety disorders.

The dialectical worldview is integral in the philosophy and practice of DBT. One fundamental theoretical underpinning is that dialectics stress the interrelatedness of different aspects of a system and different behavior patterns. Patients often need to learn skills not only for changing themselves, but also for influencing their environment (Linehan, 1993). A patient with Social Phobia, for example, may receive negative feedback from others because he lacks assertiveness and fails to positively influence other people.

A second component in DBT is that reality is based upon opposing forces and polarities, which can create tension and difficulties if only one side is adopted (Linehan, 1993). For example, a patient who engages in polarized thinking and believes that any level of anxiety will result in her spinning out of control does *not* have a dialectical balance. Linehan (1993) points out some common examples of polarities seen with patients with borderline personality disorder that are also common with patients with anxiety disorders. The first is the tension between accepting oneself as is versus the need for change. Patients benefit the most when they first accept where they are while simultaneously working on changing. The more they resist their current position and their anxiety, the more the anxiety increases. Acceptance of anxiety is a crucial step in learning how to stop fighting it by engaging in rituals and safety behaviors, and start managing it through exposure and other methods.

A second polarity in the DBT framework frequently seen in patients with anxiety disorders is the polarity between making a change that reduces anxiety versus the cost to this change. Patients will frequently need to sacrifice or lose something when they become less anxious and more competent. Take the example of Susan, the new mother with Panic and Agoraphobia. In overcoming the Panic and Agoraphobia, Susan will have to make several sacrifices. She may no longer get the attention from her husband and others. She may see family members less frequently because they don't feel that they need to be around and help her out as much. She might have to start doing undesirable errands like grocery shopping more often. In addition, there is a cost to the treatment itself since it requires exposure to the anxiety that can be difficult and unpleasant for many patients.

DBT Skills Training

DBT skills training is typically conducted in groups and each patient is also assigned an individual therapist. In the treatment of anxiety, the skills can be taught in individual therapy and clinicians can select the skills that best meet the needs of their patients. The procedure for skills training consists of three primary aims. The first is skill acquisition. In this process, the clinician provides instruction about how to begin utilizing a new skill. To effectively complete this task, clinicians must first assess their patient's skills and skill deficits to determine the skills that are needed and how to best present them. The skill acquisition phase also consists of clinician modeling via role-playing. Patients can also observe modeling in competent individuals in their lives, in films, and in videos (Linehan, 1993).

The next step in skills training is skill strengthening, which involves behavioral rehearsal and response reinforcement. Behavioral rehearsal entails practicing in vivo or in imagination. Reinforcement and feedback by the clinician is critical in helping the patient adopt new behaviors (Linehan, 1993). The third step in skills training is skill generalization. The following sections present information about the core skills training in DBT to provide an overview and some ideas about how to utilize the skills with patients with anxiety disorders. For more information on DBT, clinicians should read books and manuals or attend trainings by Marsha Linehan and her colleagues (see http://www.behavioraltech.com for more information).

Core Mindfulness Skills

DBT rests on the concept that a "wise mind" state is created when "emotional mind" (the less-rational, emotion-driven state of mind) is balanced with the "reasonable mind" (the rational, factual, intellectual state of mind). Wise mind is one's sense of personal truth. It entails intuition, deep meaning, and the sense that things are right. The first aim in the core mindfulness skills is the development of the "what" skills: observing, describing, and participating.

Observing entails noticing an experience without describing it and attaching meaning to it. Experiences are simply attended to and experienced. For example, patients can observe the feeling of the desk that they rest their hands on. Observing is sensing without words, and describing then adds words to the experience. Describing entails labeling something. It is not a judgmental process; instead, patients describe just the facts. The third "what" skill in core mindfulness training is participating. Participating involves fully putting yourself into an experience in a spontaneous and engaged manner (Linehan, 1993).

The next aim of core mindfulness training is the development of three "how" skills: Nonjudgmental, one-mindfully, and effectively. Nonjudgmental is a skill in which patients do not label something as good versus bad. There is no value assigned to a behavior. The consequences of a behavior may be harmful, but the behavior itself is not judged as good or bad.

"One-mindfully in the moment" is the skill of devoting one hundred percent of attention to whatever one is doing in that moment. This skill helps patients to combat the inattention and distractedness that often occurs with anxiety disorders. It also helps to banish mindless activity in which patients are not at all aware of their behavior. The goal is to do what you are doing in that moment. This concept goes along with the idea of exposure therapy very nicely. Exposures work best when patients focus on the exposure. In addition, exposure works because it draws patients' attention to the feared stimulus and breaks the cycle of trying to avoid thinking about or experiencing the feared stimulus.

The last core mindfulness skill that we will discuss is "effectively." This skill entails doing what works. It is not about being right or proving someone else wrong, it is about doing what will work to achieve important objectives. One does not act based on how things "should" be, rather it is most helpful to accept the situation and make it work for you. This idea can be very helpful for patients who feel that they "should" be able to stop worrying. When they focus instead on what works, they realize that what works is not to force themselves to stop worrying, but instead to accept the worry or to worry on purpose.

Interpersonal Effectiveness Skills

Interpersonal difficulties can be both a cause and a result of patients' anxiety. Many patients with anxiety are less effective in relationships than they could be because they are tense, nervous, and worried. These symptoms cause them to respond in ways that are not helpful. Recall the concept of "emotional mind" from the core mindfulness skills. When a patient is anxious, he is more likely to be in emotional mind and not in wise mind. He is then more likely to act in ways consistent with emotional mind and alienate people or create conflict. Patients with anxiety disorders may lack assertiveness, have difficulty saying no, and have trouble asking for what they need.

The first goal of interpersonal effectiveness is to nurture relationships. This entails attending to relationships, balancing your priorities versus the demands of others, balancing what you want to do with what you need to do, and building self-confidence and mastery. Anxious patients may avoid relationships and end relationships when any potential threat occurs. They may also over rely upon relationships and become dependent on others.

The second goal is to help patients accomplish their objectives in interpersonal situations. These skills involve the assertiveness skills of standing up for yourself, making requests, and saying no to unwanted requests. Patients need to determine the goal of an interpersonal situation and then tailor their responses accordingly.

According to Linehan, there are three primary goals from which to choose. The first is the outcome or objective. In this case, the patient wants to be sure to use assertiveness to create a specific outcome, like getting a raise. The next is the relationship focus. In these instances, patients' goals are to preserve or improve the relationship. Staying in the boss's favor may be more important than getting a raise. The third possible goal is self-respect. The goal in these interactions is to stay true to one's beliefs, morals, and priorities. An important message in this DBT module is that patients lose respect for themselves when they give in. Patients will thereby become more helpless and less able to engage in the activities necessary to beat anxiety.

Linehan offers the skills for Objective Effectiveness in the acronym **DEAR MAN: D**escribe (the situation), **E**xpress (your view), **A**ssert (your needs), **R**einforce (the other person for responding), (stay) **M**indful, **A**ppear confident, amd **N**egotiate to compromise when necessary.

For Relationship Effectiveness, Linehan provides the acronym **GIVE.** When the goal is to preserve the relationship, one should be **G**entle, act **I**nterested, **V**alidate the other person's views and remain nonjudgmental, use an **E**asy style of interacting and not use a harsh or intimidating style.

For Self-Respect Effectiveness, clinicians can provide patients with Linehan's acronym, **FAST.** Patients should remain **F**air because they will not feel good about themselves if they take advantage of others. Patients should not **A**pologize when they are not in the wrong. They should **S**tick to their values and be pleased that they are living in line with their own priorities. And patients should be **T**ruthful, as they will not respect themselves if they lie.

Emotion Regulation Skills

There are several reasons that patients with anxiety disorders could benefit from learning to regulate their emotions. This might be particularly true with GAD, as we discussed in Chapters 1 and 2. As we have discussed, when patients try to not experience anxiety and other troublesome emotions, they often continue to experience them, sometimes even more intensely. Linehan (1993) emphasizes the importance of utilizing the core mindfulness skill of nonjudgmental observation. Frequently the problem is not the emotion itself, but the patient's reaction to the emotion.

Clinicians can help their patients learn to accurately identify their anxiety or other emotions and then to accept them in a nonjudgmental manner. Patients can be helped to recognize the role of the emotion and the emotion-driven behaviors including any positive reinforcement that may result. This process includes identifying the prompting event, the interpretation of the event, the emotional reaction, the way that the emotion is communicated to others, and the urge to take action. Patients learn that they can observe their emotions and effectively move with them rather than against them. A discussion about the purpose of emotions can ensue. Clinicians can educate patients about how anxiety serves the purpose of communication—both to oneself and to others. The patient's expression of anxiety will give a message to others that is likely to influence the other people's behaviors. People may respond in ways that serve to enable the anxiety rather than help the patient get through it. Emotions communicate a self-validating message to one's self. Another function of emotions is to prepare for action. We have discussed how fear readies the body for adaptive fight or flight,

Because most people increase their vulnerability to negative emotions when they have not taken care of themselves, Linehan recommends self-care skills to clients to help regulate emotions. She provides the acronym **PLEASE MASTER** to remind patients of the key self-care skills. This stands for treat **P**hysica**L** illness, balance **E**ating, avoid mood-**A**ltering drugs, balance **S**leep, get **E**xercise, and build **MASTER**y.

Another important component of emotional regulation is increasing positive emotions. Patients can do this by building more pleasant events into their lives, consciously turning their attention toward positive experiences, and not destroying positive experiences by worrying about them and when they will end. As we have discussed throughout the book, a key component to the treatment of anxiety disorders is to act in a way opposite to the anxiety. To act in a way consistent with the anxiety is often to avoid something. To act opposite is to approach the anxiety and experience it.

The same concept holds true for other negative emotions. A core tenet of DBT is to "act opposite to negative emotion." If a patient is depressed, they would do the opposite of what the depressed feeling would have them do. This typically means they would get out of bed, shower, get out, and get some exercise. Clinicians treating patients with anxiety disorders should educate patients about the concept of "act opposite to negative emotion" and encourage patients to apply it in all contexts.

Distress Tolerance Skills

Some patients become very distressed while completing exposures or in other parts of their lives outside of therapy. Patients may feel more confident and competent to handle exposures if they first learn that they can control their level of distress. For this reason, some patients can benefit from learning distress tolerance skills before beginning exposure treatment. Other patients may successfully complete their exposure treatment for anxiety but continue to have difficulty self-soothing and effectively handling crises.

There are many methods for managing highly distressing, crises. The first is to reduce contact with the upsetting situation by distracting oneself. In DBT, the acronym for this is **ACCEPTS.** This stands for **A**ctivities, **C**ontributing to others' lives, **C**omparisons to show that one's situation is not so horrible, **E**motions (generating more positive emotions), **P**ushing away mentally from a troublesome situation, using other **T**houghts, and intensifying **S**ensations that can distract from the emotion.

Self-soothing using the five senses is another important skill in DBT. Many patients feel that they are not worthy or capable of soothing themselves, so they may require a good deal of practice to gain comfort with self-soothing. Another DBT skill is to **IMPROVE** the moment by **I**magery, **M**eaning, **P**rayer, **R**elaxation, **O**ne thing in the moment, **V**acation, and **E**ncouragement.

Distress tolerance is based on the principle of first accepting the moment. Some ways to do this are to observe the breath, practice a half-smile to indicate acceptance to yourself and others, and accept reality by choosing to let go of fighting the truth. Suffering occurs when people refuse to accept the pain that they experience. Patients can learn to accept the presence of the painful situation and then choose the most helpful action.

Clinicians can integrate distress tolerance and other DBT skills training into their work with patients to improve treatment outcome. Patients will already be socialized to the cognitive behavioral approach and many patients enjoy learning concrete, hands-on skills to help them improve their interpersonal relationships, regulate emotions, and tolerate distress.

Acceptance and Commitment Therapy (ACT)

ACT is another branch of cognitive behavioral therapy designed to help people end their struggles and suffering (for more information, see http://www. acceptanceandcommitmenttherapy.com). ACT is based on Relational Frame Theory (RFT). The theory and therapy rest on the idea that pain is normal, pain and suffering are two different things, and suffering can be stopped when patients learn how to accept pain. Patients can end suffering and learn to live a life they value (Hayes, 2005).

ACT shares a great deal with the general CBT and DBT concepts we have discussed thus far. Recall the notion we have presented that fighting anxiety and avoidance are the primary activities that maintain anxiety. ACT also rests on the principle of thought suppression, discussed throughout this book. To review, thought suppression refers to the phenomenon that the more a person tries *not* to think of something, the more they tend to think of it. Likewise, emotional suppression dictates that the more you try not to have an emotion, the more you have it. Like DBT, ACT includes core principles of mindfulness and willingness.

A powerful metaphor presented in *Get Out of Your Mind and Into Your Life*, an excellent self-help book for patients (Hayes, 2005), is that of getting stuck in a pool of quicksand. The patient in quicksand is likely to step up to try to get out. These actions will only cause him to sink deeper into the quicksand. The way to get out of the quicksand is quite counterintuitive. The patient needs to lie flat. He needs to actually maximize his contact with the quicksand and then roll out of it. This metaphor is similar to ones we have presented throughout the book that show that the way to handle an anxiety disorder is often the opposite of what people naturally try. Exposure to anxiety requires an initial increase in anxiety as patients confront the feared stimulus. Like the individual who struggles in quicksand and needs to do something paradoxical to get out, patients facing anxiety need to lean into their anxiety and experience it in order to get through it.

Language and Suffering

Relational Frame Theory (RFT), the theory underlying ACT, proposes that humans learn and behave based on relational frames which form the core of language and thought. Humans have the ability to relate things and feelings to one another. People are able to relate anything to anything else. Language, therefore, creates suffering. It is impossible to get rid of language because everything is related to something else. If patients tell themselves to "relax," the very word "relax" brings forth opposing words, such as panic, anxiety, stress, and so on. This is one reason why it often does not work when patients tell themselves to relax or not be nervous.

Experiential Avoidance

Stephen Hayes and other proponents of ACT strongly agree with the core principle of anxiety disorder treatment regarding the reinforcing role of avoidance, which we have discussed in detail. A powerful metaphor in ACT is that of the Chinese finger trap. The more someone pulls to get out of the finger trap, the more they will become stuck. Whereas, if someone pushes his or her finger into the trap, there will be more room. Letting go will end the struggle and create freedom.

Acceptance and Willingness

If patients are not willing to experience anxiety, they are more likely to experience it. This is why exposure therapies are effective. The reason that patients allow themselves to experience anxiety is important. Hayes says, "If you are willing to be anxious only in order to become less anxious, then you are not really willing to be anxious, and you will become even more anxious." Patients need to be willing to feel their anxiety in order to get over it. Acceptance is the key to not hanging onto thoughts and emotions. After acceptance, patients can utilize a variety of cognitive "diffusion" techniques to get through the power of the language. Hayes provides the metaphor of taking off a pair of yellow-tinted sunglasses and holding them away to see how they make the world appear yellow, rather than seeing a yellow world.

Mindfulness

Mindfulness helps patients with anxiety disorders to focus their attention completely on what they are doing in a nonjudgmental and accepting manner. Mindfulness practice can run the gamut from attentional training to intense meditation. We have counseled many patients with Social Phobia to help them shift their focus of attention away from the internal criticisms and chatter and toward the external environment. ACT further helps patients learn to shift their attention through the process of mindfulness. Patients learn mindfulness through practicing how to be where they are, walking silently, and other useful exercises. Anything can be completed mindfully, from eating a piece of fruit to doing the dishes. Meditation is also discussed in ACT as a method to become more mindful.

Living with Values

When patients' anxiety takes over their lives, they often feel forced to live in a manner that is not consistent with their core values. Several of our patients with

OCD greatly valued their relationships with others, yet their perfectionism and OCD kept them tied to their desks, unable to participate in meaningful activities that had the potential to bring them joy and fulfillment.

In *Get Out of Your Mind and Into Your Life*, Hayes (2005) describes values as chosen directions in life. The choices are between alternatives that are made based on reasons. He recommends considering values in various domains, such as family, work, spirituality, and health. The crucial step is to take committed action in line with core values.

One of the wonderful aspects of the ACT framework is that it is consistent with exposure-based therapies and can help patients to gain the motivation and courage to proceed with an exposure treatment for their anxiety disorders. When patients are inspired and committed to act along with their values, they are much more willing to engage in CBT and the therapy is likely to be effective. We have found that a patient's anxiety is often tied to something they value. If a patient is nervous about health-related concerns, he likely values his health. If a patient is worried about offending others, she probably values facilitating her social relationships. If a patient is concerned about being negatively evaluated at work, she probably values her career and the esteem of her coworkers. The patient's values are being thwarted by the anxiety disorder because it keeps them from engaging in meaningful activities. This knowledge helps the patient to maintain the motivation and dedication to pursue CBT for the anxiety disorder.

Humanistic and Existential Approaches

Carl Rogers and the Humanistic psychotherapists approached anxiety as they did any issue that the client brings forth—with empathy and positive regard. This is a critical concept that is important for clinicians to keep in mind because the therapeutic relationship is a key component in the treatment of anxiety disorders.

Humanistic psychotherapists believe that anxiety results from an incongruence between one's representation of their *ideal self* versus their *true self*. When clients' ideal selves and true selves overlap substantially, there is congruence. If there is not a high degree of overlap, individuals are different from what they want to be, and anxiety is likely to result.

The primary intervention used by Humanistic therapists is to help the client to explain the difference to themselves, using empathy, reflection, clarification, and a nonjudgmental stance. The therapist creates an environment of unconditional positive regard in which the client can find and resolve the incongruence, and therefore, anxiety. Clinicians can learn more about client-centered therapy and the application to the treatment of anxiety in books by Carl Rogers, such as *Client-Centered Therapy: Its Current Practice, Implications, and Theory*.

Another significant contribution that the Humanistic and Existential psychotherapists contributed to the treatment of anxiety is the idea that anxiety is created when people are not able to create a sense of meaning and importance in their lives. The book *Man's Search for Meaning* by Viktor E. Frankl is wonderful for both clinicians and clients to help understand the fundamental need to lead a meaningful existence.

Existential anxiety is thought to be created by the following four variables (Note: The following is a description of existential anxiety along with our application to anxiety disorders. Humanistic and Existential theory is not based on diagnoses, but we apply the concepts to various anxiety disorders):

1. Fear of death. Existential anxiety is created when people realize that they are mortal and begin thinking about their own deaths. Thoughts about death and danger are prominent in anxiety and are hallmark features of many types of OCD and Panic Disorder. A sign that a client experiences this form of existential anxiety is avoidance of free time. Clients try to occupy their time to ensure that they will not think about their own death.

2. A sense of meaninglessness. Existential anxiety is created when people grapple with their sense of purpose and struggle with the question, "Why am I here?" Clinicians might see this type of existential anxiety in clients with GAD. Sometimes patients with GAD utilize worrying as a means of avoidance. They may worry about trivial things to avoid facing a lack of purpose and meaning.

3. Fear of isolation. People fundamentally fear being alone because humans are social by nature. Some people are alone and the isolation creates anxiety, whereas others have important people in their lives, but worry that they might do something that will result in being alone. This type of fear is quite common among socially anxious patients, as well as some GAD patients who worry about their interpersonal relationships.

4. Fear of loss of freedom. People worry about whether they will lose their ability to make choices and commitments. If people don't make important commitments, they become stagnant and anxiety results. Many clients with anxiety struggle with decisions, from the mundane to the important decisions in life, perhaps because they fear a loss of freedom resulting from the wrong choice.

Clinicians practicing CBT for anxiety can benefit from the application for Humanistic and Existential theory. Clinicians can learn more about Existential therapy and Logotherapy with the books *Existential Psychotherapy* by Irvin D. Yalom and *The Will to Meaning: Foundations and Applications of Logotherapy* by Victor E. Frankl.

Integration of Treatment Approaches

We have presented some of the basics of Dialectical Behavioral Therapy (DBT), Acceptance and Commitment Therapy (ACT) and Humanistic and Existential Psychotherapy. This chapter is intended to serve as a broad overview and introduction to the application of the principles to the treatment of anxiety. Part of the art in the treatment of patients with anxiety disorders is determining when to integrate various types of conceptualization and techniques. We suggest first utilizing the basics and then looking for ways to apply additional treatment approaches. As with any type of new therapeutic practice, the best way to learn and apply new material is under the supervision of a qualified clinician.

Therefore, an effective plan for learning more about these and other treatment approaches is first to read the literature on the topic. Second, clinicians can attend trainings and seminars on the topic of interest. Third, clinicians can utilize supervision or consultation from a specialist to apply the principles to their clinical treatment of anxiety disorders.

References

Frankl, V. E. (1988). *The will to meaning: Foundations and applications of logotherapy.* New York: Plume.

Hayes, S. C. (2005). *Get out of your mind and into your life.* Oakland, CA: New Harbinger Publications.

Linehan, M. M. (1993). *Skills training manual for treating Borderline Personality Disorder.* New York: Guilford.

Yalom, I. D. (1980). *Existential psychotherapy.* New York: Basic Books.

CHAPTER 12

Treating Children and Adolescents with Anxiety Disorders

In terms of *content*, cognitive behavior therapy for anxious children and adolescents is almost identical to CBT for anxious adults. However, the *style* in which CBT is delivered to children and adults is very different. Therapists cannot expect kids to engage with CBT if they are addressed as mini-adults. Variations must be made so that they understand the treatment, can become engaged with it, and attain favorable outcomes.

At What Age Can Kids Do CBT?

There is debate regarding the question of when children can start doing CBT. Many of the major clinical trials of CBT for anxious children include patients aged 7 and above (e.g., Barrett, 1998; Barrett, Dadds, & Rapee, 1996; Spence, Donovan, Brechman, & Toussaint, 2000). Children who are younger than 7 can still benefit from CBT, albeit at times indirectly. Clinicians can work directly with parents of anxious children, educating them about the nature of anxiety and how they can help their children to get past it. Sometimes, it becomes evident that parents themselves are anxious and can benefit from their own treatment. Once they have dealt with their own anxiety, they will be able to model appropriate behaviors to their children. For example, consider a mother who seeks help for her shy five-year-old. During an initial evaluation, it becomes evident that the mother's symptoms meet criteria for Social Phobia. Because she worries about meeting new people, she has never taken her daughter to any playgroups or other organized activities. Her daughter has now started school and is worried about interacting with the other children and speaking to her teachers.

The mother knows that she should try to facilitate these interactions for her daughter, but is simply too afraid.

In this case, it was recommended that the mother seek treatment for her own social anxiety. Concurrently, she completed some sessions in parent education. She was assigned books to read about how to help her child—two great ones include Rapee et al.'s *Helping Your Anxious Child: A Step-by-Step Guide for Parents* (2000) and Chansky's *Freeing Your Child from Anxiety* (2004). She learned about avoidance and how she must help her daughter to confront her feared social situations. She and her therapist created a hierarchy for the little girl and then, with the therapist's help, mom worked through the hierarchy with her. She arranged play dates, had her daughter attend birthday parties and signed her up for a music class. When they went out to do errands, she encouraged her daughter to say "Hi" to the various clerks and answer them when spoken to. All of this was accomplished with the therapist just meeting the little girl a few times. By the end of treatment, both mother and daughter were very involved in the social world.

Many children can benefit from working directly with a therapist. Therapists skilled in working with young children can sometimes conduct therapy directly with children as young as 5 and 6. CBT with younger children will look slightly different from CBT with older children. With younger children, there should be less focus on cognitive interventions since the effectiveness of these techniques might be limited by normal cognitive development. When cognitive techniques are used with younger kids, they should be kept very simple. For example, a child with separation anxiety disorder can be taught a simple coping phrase to keep in mind when in anxiety-provoking situations (e.g., "Mom always comes back to get me."). In contrast, an older child (e.g., age 12) with separation anxiety can be taught more formal cognitive restructuring, where he examines his thoughts in anxiety-provoking situations and comes up with new ways of thinking that are more rational and adaptive.

Other developmental considerations will also impact CBT with children. Very young children might need shorter sessions than older children, and more time to play during the session. Young patients should not be given complex reading or writing assignments; rather, assignments should be altered for their developmental level. For example, self-monitoring can be done with check marks on a piece of paper (e.g., the number of times a child does a ritual during the school day), rather than in written format. Finally, younger children also require more parental involvement in CBT than older children do. We will talk more about parental involvement later in the chapter.

Establishing Rapport

When children think about going to the doctor, they think about white coats and needles! For most children, learning that they are going to meet a new doctor is quite scary. For anxious kids, the fear is even more intense. There are a few things therapists can do to set kids at ease when they walk into their offices.

On the subject of offices, it is nice for clinicians who work with children to have a kid-friendly office. It is nice to tack up pictures on the wall that were drawn by other kids (maintaining confidentiality, of course). There should be somewhere appropriate for children to sit (e.g., a chair that doesn't swallow them up). In addition, there should be stuff around that is familiar to them, like crayons and markers, paper, and toys.

The tone used in CBT with both adults and children helps to establish rapport in and of itself. CB therapists take a stance of collaborative empiricism, where the therapist and patient work together to learn about problems and how to treat them. The therapist is invested in teaching the patient to be his own therapist so that he can continue to help himself once treatment is over. If therapists are true to this stance when working with children, it is quite likely that a strong rapport will be established. Children like to feel that they are partners with adults, rather than being bossed around by adults (as they usually are!).

Much can be done to establish rapport within the first few minutes of meeting a young patient. They should be told directly what they can call the therapist. Some people prefer to be addressed formally as Dr. X, but others are completely comfortable being called by their first name or by some less formal title like Miss Deborah or Miss Larina. Often kids are too shy to call adults by any name, but knowing that the clinician is personable and approachable can make them feel more comfortable in session.

It is also nice for therapists to explain to children what they do. Therapists can say, "I'm a different kind of doctor from others that you see, like your pediatrician. I don't use needles or draw blood or anything like that! I talk to kids about what is bothering them and help them to feel better." This simple explanation will put most children at ease early on in the therapeutic interaction.

In the first few sessions, the goal is to complete an assessment and formulate a treatment plan. There is a lot to discuss and clinicians can fall into the trap of being all business. Yet, some time should be dedicated to getting to know the child, not just their symptoms. Children can be asked about their siblings, whether they have any pets, and what sorts of activities they do after school. Most children will relish telling the therapist about their dog or about their passion for the local baseball team. Furthermore, the answers to these kinds of questions can contribute important information to the case conceptualization. They help the clinician to get a sense of the extent to which the presenting problems are impacting the child's functioning.

During the assessment and throughout treatment, it can be appropriate to use a bit of self-disclosure–perhaps more than one would use with adult patients. Children will sometimes ask their therapists "personal questions" and answering them is usually preferable to explaining why one cannot. We have found that sharing a bit about a new baby or a new puppy with young patients is a great way to establish rapport. Kids also love to hear stories about adults when they were "little." It can be helpful for the therapist to share a story about something she was afraid of as a child and explain how she got over it (through exposure, of course).

Finally, a surefire way to establish rapport with young patients is to deliver treatment in a kid-friendly way. This means using analogies that are meaningful to kids, doing assignments with computers or colored pens and neat paper, and setting aside a bit of therapy time for something fun. We will discuss all of these concepts at length in this chapter. Basically, therapists need to get the job done, while making the experience of therapy as enjoyable as possible.

Selling the Rationale and Explaining the Treatment

Once the assessment is complete, children and their families must be educated about their diagnosis and how treatment will help them to feel better. John March and Karen Mulle (1998), in their treatment manual for kids with OCD, do an excellent job with this. While their manual is designed specifically for children with OCD, their general approach to explaining a disorder and how to treat it can be applied to any anxiety disorder.

Children and their families need to come away from this psychoeducation session with two important concepts. First, avoidance maintains fear. Avoidance prevents people from learning that their anxiety is manageable and that their feared outcomes are unlikely to occur. Second, in order to stop feeling anxious about a given stimuli, patients must expose themselves to it. Only in this way will patients learn that their anxiety will decrease on its own over time, that they can manage feeling anxious for as long as it lasts, and that their feared outcomes are unlikely to occur.

Does this sound familiar? It should, since it was taken directly from Chapter 7 of this book! The same concepts apply to CBT with adults and with children. The important issue when working with kids is how to make sure they understand that avoidance and anxiety are related and form a "vicious cycle." A helpful metaphor to use in explaining this is of a hungry dog:

Therapist: Do you have a pet at home?

Child: Yeah. His name is Griffy! He's a border collie. He's black and white. Do know that he knows how to herd sheep?

Therapist: Wow! That's cool. Hey, do you ever give Griffy scraps of your after school snack?

Child: Well, I am not supposed to feed him, but I do! He really likes chips!

Therapist: So, when you come in the house and sit down to do your homework with your snack, what does Griffy do?

Child: Griffy comes to sit right by me. He knows he's going to get some goodies!

Therapist: Right. Well, I want you to imagine that one day you take Griffy to the veterinarian and the vet says that Griffy is too fat and has to go on a diet. No more people food.

Child: He'd be sad.

Therapist: I bet! Now, what do you think would happen the first few days that he comes over and you know that you can't feed him anymore?

Child: Griffy would still come and sit by me. He wouldn't know.

Therapist: Exactly. So, he might be a little upset. Right? Now, how about in a week's time? What would Griffy do then?

Child: I guess he'd figure it out. He's pretty smart. Maybe when I sat down to do my homework, he'd just stay by the window in the living room where he likes to sleep.

Therapist: Oh, so Griffy would *learn* that you weren't going to feed him anymore.

Child: Yeah, poor guy.

Therapist: So, you know what? Anxiety is kind of like a hungry dog. It sounds like anxiety pesters you a lot just like Griffy does. Like, anxiety might tell you lots of times when you get to school that your mom isn't going to come back and pick you up.

Child: Yeah, that's what happens. I ask my teacher to go to the bathroom, but what I really do is call Mom to make sure she is okay and that she knows to come and pick me up.

Therapist: And how do you feel after calling?

Child: I feel better for a while. But, then at lunchtime, I want to call again. And, in the afternoon, I go to the bathroom and call again. Sometimes I just want to play with my friends and not worry about it.

Therapist: Does this happen with Griffy and the chips? Does he want one chip or more and more chips?

Child: Well, I give him one chip, but then he comes back over and over and wants more. He never seems to get full! It makes it hard to get my homework done!

Therapist: Hmmm. Kind of sounds like your anxiety barks and you feed it some chips.

Child: What?

Therapist: Well, we can picture anxiety like a dog, barking away and wanting you to do stuff for it. Sounds like when it barks, you feed it, just like it wants you to. When it tells you to be worried about mom, you call to check in on mom.

Child: Oh, I think I get it.

Therapist: What's the problem with calling once? What happened with Griffy when you give him one chip?

Child: Well, he wants more. And anxiety does too. One phone call doesn't really work so well. I get anxious again pretty soon.

Therapist: So, what would we have to do if we want anxiety to go over and just sit quietly by the window instead of bugging you all the time?

Child: Stop feeding it?!!!

Therapist: Right. But, how would we do this?

Child: Stop calling mom when I am worried?

Therapist: Right! That's exactly it! Now, remember, we thought Griffy might be confused the first few days we decided not to feed him goodies anymore. What about anxiety?

Child: Oh, it will be upset too ... that's for sure! I bet it's going to keep telling me all day at school to go and call my mom. It's going to be really hard to not listen.

Therapist: I agree. It is going to be really hard at first. But, if you can really resist giving in to anxiety for a little while, what might then happen?

Child: I guess anxiety would get very quiet like Griffy.

Therapist: Exactly. And, that's what we are going to try to do together. We are going to try to stop "feeding" your anxiety and make it become very quiet and not nearly as pesky as it is right now!

In using a child-friendly example like this, the child learns about why anxiety sticks around and learns what he or she needs to do to get rid of it. March and Mulle (1998) suggest framing OCD treatment as the child "bossing back" OCD. The aforementioned conversation, and the concept of bossing back anxiety, introduces children and parents to the idea that Anxiety Disorder is external to the child. It is an entity that child, parents, and therapist are going to fight together. Because of the nature of this, the therapist clearly communicates that fights *about* anxiety are not permitted during treatment (e.g., fights between parents and children; fights between child and therapist)—rather, anger should be directed against the anxiety since it is the "thing" causing the anger and distress in the first place.

Again drawing from March and Mulle (1998), some children, particularly young ones, might want to give their anxiety a name (like "Pesky," "Mr. Worry," or "The Voice"). It can be fun to let children draw a picture of their anxiety and put its name underneath. This can be pinned to the therapist's office wall during sessions to remind children of the major task—bossing back their anxiety. As treatment progresses, children can be asked to redraw their anxiety. Often, it gets much smaller as treatment progresses!

Self-Monitoring

Self-monitoring can be difficult for children. The information gathered via self-monitoring is very useful to treatment, so it is important to adapt the technique to young patients. For young children, writing should be kept to a minimum. Rather, they can be taught to make check marks or other marks on a page to indicate the occurrence of an experience. For example, a nine-year-old patient was asked to keep track of situations in which OCD told him to double check or redo his schoolwork. He and his therapist created a page with two columns—one for times when he "beat" OCD and one for times when OCD "beat" him. If he resisted the urge to perform these rituals, he would put a mark in his own column and if he gave in and performed the rituals, he would put a mark in OCD's column. While this method did not yield as much information as a traditional self-monitoring sheet, it allowed the clinician to see how often the patient was experiencing intrusive thoughts and how often he was doing rituals. In addition, during treatment it can become a fun game to see how much he can beat OCD. Over many weeks of treatment, the clinician was also able to see if the patient was attaining more control over his rituals.

Older children and adolescents can certainly complete traditional self-monitoring forms, but compliance can be a problem. Understandably, kids balk at the idea of homework and therefore, it should be made as fun as possible. In the case of self-monitoring, kids can choose how to complete it. Some kids like to do it on the computer. During the session, the therapist and patient can design a chart and the patient can then fill it in on a computer during the week. Other kids like to get a special journal to record things in, or like to use special pens or markers. Some kids come in with self-monitoring sheets decorated with pictures or stickers. This should be encouraged! If patients figure out a way to make their homework more fun, it is more likely that they will do it.

It is also helpful to design the self-monitoring sheet with each child, rather than handing them a set sheet. This allows for the use of the child's own language and encourages creativity. Figure 12.1 shows an example of a self-monitoring sheet designed by a child with separation anxiety disorder.

Making a Hierarchy

Similar to self-monitoring, clinicians should try to make the process of creating the hierarchy fun. Most children have done brainstorming in school and like the idea of generating things that they need to work on to beat their anxiety. The clinician can come prepared with notes of items that should be on the hierarchy based on their earlier interactions with the child. This ensures that important items will not be overlooked. As with adults, these items can be placed in a table on the computer, with an adjacent column for SUDS ratings. Pictures can be used to decorate the hierarchy. Since the word "hierarchy" is a big word for many

Lindsey's Monitoring Sheet

Date/Time	What was happening?	What was I thinking about?	What did I do?	What ended up happening?	What did I learn?
Thursday 9 AM	I am taking a spelling test.	Something bad happened to Mom. I need to call her.	I called Mom.	Mom was fine. I got a bad grade on my test.	Listening to my anxiety made me mess up my test.
Friday 11 AM	I am eating lunch with my friends.	Something bad happened to Mom. I need to call her.	I called Mom.	Mom was fine. Everyone was laughing when I got back and I felt left out.	Anxiety gets in the way of things with my friends.
Monday 4 PM	Waiting for Mom to get me from school.	Something bad happened to Mom. I need to call her.	I called Mom.	Mom was stuck in a bit of traffic. She came at 4:03 PM.	There's a lot of traffic near school. I should know that everything is fine with Mom.

FIGURE 12.1 *Sample Self-Monitoring Sheet for Patient with Separation Anxiety Disorder*

kids, therapists can call it a fear ladder or worry steps and draw a picture of a ladder or steps.

As is the case with adults, children will often balk at putting items on the hierarchy that seem impossible to confront. The same rationale for including these items can be used. As they confront items lower on the hierarchy, it is likely that the higher up items will become easier. Socratic questioning can be used to help kids arrive at this conclusion. Metaphors can also be helpful. For example, when kids first learn to read, just reading one word is hard. It seems impossible to read a whole storybook. However, with practice, this becomes manageable. With even more practice, kids can read chapter books too.

Once all of the items are generated, SUDS ratings should be assigned. SUDS ratings can be tricky for young patients, especially one that uses a 0–100 point scale. Instead, a fear thermometer can be used with children and adolescents. Clinicians can introduce the fear thermometer (Figure 12.2) by saying, "Do you know how you use a thermometer to take your temperature when you are sick? Well, here, we have a special thermometer to measure how scared something makes you. The thermometer starts at 0, meaning you are not scared at all. It ends at 10, meaning the most frightened you can ever imagine being. Right here in the middle is 5, where you feel pretty scared, but not so scared that you would have to run away." This thermometer is then used to help children assign SUDS ratings to hierarchy items. Some children have a difficult time with numerical ratings. Instead, clinicians can give them a scale of a little scary, scary, and very scary (or some other adjective that matches their language) and do verbal ratings instead of numeric ones.

When children have fears in different domains, it can sometimes be helpful to create separate hierarchies for each domain. For example, a child with OCD who has both washing and checking obsessions/compulsions could create two hierarchies—one for each symptoms cluster. Focus in treatment can be placed first on one hierarchy before moving on to the other. See Figure 12.3 for a sample hierarchy.

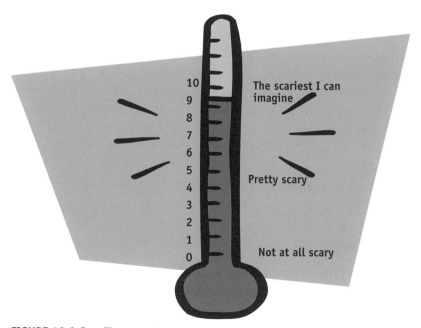

FIGURE 12.2 *Fear Thermometer*

Item	SUDS
Taking the bus to school	5
Sleeping overnight at Grandma's	6
Going to ballet class	7
Having a playdate with my best friend at her house	7
Going to my best friend's birthday party	8
Being upstairs alone when Mom and Dad are downstairs	8
Having a babysitter	8
Going to a girl's birthday party who I don't know well	10
Having a playdate with a friend who I don't know well, at her house	10

FIGURE 12.3 *Sample Hierarchy for Patient with Separation Anxiety Disorder*

Carrying Out CBT with Young Patients

Cognitive Work

As we noted earlier, cognitive work must be kept very simple for younger clients. Older teenagers can do cognitive restructuring in much the same way as adults. With younger clients, simple questioning can be used to help kids see that there are different explanations for one situation. It can be helpful to arrive at one simple coping statement that children can carry with them into the feared situation. Here is an example of some cognitive work with an 8-year-old patient with separation anxiety disorder:

> **Therapist:** So, what are you worried will happen at the play date with your friend Jane?
>
> **Patient:** I'll be scared.
>
> **Therapist:** Okay. What will you be scared of?
>
> **Patient:** I'll be scared that mom won't come to get me.
>
> **Therapist:** Ah. Gee, I kind of remember you thinking that before. Do you?
>
> **Patient:** Yeah.
>
> **Therapist:** When?

Patient: Well, I worried about it all night at Grandma's. And, the first few times I went to ballet, I worried about it too.

Therapist: Yeah! I remember that. What happened at Grandma's?

Patient: Mom came in the morning to get me, just like she said she would. She came and had breakfast with me and Grandma.

Therapist: That sounds like fun. And what happens at ballet?

Patient: Mom always comes to get me. I've gone lots of times now and she has always come.

Therapist: Do you still worry about it every time you go to class?

Patient: Well, a little. But, I don't cry like I did the first week.

Therapist: Maybe because it has happened so many times now? You went to ballet and Mom came to get you?

Patient: Yeah!

Therapist: So, is this something you can think of at Jane's house?

Patient: Yeah! I can remind myself when I am scared that Mom will come back because she always does.

Therapist: I think that is a great idea. Let's write it down.

Together, the therapist and patient wrote this mantra down on a cue card—"Mom will come back. She always does." The patient could put this card in her pocket so that she could use it as a reminder if she began to feel anxious at her friend's house.

Rapee and colleagues (2000), in their book, *Helping Your Anxious Child,* include an excellent way to do cognitive restructuring with slightly older kids. While very young children do best with mostly verbal dialogue, older children can do some writing. Their detective-thinking worksheets pose three questions for each problematic event:

1. What am I worried about?
2. What is the evidence?
3. What is my calm thought?

The first question helps children to capture their automatic thoughts and the second question helps children to challenge their thoughts. Rapee et al. (2000) suggests some follow-up questions for challenging thoughts, including "What happened when I was worried before?" and "What else could happen?" Much like in our example with a very young CBT patient, the final question on the detective worksheet prompts children to come up with a coping statement to take with them into a situation. The worksheet is simple enough that kids can work through it on their own between sessions or mentally ask themselves the three questions when they are actually in a stressful situation.

Teenagers can be taught cognitive restructuring in the same way as adults. Again, they should be encouraged to do cognitive restructuring in their own style. Some like a formal chart, some like to write out an anxious self/coping self dialog, and some enjoy journaling. What is most important is that teenagers understand the *spirit* of cognitive restructuring—the idea that anxious thoughts do not need to be taken as truths, but rather should be questioned carefully and reframed as necessary.

Behavioral Work

Behavioral work with children and adolescents looks much the same as with adults. Exposure to feared situations is completed during sessions and then assigned for homework. Exposures are guided by the hierarchy, working from least to most anxiety provoking. As with adults, the most essential part of exposure work is that children *learn* something in the process. As such, it is important to ask children for their predictions of what might happen during the exposure and then to evaluate the predictions once the exposure is completed. The key is to use exposure to demonstrate to kids that their feared consequences are unlikely to occur and that anxiety is manageable.

A few caveats deserve mention with respect to doing imaginal exposure with kids. Young children often have difficulties separating reality from fantasy. As such, vivid imaginal exposures are often not a good idea with young kids. Consider a child with OCD who fears going to hell. His fear is triggered by intrusive thoughts about accidentally harming his family members. A common trigger is helping his mom prepare dinner. Since he is 12, his mother allows him to help her chop things up for dinner with a relatively sharp knife. He worries that he will accidentally use the knife to stab his mother and will end up in hell. He is so concerned about hell and the devil that he can't say words that sound similar (like deviled eggs or hello). He worries that if he says these words, the devil will think he is trying to befriend him, causing him to go directly to hell when he dies.

With an adult patient with similar concerns, imaginal exposure would be used. The patient would be asked to vividly imagine stabbing his loved one and ending up in hell. This is probably not advisable with a child who might have a hard time separating fact from fiction. Therapists must be creative and come up with other exposures that would still target the same fears. For example, simply imagining, saying, and writing the word "hell" can be helpful for a child who refuses to say any word beginning with "h" for fear of accidentally saying hell. A child who is scared of going to hell could also tell stories about hell to the therapist. The child and therapist could snack on deviled eggs or devil's food cake. The therapist could ask the child to tell him what it would be like to have a snack with the devil. This seems like a silly exposure, but it accomplishes the goal of having the child confront his feared stimuli (thoughts of the devil), with a bit of lightness and humor that can be so helpful when working with kids.

It is important that parents are on board with exposures. When exposures are somewhat over the top, parents should be consulted and the rationale for treatment should be reviewed so that they understand the importance of the activity. For example, the same child described previously would not swear for fear of going to the devil. His parents were consulted about whether they were okay with having some exposure sessions in which the child would have to write and say curse words. These particular parents completely understood the importance of the exercise and were supportive. When parents refuse, however, therapists must either come up with other exposures or spend some more time discussing the rationale with parents and hoping that they will eventually agree.

Homework

Children get plenty of homework at school and are often not keen to be assigned more in the context of therapy. They must understand the rationale for why homework is used as a part of CBT. First, practice makes perfect! The more frequently kids can work on their anxiety, the sooner their anxiety will no longer be a problem. Children like to hear this because while many don't mind coming to therapy, they would rather be playing with friends or watching TV or going to ballet class! Second, when kids do an exposure with the therapist, they often chalk up their success to the therapist's presence. A teenager with Panic Disorder felt fine doing interoceptive exposure at the therapist's office because she knew that if she had a heart attack, the therapist would call 911. It was much more difficult for her to do her exposures after school, when she was home alone. On a similar note, when a therapist does an exposure with a child, the child often assumes its "okay" for him to do it too since the therapist felt safe doing it. If the therapist touches a doorknob and then eats a snack, a child can tell himself, "It must be safe, or Dr. Ledley wouldn't be doing it." Doing it alone, without reassurance, is much harder.

When kids understand the rationale for homework, they are usually fairly agreeable about doing it. Therapists should keep assignments simple and be mindful that kids do have a lot on their plates and that assignments should not be terribly time consuming. Children should know that if they have trouble with homework during the week, they (or their parents) can call and speak to the therapist rather than waiting until the scheduled session. Speaking to the therapist midweek and designing an easier homework assignment that is "doable" is much more productive than not doing any homework at all. As we have alluded to throughout the chapter, homework should also be fun. Kids should be encouraged to do written work in any way that is enjoyable for them. While exposures just need to be done (there is no "fun" way to touch a toilet seat!), kids can be encouraged to reward themselves once they complete a difficult exposure. For example, they can plan to do their exposure homework in the half hour prior to their favorite TV show and use that as a reward for their hard work. A formal reward schedule that the patient, parent, and therapist co-create can also help boost motivation.

Termination and Relapse Prevention

As with adult patients (see Chapter 10), it is essential that children complete treatment with a sense of their accomplishments and with the knowledge that they need to continue being their own therapists once treatment is over. One of the best ways to help children see their accomplishments is to re-rate their hierarchy near the end of treatment. They will see that the stimuli that used to elicit extreme anxiety now elicits little, if any, anxiety.

From there, it is important for children to be able to articulate how they made the progress that they did. It is helpful to have children make a list of "Helpful Tips" that they can take home with them. This list encapsulates what they learned in therapy and can be referred to after treatment is over when the anxiety pops up again. Figure 12.4 shows a sample "Helpful Tips" sheet for a child with separation anxiety disorder.

A related point is that children (and their parents) should leave therapy with reasonable expectations. They should know that anxiety can pop up in the future at any time. It can be about the same things they were anxious about when they came to treatment, or it can be about completely new things. The most important point is that children understand that they know how to fight anxiety, regardless of how it presents itself. The "Helpful Tips" sheet should be broad enough that the tips can apply to any anxiety-provoking situation.

Finally, children can be helped to set goals at the end of treatment. Since CBT is time-limited, children might not be able to confront all of their fears during the course of treatment. Therapists can help children to list situations that they still want to work on, and to specify when they would like to work on these items. Children are more likely to carry out a very specific plan (e.g., "I will volunteer to read at school assembly in June.") than one that is open-ended (e.g., "At some point, I should do some public speaking.").

❀ Avoid avoiding!!!!

❀ The more times you do something, the easier it gets.

❀ There are a lot of different ways of thinking about a situation. You don't have to

believe the first thought that pops into your head.

❀ Just because I feel nervous, doesn't mean something bad has happened.

❀ Checking just makes my anxiety stick around. Even when I get the urge to check,

I can't do it! I need to get busy with something else.

❀ If it gets hard to deal with anxiety again, I need to tell my parents or call my

therapist. Her number is 555-5555.

FIGURE 12.4 *Sample "Helpful Tip Sheet"*

What About Parents?

The ideal model for CBT with kids is to set a collaborative tone between parents, the child, and the therapist. In the great majority of cases, parents understand CBT, support the therapist's effort, and help along their child's progress in an appropriate way. With very young patients, it can be helpful to have the parent in the room during sessions since they will serve as the child's coach in between sessions. The focus of sessions should most definitely be on the child, with parents listening and learning. With older kids, sessions can occur one-on-one with the therapist and child. Parents can be brought in at the beginning and/or end of the session to bring up concerns, hear about the session, and learn what the plan is for homework. Parents also play a variable role in homework depending on age, with greater involvement for younger kids. Parents might also have to facilitate homework in other ways, like setting up play dates, taking the child to the zoo to see a feared animal, or going to the mall to confront germs in a public place. Therapists must directly instruct parents on how to behave during exposures. Most importantly, they need to understand that providing reassurance maintains anxiety. They need to remind the child in a friendly way that they will not provide reassurance anymore. When a mom drops a child with separation anxiety disorder off for a play date, she is likely going to ask a million questions about when her mom is going to come back to get her, where she is going to be in the interim, what she should do if she doesn't come back, and so on. Parents need to have a set response to these questions: "That sounds like your anxiety talking. I want your anxiety to go away, so I am not going to answer."

Parents can also be taught to help their kids get busy with something else. On the way to the play date, mother and daughter can listen to a book on tape, or sing a song, or decide what to have for dinner. This does not mean they are *avoiding* anxiety—they are just trying to go about their business *despite* anxiety. Decisions about homework and about parents' responses to anxiety should always be made collaboratively during the session between parents, kids, and therapists. Parents should *not* design their own homework assignments or surprise their kids with exposures. Progress is best made when children feel that they are in control of the therapy process.

Sometimes, it is best for parents to have a minimal role in their children's treatment. This comes up in two cases. First, some parents deliberately sabotage their children's treatment or belittle their children about anxiety and being in therapy. While some criticism is natural prior to therapy, once parents hear the rationale for the maintenance and treatment of anxiety, it is unacceptable to continue in this critical stance. When confronted with critical parents, therapists should plan some separate sessions with them to discuss how their stance will have a negative impact on the treatment and on the child's mental health in general. If they continue to be critical, unsupportive, and unhelpful, it is worth considering whether there is some other trusted adult who can help the child with their treatment. Sometimes, an aunt or a grandfather or an older sibling can be a better therapy coach than a parent. Furthermore, parents who don't "get" anxiety often feel relieved when this responsibility is taken from them.

A more common scenario is when parents' own anxiety interferes in their child's treatment. For example, a father who himself has OCD might not allow his child to touch contaminated objects as part of treatment. This dad might truly believe that his child will get sick from such exposures and even worse, will spread contamination to the rest of the family. The first course of action in such a situation is to set a separate session with the father and review the rationale for treatment. Often, when parents are reminded of the rationale behind why their children are being asked to do certain things, they will be supportive of the activity. In cases where they continue to resist, therapists can recommend that parents pursue their own treatment. In a private session (without the child), therapists can explain to parents how their own anxiety will serve to maintain their child's anxiety. Therapists can facilitate a good referral for the parents so that they can work on their own difficulties at the same time as their child.

Another "selling" point for resistant parents is to remind them that their child is going to be doing some unusual things in the context of treatment in the service of being able to lead a normal life after treatment. There is not the expectation that he will walk around touching toilet seats everywhere he goes for the rest of his life! There is only the expectation that he will be able to use a public restroom when he needs to. Thinking in this way (short-term pain leads to long-term gain) sometimes helps anxious parents.

It is worth noting that parents can also sabotage their children's treatment by a simple lack of organization. Some parents struggle with time management and organizing their lives. As a result, patients sometimes miss sessions, patients do not get the materials they need to complete assessments, parents do not set up play dates for exposures, and so on. The best way to deal with parental disorganization is for the clinician to meet separately with the parent to let them know how important it is that patients have consistency and repetition in their anxiety disorder treatment. Clinicians should try to reinforce all the things that parents have done well and take a collaborative approach to solving the areas that need work. Using empathy can be very helpful. For example, "I know that life is extremely busy with four kids and that it has been difficult to go to the store to get the supplies for your son's exposures. Can we put our heads together to find a way to get those supplies before next week's session?"

A much more frequent problem is when parents cannot tolerate seeing their kids exhibit anxiety. Often this factor contributed to the child's anxiety in the first place. Dr. Ledley recently had an experience that showed how a child can develop a fear. She was giving her 8-month-old baby a bath and thought it would be helpful to use the showerhead to quickly rinse the baby's hair. The first time she showed the baby the showerhead, she held it next to the baby's tub (which sat inside the bathtub) and the baby studied it with a puzzled look. She very gently placed her hand in the stream of water and quickly drew her hand back with a look of fear. She looked up at mom, wanting to know how to react. Mom giggled, and so did the baby. The next day, the exact same thing happened–the baby looked rather frightened of the showerhead, looked to mom to figure out what to do, and giggled as mom did. On the third day, the baby stuck her hand right into the stream of water, leaning forward so that mom would spray her. Mom did, the baby laughed, and now they have an efficient way to rinse off the shampoo and soap. Things could have turned out differently though had mom reacted to the baby's fear with discomfort. She could have very well thought, "This is too scary for the baby" and stopped using the showerhead. This does not seem like a big deal, unless of course the baby grew into a child who was scared of getting water in her face. This is a silly example, but one that shows how a parent's own discomfort with a child's reaction to a range of novel stimuli could contribute to a very fearful child.

This problem, while very common in working with anxious children, is very easy to remedy through some psychoeducation and a bit of reassurance. Parents need to understand that their children must first feel anxious before becoming less anxious. They must also understand that anxiety is not dangerous or damaging to the child's psyche. Again, they have to realize that the short-term pain of anxiety will lead to the long-term gain of a calmer child. The motto, "Invest anxiety in a calmer future" (Hope et al., 2000) can be very helpful for parents to keep in mind when they feel anxious about seeing their child feel anxious!

Reward Systems

Prior to treatment, parents often use reward and punishment with anxious children. When their children will do something that makes them anxious, they give them a treat and when they refuse, they take a special privilege away or punish them. When parents come for treatment, they often ask if this is "okay." It is best to start treatment with no reward or punishment tied to the tasks of treatment. Children should *not* be punished when anxiety gets in the way of them doing something. Parents should direct their anger against the anxiety and help children in any way they can to do the same. Rewards are also not a necessary part of treatment. For many children, treatment can be intrinsically rewarding. A child with Social Phobia might feel a great sense of accomplishment at being able to attend a birthday party. A child with separation anxiety might feel very relieved at being able to go to a friend's house for a sleepover. Intrinsic rewards like these are much more powerful than material rewards like stickers or candy.

With that being said, reward systems do have their place in treatment programs. If after a few weeks of treatment, children are not able to engage in the tasks of therapy, a reward system should be considered. This can sometimes serve as the essential motivator to get kids started and help them to see that anxiety is manageable and that feared outcomes are unlikely to occur.

One of our patients had severe Social Phobia and excessive perfectionism, both of which had a significant impact on her school performance. Her therapist, mom, and teacher all worked together to set her up on a reward system. Four target behaviors were selected at a time. For example, during one time period, the four target behaviors were: saying good morning to Mrs. Jones; writing four lines in creative writing; reading four lines out loud to Mrs. Jones; and asking Mrs. Jones a question. Mrs. Jones kept track of these behaviors and gave the patient a sticker on her sticker chart each time she accomplished one. At the end of the week, she gave the sticker chart to the patient's mom. If the patient had received 80 percent of the possible stickers for the week, the patient got a reward that she and her mom had agreed on at the beginning of the week. Rewards should not be expensive or fancy, but rather something simple that the child enjoys. In this case, the child got to pick the family's Saturday night dinner or select a video for the family to watch over the weekend. This reward system was very motivating to the patient, relatively simple for the teacher to implement, and inexpensive for the mother. It very much helped the patient move past her severe anxieties.

References

Barrett, P. M. (1998). Evaluation of cognitive-behavioral group treatments for childhood anxiety disorders. *Journal of Clinical Child Psychology, 27,* 459–468.

Barrett, P. M., Dadds, M. R., & Rapee, R. M. (1996). Family treatment of childhood anxiety: A controlled trial. *Journal of Consulting and Clinical Psychology, 64,* 333–342.

Chansky, T. (2004). *Freeing your child from anxiety: Powerful, practical solutions to overcome your child's fears, worries and phobias.* New York: Broadway Books.

Hope, D. A., Heimberg, R. G., Juster, H. R., & Turk, C. L. (2000). *Managing social anxiety: A cognitive-behavioral therapy approach.* San Antonio, TX: The Psychological Corporation.

March, J., & Mulle, K. (1998). *OCD in children and adolescents: A cognitive-behavioral treatment manual.* New York: Guilford.

Rapee, R. M., Spence, S. H., Cobham, V., & Wignall, A. M. (2000). *Helping your anxious child: A step-by-step guide for parents.* Oakland, CA: New Harbinger Publications.

Spence, S. H., Donovan, C., & Brechman-Toussaint, M. (2000). The treatment of childhood Social Phobia: The effectiveness of a social skills training-based cognitive-behavioural intervention with and without parental involvement. *Journal of Child Psychology and Psychiatry and Allied Disciplines, 41,* 713–726.

CHAPTER 13

Consultation and Collaboration with Multidisciplinary Professionals

C BT, like many forms of therapy for anxiety disorders, is enhanced through collaboration and consultation with multidisciplinary professionals. Consultation is an integral part of CBT that can significantly increase its effectiveness.

Clinicians treating anxiety disorders can take on the role of consultant and educate and guide consultees (typically other professionals who work with the same patient) on how to best help the patient overcome anxiety. Clinicians will often find that different professionals will greatly want to help the patient, but they simply do not know how to do so. For this reason, they are appreciative of consultation provided by the clinician.

This chapter will outline the primary models for consultation that clinicians can utilize to improve anxiety disorder treatment. We will then provide some examples of professionals with whom to collaborate and ways to give and receive consultation. Finally, we will outline some of the methods to provide information and consultation.

Types of Consultation

Caplan (1970) describes four types of mental health consultation. These are: client-centered case consultation, consultee-centered case consultation, program-centered administrative consultation, and consultee-centered administrative consultation. We will focus on the first two in this chapter, client-centered case consultation and consultee-centered case consultation. These two types are aimed at helping the consultee (or other professional) to improve his or her skills to best help a particular patient or better help patients in general.

The other consultation types are also very useful to consider. A clinician can provide program-centered administrative consultation to create or improve a program to help people overcome anxiety or stress amongst staff members in an organization. Consultee-centered administrative consultation would help a consultee improve his or her skills in managing organizational difficulties. A consultant could, for example, help a sales manager who has noticed that many of her sales representatives are nervous about placing calls to new prospects. The consultant would focus on helping the manager improve her administrative skills by learning how to work with the anxiety.

Client-Centered Case Consultation

The focus in this type of consultation is to advise others how to best help an individual patient. Clinicians should consider how they can best provide and utilize client-centered case consultation. In providing consultation, clinicians can offer recommendations to teachers, physicians, or other care providers regarding how to best help a patient.

In requesting a consultation, clinicians should think about what information could be useful to the patient. If, for example, the clinician suspected an additional diagnosis, she could make a referral for testing or assessment. A clinician might think that his or her patient has adult ADHD. The clinician could refer to a psychologist who specializes in the assessment of ADHD in adults. If results show that the patient does have ADHD, then the patient may wish to consult with a psychiatrist to consider the commencement of stimulant medication.

As another example, if a clinician notices that a young patient has evidence of a learning disability, she can refer to a psychologist who conducts batteries of learning disability tests. If the patient does in fact have some type of learning disability, he or she can receive appropriate accommodations in school to help improve school performance.

Another common type of client-centered case consultation that clinicians request is a medical opinion from a physician. A clinician may have concerns about a patient's lack of energy, sleepiness, and depressed mood. The clinician should recommend that the patient get a physical examination to rule out hypothyroidism, anemia, or other medical difficulties that might play a role in the patient's symptoms. The physician then conducts an examination, runs appropriate tests, and provides consultation to the clinician regarding the patient's condition and how to best help the patient.

Consultee-Centered Case Consultation

Clinicians treating anxiety disorders can also give or receive consultee-centered case consultation. With consultee-centered case consultation, the clinician would probably not meet with the consultee's patient directly, rather they would help the consultee to pinpoint difficulties and build new skills (Brown, Pryzwansky, & Schulte, 2001). When a clinician gives consultee-centered case consultation, the focus is on improving the consultee's skills. The process is similar to or may include supervision and training. Likewise, clinicians can also request case consultation. Reasons that a consultee pursues case consultation include lack of knowledge, lack of skill, lack of confidence, and lack of objectivity within the client-clinician relationship (Brown, Pryzwansky, & Schulte, 2001).

We frequently provide trainings and consultation to other clinicians who are working to develop their skills and expertise in the treatment of anxiety disorders. This can be done one-on-one or in groups. In a group format, we would be the providers of the consultation and the audience members of a seminar or training would be the consultees. When we work one-on-one with other clinicians, the individual clinicians are the consultees. The trainings (that we give) do not involve direct supervision, but rather involve general consultation on the treatment approach to various types of anxiety disorders. Seminar or consultation meetings are geared towards teaching and explaining the approach in detail and answering questions.

Supervision (which is described in more detail in Chapter 15) is another excellent method of consultee-centered case consultation. The consultee is the supervisee who seeks to build up skills in a particular area. For example, a supervisee may wish to build a practice specializing in Panic Disorder. The supervisee would get as many referrals for patients with Panic Disorder as possible and then work directly with a supervisor who is an expert in the treatment of Panic Disorder. The supervisee may be a student, a post-doctoral intern, or a licensed clinician interested in building an area of specialty. Supervision is one of the best ways to build new skills because the clinician will receive specific feedback on his or her cases and how to improve skills (and treatment outcome) with those clients. Supervision can also be considered client-centered case consultation if the purpose of the supervision is to assist with a specific case and optimally help the client.

Professionals with Whom to Collaborate

Teachers

When clinicians work with children and adolescents with anxiety disorders, there is likely to be some consultation and collaboration with the patient's teachers or other administrators within the child's school. The multidisciplinary team approach of clinicians plus teachers, school counselors, school psychologists, and administrators can be very helpful for the anxious child.

What Information to Share

Clinicians can provide consultation to teachers, collaborate with school personnel, and gain information about the child's performance in the classroom in several ways. The extent of the collaboration depends on the consent given by the parents and patient. Parents or patients may only want the clinician to solicit information from the teacher without going into detail about the patient's anxiety disorder. Other parents and patients would like the clinician to share as much as needed to help the teacher.

A problem arises when parents' ideal level of disclosure differs from the patient's desired disclosure. One patient with OCD did not want her diagnosis shared with her teachers because she felt that she would be using it as an excuse or taking the easy way out. She also did not want to be seen as different from other students and was concerned that once the word about her OCD got out, other students would look at her differently. This patient was, however, having some difficulties in the classroom based on her anxiety. Her parents did not want the problems to affect her grades so they wanted to tell the teacher. The patient's clinician met with her separately to go through the pros and cons of describing the OCD to her teacher. The patient agreed that she did not want her grades to go down while she worked on her OCD. The patient decided that she would be most comfortable with her parents speaking with the teacher, so the parents met briefly with the clinician to come up with a plan for this meeting.

Gather Information

Clinicians can glean valuable information from the teachers of their young patients. Parent and patient reports of what happens in the classroom will not be as specific and informative as direct teacher observations. When clinicians meet with teachers they can gather specific information about how the student functions in the classroom. Some children, adolescents, and college students are able to keep their anxiety under control while in the classroom and show few or no signs of anxiety. Others become highly nervous and agitated in the stressful environment of school. Information about how a student behaves in school is very helpful to the clinician in treatment planning.

Provide Recommendations

There are many ways that anxiety comes up in the classroom. Often teachers will not know how to handle the patient's anxiety and will be greatly appreciative of any recommendations that the clinicians can provide.

A young patient with OCD was concerned that he would get sick from touching one of his classmates. The teacher had no idea why he would not go near the other kids in the class. The young patient refused to sit next to other kids, use the bathroom at school, play sports during recess, or walk in a line behind another child. The teacher viewed these behaviors as oppositional, and the patient was frequently punished.

With patient and parental consent, the patient's clinician contacted the teacher and educated him about OCD and his student's unique obsessions and compulsions. The teacher was extremely relieved to speak to the clinician—he frequently punished this student, but had a feeling that he might be missing what was causing the odd behaviors. Once he was told that the student's odd behaviors were because of OCD, he was able to view the situation in a completely different way.

The clinician shared a copy of the student's hierarchy with the teacher and opened up a weekly dialog in which the teacher was informed about which item on the hierarchy they were currently working on. For example, when the patient was working on sitting at his desk next to a classmate, the teacher understood that the student needed to spend a few weeks sitting next to a "less contaminated" child before confronting the most contaminated children. This information allowed the teacher to facilitate these different seating arrangements. The clinician also provided the teacher with tips about how to coach the student through exposures. He and the patient decided on a special hand signal that cued the patient to adhere to his exposure work when the teacher noticed him gradually moving his desk away from the other child's desk.

It is important to note that in this sort of situation, the therapist should not "lay down the law" without input from the teacher. Teachers are therapists' eyes into the classroom. They will be able to report whether or not a student is succeeding with exposure to a particular item on his hierarchy. This information will impact the treatment plan. If an item still appears to be problematic, this would suggest to the therapist that it needs more work. If the item appears to no longer provoke avoidance or distress, the therapist and teacher can discuss what the next step in treatment should be.

As another example, the student described at the end of Chapter 12 with social anxiety and perfectionism was reluctant to talk in class and refused to read aloud or answer questions. Her teacher was confused by this at the beginning of the year, because the student's written work suggested that she was very intelligent. A few weeks into the school year, the teacher had come to the conclusion that the patient was shy and she simply decided to stop asking her questions.

Once she was brought into the treatment process, the teacher learned that she was facilitating the student's avoidance. The therapist provided her with recommendations about how to gradually expose the patient to speaking up in class. She suggested that the teacher begin by asking her easier questions, specifically those with an objective answer (such as an answer like "two times"). Later in treatment, they would move onto questions that required a more comprehensive answer or an answer of a more personal nature (such as an answer like, "Well, I think that the moral of the story is ..."). The clinician encouraged the teacher to contact her whenever she needed guidance on how to best help the student overcome anxiety and function better in school.

Finally, consider the case of a little girl who always seemed to be off in her own world during class. Her teacher started to wonder if the child had Attention Deficit Disorder. In reality, the patient was constantly worrying. She most often worried about understanding her work and doing well in school. Worrying resulted in many physical symptoms and as soon as she began to feel a headache coming on or knots in her stomach, she started to worry about a completely new thing–getting sick in school. When she felt sick, she really wanted to go and see the school nurse, but this decision was also fraught with worry. She worried that she could become even sicker by going to the nurse, since other sick kids went there. She worried about whether she would tell her teacher if she were to become sick, and about the negative impact on her grades that could result from missing schoolwork because of illness. As with many people with GAD, she was thinking of all the negative ramifications of being sick, including missing school, not getting into a good college, and not being able to pursue her dream of being a lawyer. Not surprisingly, all of these worries just made her feel sicker.

Her clinician spoke with her teacher and recommended that the student let the teacher know if she needed to go to the nurse based on some agreed-upon criteria (feverish, nausea at a level of 7 or above on a scale of 0–10, etc.). The clinician also recommended that the teacher help engage the student in class to keep her focused externally rather than focused on her internal struggles. When the student became more engaged in class, her nausea decreased. As her nausea decreased, she became less nervous and worried.

Education and Referrals

When teachers are educated about how anxiety can present in the classroom, they are able to make appropriate referrals. Clinicians can make it their duty to begin a vital education campaign. It is useful to educate other professionals as much as possible and to encourage them to share the information with their colleagues. The education and knowledge offered by the clinician will spread. Clinicians can serve as consultants to educate other professionals regarding how to best help current patients or to help professionals make appropriate referrals for treatment in the future.

A college professor of religious studies noticed that one of her students was becoming increasingly distressed in the classroom. The behavior appeared abnormal and the professor was concerned. Several other professors had expressed concern that the student may have a serious mental illness like psychosis because she appeared to be absorbed in and responding to her own thoughts. This professor had recently attended an in-service presentation about anxiety in the classroom and wondered if the student's unusual behavior may actually be a manifestation of anxiety. She provided an appropriate referral to the student for an anxiety treatment center. The student attended an evaluation and it turned out that she had OCD with scrupulosity or religious concerns. The student was a devout Christian and she was obsessed with learning about other religions in her religions class. She was afraid that she would like another religion better, or worse, that she would decide she was not religious, and would no longer be a "good Christian," in her words. The unusual behavior observed by the professor was the student repeating to herself mental reassurances, such as "I'm a good Christian, I go to church every week" or "I love God and God loves me." She would also pray to herself to show herself that she remembered the right prayers.

Clinicians working with schools or college counseling centers can provide training to staff and faculty on the signs and symptoms of anxiety disorders, how to refer students, and how to best help the students in their classes. Many teachers and professors are reluctant to provide a referral because they do not know how to phrase the recommendation and are nervous about offending the student. Clinicians can explain that it is not a good idea to approach someone and say, "You seem nervous, here's a referral." Instead, they can set up a private meeting with the student (or the parents of younger children) to discuss grades or classroom behavior. In the discussion, they can say that it seems that the student's grades have been dropping or it seems that the student has had difficulty concentrating lately, and ask the student what he or she makes of it. The professor can normalize the student's difficulties and inspire hope that the student can make a positive change. After a dialogue about the student's difficulties, the teacher or professor can emphasize the student's potential for academic excellence and provide a referral for a clinician specializing in anxiety.

Special Issues on Consultation and Collaboration with Teachers

Clinicians should be aware of and sensitive to some of the constraints that teachers face that can limit their ability to receive consultation or collaborate with clinicians. If a clinician overlooks these variables, they run the risk of making assumptions about the teacher that are not true. First, teachers have limited time in their day during which to collaborate. They cannot leave their classrooms to take a phone call. Many teachers have a planning period, but need that period for lesson planning or other administrative duties. A good solution to this time problem is to gain administrative support and build in time for the collaboration. Arranging times to speak by phone during planning periods or before or after the school day can be helpful (Brown, Pryzwansky, & Schulte, 2001). If teachers utilize e-mail, then e-mail can be used to set up these contacts. Teachers may also have an erroneous understanding of the role of the school psychologist. They may not see the need for an external consultant when the school has a psychologist. In this case, it can be helpful to include the school psychologist in the conversations since she or he may have an additional viewpoint to share that can benefit the patient.

Another model for consultation to teachers is speaking to groups of school personnel. A primary advantage is that the consultant can help multiple school professionals in a limited amount of time. With administrative support, this approach can be very helpful. There is research showing that this approach has been effective in improving knowledge of consultees, reducing the need for student referrals, and improving communication among school personnel (Cohen & Osterweil, 1986). A case study focused approach can be used where the clinician educates the teachers and other school personnel on how to handle a specific case. The clinician can then generalize the experiences learned through the case study to show school personnel how to best manage additional situations that may arise in the future.

Physicians

It is also useful to consult and collaborate with patients' physicians. The most common physicians for clinicians to collaborate with are primary care physicians (internists, family medicine doctors) and psychiatrists. Again, clinicians can both educate and gather valuable information. Primary care physicians who have worked with the patient for a long period of time are able to provide background information, family history, medical history, and many important sources of data that can aid in the patient's treatment. Physicians can educate therapists on how particular medical conditions impact the patient's mental and physical health. Psychiatrists or primary care physicians who prescribe psychotropic medications can advise the therapist on potential side effects that they have seen in their patients.

Clinicians can also advise physicians on the process of CBT for anxiety disorders and how they can best support the treatment. Many patients with anxiety disorders experience frequent medical complaints. They may worry about the significance of their medical concerns and seek frequent reassurance from their physicians. Their physicians have likely noticed this reassurance-seeking behavior. Clinicians will work with their patients on reducing their safety behaviors and rituals, including reassurance seeking. Clinicians and physicians can together decide how to best address any ongoing reassurance seeking that the patient engages in.

Clearly there will be times when clinicians seek out consultation from physicians. One patient with Panic Disorder also had a heart condition. The clinician spoke with her cardiologist before beginning any exposures. As a result of speaking with the patient's cardiologist, the clinician learned more about the patient's heart condition and received advice to go ahead with interoceptive exposures. The clinician and cardiologist both supported the use of CBT and the patient was able to overcome her Panic Disorder in 12 sessions.

Other Therapists and Counselors

Clinicians can also collaborate and provide consultation to other therapists. These include couples therapists, family therapists, pastoral counselors, social workers, counselors, psychologists, and neuropsychologists.

Collaboration and Multiple Therapists

Patients with anxiety disorders may sometimes have other therapists or counselors whom they see for treatment. Some patients are engaged in marital or family therapy. Others have been working with a clinician on a long-term issue and would like CBT for anxiety in addition to their long-term work. When this is the case, it is helpful for the clinician to get a release of information to collaborate with the other treatment providers and to provide information on the patient's anxiety disorder treatment. It would be highly counterproductive for one clinician to help the patient with relaxation, distraction, and avoidance of anxiety, while the other clinician is sending messages about the importance of confronting anxiety and doing exposures–the patient would get a mixed message.

A clinician may recommend that the patient put a temporary hold on other therapies. Alternatively, the patient and therapist could agree that the patient will only focus on anxiety in the CBT for anxiety treatment and could focus on other relationship or life issues in the other form of therapy.

Clinicians can collaborate with other treatment providers to offer comprehensive and consistent treatment approaches. Information brought up in individual therapy for anxiety can be important for the patient's family or couples therapy. For example, a patient may discuss the negative impact that her anxiety has had on her relationship with her fiancée. The clinician could provide information to the couple's therapist to help him understand the role that anxiety has played in the relationship and how the patient's anxiety is currently being addressed. The clinician could also request consultation from the couple's therapist regarding whether or not the fiancée would be the right person to serve as the patient's coach or primary support person for the anxiety treatment.

Consultation

Clinicians specializing in the treatment of anxiety disorders can provide consultation to other mental health professionals through trainings, mentoring, supervision, consultation, and writing. These methods are discussed in the next section. In addition, clinicians who seek to enhance their skills in the treatment of anxiety disorders can request consultation from other experts.

Methods to Provide Information

There are many ways that clinicians can provide information to consultees and other professionals. Clinicians can decide what method or combination of methods would work best for the aim of the consultation. Remember that people do not typically remember most of what they learn verbally without some form of visual reminder.

Trainings and Seminars

Clinicians can provide training to groups of mental health professionals and allied healthcare professionals on the assessment, diagnosis, and treatment of anxiety disorders. These trainings are typically psychoeducational in nature and vary from formal lectures to informal case presentations and question-and-answer sessions. The primary benefit is the dissemination of information to multiple professionals at once. The primary drawback is that audience members are unlikely to receive extensive specific case consultation on their cases from the presenter.

In-Person or Telephone Discussions

A common form of consultation entails in person or over the telephone conversations. The primary advantage to this method is that consultees can ask whatever questions come to mind and will receive specific and relevant answers. The consultation will be highly customized to the needs and concerns of the consultee, and can be designed to greatly benefit the patient. The primary disadvantage of this method for consultation is that the consultee will not have a written record of the conversation and therefore may forget some of the important information discussed. There are several solutions to this problem. The first is to record conversations and then have the conversation transcribed. Assuming that patient confidentiality is maintained, the written record of the consultation can be distributed to other professionals who could benefit from the information provided. Another option is to suggest that the consultee take notes or for the clinician to offer to take notes and e-mail them to the consultee. A third option is to set up a brief follow-up meeting or phone conversation to reinforce the material discussed during the initial conversation.

E-mail

E-mail is a viable option for consultation and is preferred by many because of its ease of use. People can read and respond to e-mails when time permits within their schedules. This works well for professionals who work different hours during the day. A clinician who specializes in working with children is likely to work afternoons and evenings while teachers usually work in the mornings and early afternoon, so it can be difficult to connect. The main caution to the use of e-mail is that it is not a secure method of relaying confidential information. Fortunately, consultation can often be conducted without including identifying information. E-mail is also useful for setting up telephone or in person meetings, following up with questions or observations, and sending articles, book recommendations, and other referrals.

Brochures

Clinicians can develop or distribute already developed brochures that provide education on the various anxiety disorders and implications for patients. These brochures are powerful marketing materials, and offer great information for professionals and their patients. Informative brochures should provide information such as:

- Description of the specific signs and symptoms of a particular anxiety disorder or anxiety disorders in general.

- Ways in which the anxiety disorder may present in the setting for which the brochure is designed (e.g., school, physicians office).
- Brief description of the effectiveness of treatments for the anxiety disorder.
- Information on when to seek treatment and how to find a clinician who specializes in the anxiety disorder.
- Additional resources, including recommended books and web sites.

Articles

Clinicians who write articles that can be useful to other professionals can pass them out if they have redistribution rights. If you cannot reprint articles due to copyright, you can create your own article and retain copyright to distribute however you would like. Articles are an excellent way to provide a great deal of information that can be accessed quickly and easily. Articles can also build credibility and lead to more comprehensive forms of consultation later.

Articles can be particularly helpful when they serve the dual purpose of educating both professionals and potential patients or their family members. An article, for example, on how OCD affects children's school performance could be very beneficial to school personnel and also to the parents of children with OCD. Articles can also provide information regarding the effectiveness of treatments for anxiety disorders that can help to encourage reluctant patients or parents to pursue a clinical evaluation.

Articles should be written in layperson language and avoid the extensive use of psychological jargon. The purpose of the article should be to inform and educate. The information should be limited to that which would be most understandable and helpful to other professionals and patients, and limit extraneous information. Tables, graphs, and charts can display key statistics and help to break up the text.

Web sites

Clinicians or organizations can easily and inexpensively create information-packed web sites. The wonderful thing about web sites is that they can be accessed by anyone, anywhere in the world, anytime. Clinicians can collect frequently asked questions and post the questions and answers on their web sites. Other valuable information to include is:

1. Signs and symptoms of anxiety
2. Information about the different disorders
3. The basics of cognitive behavioral therapy for anxiety disorders
4. Medication and other forms for treatment
5. Recommended readings
6. Referrals and resources

The web site can also include live links to organizations that offer additional information on anxiety disorders such as The Obsessive Compulsive Foundation (http://www.ocfoundation.org) and the Anxiety Disorders Association of America (http://www.adaa.org).

One-Page Documents

Clinicians can easily create a one-page document (often called a white paper) that outlines some very specific information on topics of interest for the professionals with whom they collaborate. Because these documents are just one page, outlining basic information, they can be highly tailored to the setting and collaborating professional. Clinicians can easily update them. For example, a white paper could be written for school psychologists and counselors. This document could then be easily modified for teachers, principals, and parents. Clinicians can create the document using a word processing program and then turn it into a PDF file for electronic distribution, or print it out to distribute hard copies.

The best information to include in a one-page document is specific FAQs, signs to look for, tips, or hands-on advice. The page can also include contact information for the clinician with ongoing questions or future requests for consultation.

References

Brown, D., Pryzwansky, W. B., & Schulte, A. C. (2001). *Psychological consultation: Introduction to theory and practice* (5th ed.). Needham Heights, MA: Allyn & Bacon.

Caplan, G. (1970). *The theory and practice of mental health consultation.* New York: Basic Books.

Cohen, E., & Osterweil, Z. (1986). An "issue-focused" model for mental health consultation with groups of teachers. *Journal of School Psychology, 24,* 243–256.

CHAPTER **14**

Group, Family, and Couples Therapy

There are many ways to include others in the treatment of anxiety disorders. It is a misconception that cognitive behavioral treatments focus solely on an individual patient, and neglect social supports.

The first method that will be presented in this chapter is therapy aimed at groups rather than individuals. These groups can be general anxiety groups or anxiety-specific groups. The second method is to involve family members, friends, and significant others in various ways with the patient's treatment. The third method is to refer patients and family members or significant others to family therapy or couples therapy to provide an important adjunct to the patient's therapy for anxiety.

Group Therapy for Anxiety Disorders

There are many benefits to group therapy. The first benefit is simple logistics— clinicians can help more people in less time. If clinicians are qualified to treat a disorder or type of disorders (such as anxiety disorders), it is likely that the need for services exceeds the amount of time they have available. Group therapy addresses both of these issues because clinicians can help ten or more people in the same amount of time that they would see one or two individual patients. A nice benefit for patients is that groups are often a more affordable option than individual therapy.

Clinically, participating in a therapy group helps patients to see that they are not alone in their problems and that others struggle with similar concerns and difficulties. Patients in individual therapy will hear about how others struggle with similar issues from their therapists, but it can be even more powerful to talk to other patients directly. Another benefit of group therapy is that members are able to benefit from the experience of others in their groups. Their own motivation and commitment to overcoming anxiety can increase when they see other patients confronting their fears and habituating. Group members can also help one another with exposures. In a Social Phobia group, one patient can make a speech in front of an "audience" of other group members. The group members can offer support and provide valuable feedback in a safe environment. A final benefit to group therapy is that patients feel a sense of accountability to the other group members as well as to themselves and the therapist or therapists who run the group. This can improve compliance with homework assignments and therapy attendance.

General Anxiety Groups

One of the ways to help patients who experience anxiety is to offer general anxiety groups for patients with various forms of anxiety difficulties. This format can be particularly helpful in clinics and settings where patients have multiple diagnoses and difficulties. For example, patients can go to individual therapy within the clinic to work on relationship issues, domestic violence or a history of abuse, substance dependence, chronic pain, or whatever issues bring them in for treatment. Their clinicians may also identify anxiety as a problem. The patients can then attend a group geared toward the treatment of anxiety and remain in individual treatment with their therapist.

Patients who have severe anxiety disorders, psychosis, or other factors requiring more focused treatment are inappropriate candidates for a general anxiety group. Rather, these groups work best for those with mild to moderate anxiety.

The downside to a general anxiety group is that patients will not receive the detailed education and assistance with their particular form of anxiety. There are some aspects to treatment that are disorder specific, such as interoceptive exposure for Panic Disorder and video feedback for Social Phobia. It can also be difficult to practice exposures in a group setting because each group member will need to confront unique triggers for their anxiety. It is quite likely that general anxiety groups will yield poorer outcomes than groups tailored to a specific anxiety disorder.

With that being said, participating in a general anxiety group is an excellent alternative to no treatment or to one that has no proven efficacy for the treatment of anxiety disorders. General anxiety groups typically have a significant psychoeducation component and are useful for teaching techniques that are common to all anxiety disorder treatment, such as relaxation, exposure, and cognitive restructuring. Patients are likely to learn and begin applying key principles discussed in the group. A potential structure for a ten-session group is as follows:

Group 1—Introduction, Education, and Goal Setting

New group members will meet one another and the therapist or therapists running the group. Group members identify areas in which anxiety interferes with their lives and set goals for change. An agenda for the group is distributed and group policies and procedures are agreed upon. Confidentiality is emphasized and members must sign the consent forms to continue in the group. The clinician normalizes anxiety and discusses its prevalence and interference in the lives of millions. The clinician then introduces some of the key concepts in understanding anxiety and provides psychoeducation. The clinician uses metaphors and descriptions to help patients see how their anxiety disorders have been maintained in their lives and then distributes articles on anxiety and its effective treatments.

Group 2—Education: CBT Model with Anxiety
In the second group, the clinician and patients construct the CBT model to show the interconnection of thoughts, behaviors, physical symptoms, and mood in the context of the specific situation or environment. Patients complete their own model. A brief introduction to cognitive therapy is given and patients are asked to complete thought records for homework.

Group 3—The Role of Thoughts
The clinician teaches patients about the role cognitive distortions play and how they create and maintain anxiety. The clinician provides examples of some of the most common cognitive distortions, such as all-or-none thinking, mind reading, and magnification. Patients then review their self-monitoring and note if any cognitive distortions are present. For homework, patients are asked to continue monitoring thoughts and recognize when cognitive errors occur.

Group 4—Cognitive Restructuring
In session four, clinicians introduce the concept and method of cognitive restructuring. Patients learn to challenge their thoughts and test the evidence. Patients can share their homework with group members and role-play with a partner. One person can voice their anxious thoughts and the other person can suggest coping thoughts. Patients are given cognitive restructuring homework to work on probability overestimation and catastrophizing.

Group 5—Relaxation: Deep Breathing, Muscle Relaxation, and Guided Imagery
In this session, the clinician introduces the concept of relaxation. The key point to get across is when to use relaxation and when not to. The clinician then introduces the idea that there are many forms of relaxation. The first step for patients is to learn what works best for them. This often means trying out different strategies to see which ones are more or less effective. The next step is actually using the relaxation strategies on a regular basis. The clinician can introduce deep breathing and guided imagery as two types of relaxation strategies. The patients can then be walked through a deep breathing exercise, and then a guided imagery exercise to experientially get a sense for how they can be used to achieve a state of calm. The patients can be given the homework assignment of practicing the breathing and imagery exercises on their own.

Group 6—Relaxation: Progressive Muscle Relaxation (PMR)

The session begins by discussing the patient's use of breathing and imagery exercises during the week. Patients report what worked for them and the difficulties they experienced. The group can brainstorm how to address difficulties that were brought up. The clinician then introduces PMR. Patients are walked through PMR training for about 30–40 minutes. Afterwards, patients process the experience and discuss how they can use it. Patients practice PMR daily for homework.

Group 7—Introduction to In Vivo Exposure

Patients will be familiar with the concept of exposure from earlier sessions. In session 7, the clinician describes the SUDS scale and the hierarchy for exposures. Patients create their hierarchies in session. They get assistance and share with one another to create in vivo exposure hierarchies. Patients are encouraged to begin exposures on their own (after group) to items that have a SUDS rating around 40–50. Patients are given a handout to record homework exposures that will ensure that they carry out the exposure in such a way that they learn something from the experience.

Group 8—In Vivo Exposure Continued

In this session, patients describe any exposures that they did between group and discuss the lessons they learned from the exposure. If a patient did not habituate, the clinician and group can brainstorm explanations for the lack of habituation and ways of doing the exposure differently. If any exposures can or should be done in the group, they are done this day and group members serve as participants or confederates to help the patient with his or her exposure. For homework, patients are encouraged to move up their hierarchies and do exposures to items that have a SUDS rating around 60–70.

Group 9—In Vivo Continued, Imaginal, and Interoceptive Exposure

This session can continue with in vivo exposures, and introduce imaginal and interoceptive exposure. If the clinicians realize that no one in their group seems to need interoceptive exposure, they can omit this material. The clinician can provide the rationale for imaginal exposure. Patients then take some time to write down their own imaginal exposures. The clinician walks around and helps patients to create their imaginals. Patients can record the imaginal for homework and listen to it everyday. Patients for whom imaginal exposure is not appropriate or needed can continue with in vivo exposures during this group and over the following week.

Group 10—Group Summary and Wrap-Up

In the final group, patients discuss their progress and the lessons they have learned from treatment. This group is powerful for patients because they get to think about not only what they learned and how they changed, but also how the other group members have progressed. A discussion of "What's next?" can occur and patients can describe their ongoing goals and next steps towards anxiety reduction. Clinicians provide patients with a list of resources for future reference, including how to find a cognitive behavioral therapist for individual therapy, and how to find a psychiatry referral.

Disorder Specific Groups

Groups can also be offered for specific disorders, such as for Obsessive-Compulsive Disorder or Social Phobia (see Heimberg & Becker, 2002, for an excellent group Social Phobia treatment manual). These groups provide similar benefits to those described above. Patients see that they are not alone, gain support from group members, have an increased sense of accountability, find opportunities for exposures with other people, and learn from the treatment progress of other group members. For some types of presenting issues, such as Social Phobia, a group format can create an audience for exposures, which solves the problem that many individual therapists face regarding how to find confederates for exposures.

The primary drawback to the anxiety disorder specific group treatment modality is the loss of personalization. Patients may have the same diagnosis but very different presenting issues. For example, within an OCD group, clinicians may find some patients with contamination concerns, some patients with the fear of acting on an unwanted impulse, and some patients who have scrupulosity concerns (religious preoccupations and compulsions). To help those with contamination fears, the clinician would plan exposures outside, picking up items off the ground or in the public restroom, touching doorknobs and stall doors. These exposures are likely to help those patients with OCD regarding contamination, but they are not likely to do much for those with fears about acting on their impulses or offending a religious object. A solution to this problem is to run fear-specific, anxiety disorder-specific groups. This is often not a viable option, however, because of logistics. Filling groups to begin in a timely matter is a difficult task that would be made even more difficult if the groups were highly specific. Another option is to run a mixed group-individual treatment where the bulk of treatment is done in a group setting, but patients also meet one-on-one with therapists for very specific exposures or to process very personal issues.

Involvement of Others in Treatment

There are two ways to involve family members and significant others in treatment. The first is to involve family members as supports in an individual's anxiety disorder treatment. The second method is to recommend family and couples therapy as an adjunct or primary treatment.

Psychoeducation with Family Members and Significant Others

Patients do not live in a bubble. The lives of most people involve frequent interactions with others. They may live with family members or their significant other, or regularly see important people in their lives. These important people have a strong influence on the patient's life and are likely to also have a major influence in the evolution and maintenance of the patient's anxiety. Clinicians can best help patients when they are able to appropriately include family members in treatment.

Some patients do not have family members or are isolated, and they will need different types of support. Clinicians can help patients to build support systems and decrease their isolation. If patients have family members with whom they are estranged or with whom relationships are strained, patients and family members can be encouraged to pursue family therapy and the clinician can provide a referral.

It is common for patients to have family members who have many questions regarding the patient's anxiety. Many patients will tell their clinicians that their spouse, parent, or significant other would like to know how to help. Often, however, patients will not describe their family members to their clinicians. They may think that they are not supposed to discuss their relationships or they assume that if it is important, their clinician will ask them. For these reasons, it is important that clinicians ask patients about the role of family members and significant others.

Towards the beginning of treatment, the clinician can inquire about the role of family members with questions such as:

- How has the anxiety affected your family?
- Has your partner tried to help out? If so, how?
- Where do you find support for these difficulties?
- Do you worry about the impact that your anxiety has had on anyone?
- Is there someone in your life who you think would like to learn how to best help you overcome your anxiety? If so, who? Would you like them to be involved in your treatment?
- Do you think that you could be better supported in your treatment if someone understood more about what you're going through with your anxiety?

It is important to clarify that the goal of including a significant other in treatment is to improve the effectiveness of the therapy. It can be difficult for clinicians to remember that bringing a spouse in for a treatment session is not the same as conducting a couples therapy session. The couple, when in the room together, may begin bringing up couples therapy types of issues. If this is the case, the clinician may decide to provide a referral so the patient and their significant other have a place to do couples work.

The session with the support person is dedicated to helping the patient. Before bringing someone else into treatment, be sure to have the patient sign a release of information (unless the patient is a minor and the support person is his or her custodial guardian who consented to treatment). It is also important to clarify with the patient the extent to which they would like the support person to be involved and what information the clinician should share. When in doubt, the clinician can ask the patient to describe situations or relay information so the clinician does not disclose anything that the patient does not want shared.

The clinician and patient can decide ahead of time whether they would like to have the support person return at a later time in treatment. If so, the first session may be geared specifically towards education. This may take around 15 or 20 minutes, so the patient can have the rest of his or her regular treatment session. A later session could be dedicated to helping the support person learn the best methods for coaching the patient.

In a session with a spouse, other family member, or significant other, the primary objective is psychoeducation. The clinician should begin the session (or part of the session) by introducing the purpose of the involvement and thanking the support person for participating. The clinician can then provide education about anxiety, the patient's particular anxiety disorder, and the treatment approach. An important point to flesh out during the psychoeducation component is what behaviors are related to anxiety and what behaviors are related to nonanxiety emotions and thoughts. This is important because support people may want to respond differently to anxiety than they would to stubbornness, spite, or other factors. The best way to respond to anxiety is with empathy and encouragement. As the clinician presents this information, the patient and the support person should be asked if they have any questions or comments.

There are several important points for a support person to learn. One way that a supportive family member or significant other can assist in the treatment is by providing positive encouragement. Support people should be prepared for the patient to experience some emotional distress during the treatment. When discussing the process of exposure therapy and habituation, the clinician would explain that it is likely that the patient will experience distress as he begins to work his way up his hierarchy. Clinicians can also let patients and family members know that an "extinction burst" can occur. This is a temporary increase in the undesirable behavior when the reinforcement is first removed. When these initial increases in anxiety occur in session, clinicians know how to handle them. When, however, they occur outside of session, patients can be helped by support people who expect the increase in anxiety and know how to handle it. The messages to communicate to the support person include:

1. Anxiety is a good thing when it arises during an exposure. It means that the patient is confronting his or her fears and overcoming the anxiety.

2. Keep the long-term perspective in mind. Helping the patient to surf the urge to engage in a ritual or avoidance will help them overcome their anxiety in the long-term.

3. Positive encouragement is a great thing. Let patients know that they are being courageous and can get through the anxiety if they stick with it. Be careful, however, not to engage in reassurance (see below).

4. Habituation WILL occur. Even if it seems that the patient is "out of control" or "losing it," he or she will habituate if there are no rituals or safety behaviors. This may need to be accepted on faith at first if the support person has not yet seen the patient face and habituate to his anxiety.

5. When in doubt, ask the patient what to do to help. Patients will know how they can best be helped. Or just let them know that you are there for support.

6. If patients have agreed to have support people give them reminders (to complete self monitoring or exposure homework, eliminate rituals, and so on), then do so whenever appropriate.

Stopping Reassurance

One of the things that family members struggle with the most is reassurance. It is very hard to watch your loved one struggle. It is, therefore, very natural to want to reassure someone who is in distress. Many family members do not realize that the reassurance they give actually helps to maintain the anxiety, and does not help the patient. The intentions of family members are good, but the practice of enabling the anxiety is not good.

The first step in helping family members to properly deal with anxiety is to have the patient agree to stop seeking reassurance. The patient can explain to family members (with the assistance of the clinician) how reassurance serves as a ritual or anxiety-increasing behavior and it needs to be stopped. Once the patient agrees to stop reassurance seeking, family members can agree to stop reassurance giving. The most effective way to end reassurance is by having the patient agree to stop asking and the family members agree to stop giving reassurance.

Family members can typically identify with the idea that reassurance is only a very short-term fix and that anxiety is likely to pop back up. Many family members come in and say, "My daughter asks a million questions. It's as if she isn't satisfied with any of the answers I give her. Even if I reassure her, she's asking again in a couple minutes." When clinicians engage family members and help them to see that the reassurance is not helping, it will be easier for them to give it up.

The clinician can spend a few minutes with the family members to go through any fears they think might occur if they do not provide reassurance. Some family members will express concern that the patient's anxiety will continue to escalate uncontrollably. If this is the case, clinicians can explain the principal of habituation and recommend that they try to help patients experience and habituate to the anxiety rather than escape from it.

Some family members express concern that the patient will become angry with them or lash out if they do not receive reassurance. Clinicians should first determine whether there is evidence that this concern is valid. If patients do have a history of becoming verbally or physically aggressive with someone who did not provide reassurance, this issue needs to be addressed right away. Clinicians should ask patients to provide written and verbal consent that the support person can notify the clinician if aggressive behavior occurs. The therapist can help the patient to manage anxiety without acting on it and to substitute nonaggressive behaviors (such as exercise) when particularly distressed. Clinicians can also encourage patients to call them when they are having a hard time managing anxiety without lashing out. If there is no evidence that the patient will become abusive, but the support person has this concern, then the clinician can encourage him or her to try it out to see what happens. The clinician can explain that the patient has several strategies to manage anxiety and that acting out is unlikely to occur.

Clinicians can also educate support people about the idea that temporary frustration when a patient is anxious is normal. It does not mean that they hate or are angry with the support person. In fact, over time the patient will come to truly appreciate the steadfast responses that the support person offers. As the patient's anxiety decreases, there will be less asking for reassurance and more recognition of the important role that the support person plays in reducing the anxiety (by not giving reassurance).

Family Members Who Sabotage Treatment

A difficult issue that clinicians sometimes face is when people (other than the patients themselves) seem to sabotage the patient's progress in treatment. Family members may negatively impact treatment in subtle or overt ways. They are often unaware of their role or place blame on the patient for not improving quickly enough.

In Chapter 12, we discussed how parents can sabotage their child's anxiety treatment. Adult patients also find that significant people in their lives can sabotage their treatment progress. Clinicians may learn about difficulties with family members or significant others because patients complain about the problems. For example, a patient may say, "My spouse makes requests of me during the time I set aside to do my homework assignments." Or, "My partner complains about the time I take off to come into therapy because it's about three hours a week with the drive, and childcare is a problem." Sometimes patients feel misunderstood and unsupported by a loved one. Patients may say, "My girlfriend doesn't think I need to be in therapy," or "My husband says that my anxiety is the least of my problems."

It is important to ask patients about the roles that the key people in their lives play in their treatment because they might not spontaneously bring up this information. Some patients feel that the person sabotaging treatment is right and feel guilty about being "selfish" and taking the time for anxiety treatment. If this is the case, it is important to address the patients' concerns.

Significant others do not always understand or respect the fact that therapy is a significant investment of time and energy. They may be frustrated with the difficulties that the patient's anxiety has caused, or they may have problems with compromising and "picking up the slack" while the patient focuses on overcoming his or her anxiety. Clinicians can explain the expectations of the patient, which typically include regular attendance at sessions and daily practice between sessions. After the education component, clinicians can help the patient and significant other to negotiate a temporary change in activities during the course of treatment. Clinicians should emphasize that CBT for anxiety is a short-term approach, so the sacrifices that the significant other makes will likely be for only a limited period of time. When meeting with significant others and family members, clinicians can also elicit their views about what will improve once the patient has overcome anxiety. Thinking about the changes and benefits will help them to feel motivated to better support the process.

The other way in which family members can interfere with the treatment process is by supporting the patient's rituals or safety behaviors. People sometimes have difficulty managing the patient's anxiety and look for a quick fix. When family members are having a difficult day or feel stressed themselves, it will be hard for them to encourage patients to stick with their anxiety. They will be tempted to focus on helping the patient to feel better in the short-term, which often involves engaging in a ritual, safety behavior, or avoidance.

Clinicians can help support people to see how even in the short-term these behaviors are unlikely to be effective and how a key component of treatment is to eliminate them, even though it is difficult to do so. Clinicians can help support people come up with a script or a response to use when patients are tempted to engage in a safety behavior. Clinicians can also coach their patients to acknowledge and thank support people (at a later point in time) for being firm and supporting them in overcoming their anxiety.

Family and Couples Therapy

Family therapy or couples therapy is often useful as an adjunct to CBT for anxiety disorders. While clinicians will frequently include family members and significant others in their individual patients' treatment, there are times when family or couples therapy will be indicated. It is generally a good idea to refer out for these types of therapy since conducting both family therapy and individual therapy with one of the family members can create dual relationships and a conflict of interest for the therapist. Clinicians should network with other therapists to build a solid database of referrals for family and couples therapists.

Family Therapy

There are several situations where a referral to family therapy can be a good idea. The first scenario is when an individual in treatment reveals family issues that are creating an increase in stress or anxiety for the patient. For example, a patient with Generalized Anxiety Disorder worried about many issues related to her family. Many of her worries were due to GAD, but some of them were due to real stress and discord that the family faced. Family therapy can address the latter issues, and help to reduce conflict and stress for all family members.

The second scenario is when family members are serving as impediments to treatment. When this is the case, the clinician should consider whether an individual therapy referral (for the person sabotaging treatment) or a family therapy referral might be needed. Family therapy can address the conflicts that likely underlie the sabotaging behavior and enable the patient to focus on her anxiety treatment.

In a third scenario, a patient presents with an anxiety disorder that is serving a particular function within the family system. When the patient starts to reduce his anxiety disorder the family system shifts. It may be that the family was focused on the patient's anxiety disorder as the problem and neglected to view other difficulties in the family system. As a result, the family issues that were kept at bay by focusing on the patient's anxiety rise to the surface and family therapy can be helpful.

Another scenario in which family therapy can serve as a useful adjunct to treatment is when damage within the family has occurred as a result of the patient's anxiety. For example, when a young patient had severe anxiety, he lashed out at his parents out of frustration. His parents found this behavior unacceptable and yelled back at him. An angry, accusatory family environment was created as a result of the patient's anxiety. Family therapy can help mend the hurt feelings that occurred during the time of the patient's acute anxiety. The family therapy referral can be made during or at the end of treatment.

A final scenario is family therapy to reconstruct the family hierarchy. Anxious individuals often call the shots in the family. Children may be demanding about what they need and parents acquiesce. Children make the rules and parents follow—the balance of power is turned upside down. Typically, the parents do decision making and rule setting; however parents sometimes feel paralyzed by their children's anxiety and are unable to maintain the parental role. Children get used to calling the shots and it can be a difficult transition when the children's anxiety is no longer in the picture. In situations like this one, clinicians should make a referral to a good family therapist who follows a structural family therapy model. Structural family therapy is an approach with a strong body of research behind it. The focus of structural family therapy is on the patterns and organization of the family system. Structural family therapy was developed in large part by Salvador Minuchin who theorized that there must be an effective hierarchical structure in which parents have authority (Becvar & Becvar, 2000). This approach can be very effective with families that have lost balance and organization due to a family member with an anxiety disorder.

Couples Therapy

Like family therapy, there are several indications that a referral to couples therapy may be necessary. With adult individual clients, clinicians often hear about relationship difficulties. It may be clear that the patients' spouses do not support them in most of their endeavors. It may become obvious that the patient has many concerns about their marriage. Some patients report communication difficulties with their significant other. Patients may begin to recognize how cognitive distortions like mind reading arise in their relationships and cause misunderstandings (Beck, 1988). These are all situations in which a referral for couples therapy can be helpful. Clinicians can give the referral to their patients or discuss the referral with both parties present.

There may be times when the couple the clinician refers to couples therapy does not include the clinician's patient. Clinicians working with children sometimes notice marital problems with the children's parents. Clinicians may be concerned about the impact that the marital issues have on their patients and the patients' ability to engage in treatment for anxiety given the couple's problems. If clinicians are concerned that the parents' relationship problems negatively affect their patients, then a referral may be necessary. In these situations, clinicians can meet with the parents separately, explain the potential impact of the parental discord on the child, and provide the referral.

In all of these situations, clinicians should remember that they have an obligation and professional responsibility to make the referral when they deem it necessary. When unsure, clinicians should consult with colleagues and supervisors to see if they feel a referral should be given. Clinicians must realize that they can only provide a referral (or several referrals in case other providers are not taking new patients or do not have the availability the patient needs). They cannot make people follow through. If, however, a clinician feels particularly strongly that follow through is needed, she can say that the family or couples therapy is necessary for continuation with individual therapy. Clinicians should have patients sign release of information forms to communicate with the other treatment providers.

References

Beck, A. T. (1988). *Love is never enough: How couples can overcome misunderstandings, resolve conflicts, and solve relationship problems through cognitive therapy.* New York: Harper Perennial.

Becvar, D. S., & Becvar, R. J. (2000). *Family therapy: A systematic integration (4th ed.).* Needham Heights, MA: Allyn & Bacon.

Heimberg, R. G., & Becker, R. E. (2002). *Cognitive-behavioral group therapy for Social Phobia: Basic mechanisms and clinical applications.* New York: Guilford.

CHAPTER 15

Supervision

Supervision is typically associated with unlicensed, beginning therapists. In this chapter, we will certainly discuss issues relevant to this group of people. We will also discuss how experienced therapists of different orientations can learn to be competent cognitive-behavioral therapists and how experienced cognitive-behavioral therapists can continue to benefit from supervision over the course of their careers. Supervision, regardless of the stage one is at in their professional development, can greatly improve the quality of treatment that we provide to our patients.

Experienced Therapists Who Want To Learn CBT

Therapists sometimes want to learn CBT after years of providing treatment from a different therapeutic orientation. Some therapists decide that CBT is a superior form of treatment for certain disorders after reading the research or hearing presentations at professional conferences. Other therapists want to continue practicing from another orientation, but believe that cognitive-behavioral techniques might be a useful adjunct to their existing approach.

Self Study

There are many ways for experienced therapists to learn about CBT. Perhaps the most efficient way is to read—both books about the theory underlying CBT and treatment manuals for specific disorders. An excellent place to start is with *Cognitive Therapy of Depression*, Beck and colleagues' classic 1979 book that first introduced cognitive therapy. Beck's *Cognitive Therapy and the Emotional Disorders* (1979) is also a must-read. While there are certainly more recently written books that cover the theory underlying CBT, these two books provide the theoretical framework that all cognitive-behavioral therapists should have.

Next, therapists should do some reading on the basics of CBT technique—how to actually *do* the treatment. An excellent resource is Judith Beck's *Cognitive Therapy: Basics and Beyond* (1995). Again, there are many books written on how to do CBT, but if people are pressed for time and want to gain a maximum amount of knowledge from one book, this is an excellent resource.

Most therapists want to learn how to use CBT with a particular population of patients. Again, it is important to learn about both theory and application. In the case of anxiety disorders, it is essential for clinicians to understand the maintenance and treatment of anxiety from a CB perspective. A great resource is David Barlow's *Anxiety and Its Disorders, Second Edition: The Nature and Treatment of Anxiety and Panic* (1994). In the Appendix, we include a listing of books that cover the treatment of specific anxiety disorders that might be helpful to readers of this book.

Beyond reading, experienced therapists should try to attend workshops or lectures on the application of CBT. Since workshops often include demonstrations, video clips of actual treatment, and opportunities to role-play, they allow therapists to actually see and practice CBT. Good resources for this kind of training include the annual conferences of the Association of Behavioral and Cognitive Therapies (ABCT) and the Anxiety Disorders Association of America (ADAA). The web site for the Academy of Cognitive Therapy (http://www.academyofcognitivetherapy.org) also maintains a listing of upcoming workshops (including audio workshops that can be done at home), as well as a listing of cognitive therapy training programs for professionals.

Seeking Out Clinical Supervision

Finally, experienced therapists can seek out supervision from CB therapists. The nature of the supervision can vary. Some supervisors will meet in person or by phone to discuss cases. Supervision should involve case conceptualization, treatment planning, and carrying out the treatment. People new to CBT can gain a lot from having an experienced cognitive-behavioral therapist help them to design hierarchies, plan exposures, and discuss how to do pre- and post-processing of exposures.

Some supervisors watch or listen to tapes of treatment sessions prior to supervision meetings. The quality of supervision can be greatly enhanced by actually seeing someone do therapy. Supervisors can pick up on important subtleties, such as the therapist providing reassurance to the patient or the patient using rituals during exposures. The supervisee can also watch tapes of the supervisor providing therapy. Patients must provide consent to be audio/videotaped and must be aware of who will be viewing these tapes, how they will be mailed and stored, and how they will be destroyed once they are no longer needed. A good way to find a cognitive-behavioral therapist in your area is to look on the web sites for ABCT (www.abct.org) or ADAA (www.adaa.org). The Academy of Cognitive Therapy also maintains a list of certified cognitive therapists on their web site.

Experienced CBT Therapists

Even therapists who have been doing CBT for many years can benefit from supervision. Supervision can be casual—simply contacting a colleague on an as-needed basis to discuss a case. This might involve discussing the conceptualization of a particularly complex case or even discussing how to set up an exposure to precisely target a unique fear.

Supervision can also be more formalized. A few colleagues can form a supervision group and meet on a set schedule to discuss cases and other issues. This can serve as an excellent way to get help with difficult cases, as well as a forum to discuss relevant issues. An excellent benefit of a peer supervision group is that clinicians benefit from multiple perspectives on their cases. Clinicians can experiment to find the optimal number of clinicians to be involved in the supervision group. More clinicians leads to additional perspectives and ideas; however too many members precludes all clinicians from presenting their cases.

In addition to clinical supervision, members of peer supervision groups can share information on upcoming workshops and lectures, discuss marketing strategies for growing one's practice, and share the names of good referral sources. Perhaps most importantly, clinicians can seek support during difficult times (e.g., during a stretch of time when one's practice is filled with extremely severe and hard-to-treat patients).

Two ethical/legal issues are important to mention here. First, confidentiality must be maintained when discussing cases with colleagues. It is certainly fine to describe cases, but identifying information should not be shared. Clinicians may choose to tell their patients that they are involved in peer supervision, even if identifying information will not be shared, and obtain patient consent to discuss their cases. Patients are typically pleased to know that they are getting two (or more) minds for the price of one.

Second, when faced with clinical challenges, therapists should note in the patient's chart that they consulted with a colleague. For example, we are all faced from time to time with the decision of whether or not to hospitalize a suicidal patient. At these times, it is good clinical practice to consult with a colleague. It can be very helpful to get the views of someone removed from the case who does not have a relationship with the patient. While the protection of the patient must be forefront in our minds, it is also important during these difficult times to also protect oneself with proper documentation. Noting a consultation in the chart can serve clinicians very well if they are faced with disciplinary action. It shows that they took the patient seriously, got feedback from trusted colleagues on a course of action, and acted in accordance not only with their own judgment, but also that of another competent colleague.

Beginning Therapists

Supervision is of course most important when individuals are just learning to do therapy. Unlicensed therapists must practice under the supervision of a licensed individual. Yes, this is the law—but it is also essential to the learning process. While warmth and empathy might be inborn qualities, therapy is a skill and must be learned gradually, just as we learn to speak a new language. This can only be accomplished with a competent teacher (or teachers).

Picking a Supervisor

The first step in establishing a supervisory relationship is to select a supervisor. In training programs, this decision is sometimes made for students. Often though, as students become more senior, they can select supervisors within their department or in the community. For students who are interested in learning CBT, it is important to seek out some cognitive-behaviorally oriented supervisors. But, it can also be very helpful to seek supervision from people of other orientations. One criticism that is sometimes directed at CBT is that it is more about technique than process. To some degree, this is probably true. Most trainees can benefit from working with a clinician who is more process-oriented, such as a psychodynamic therapist. This might help the student to learn more about the interpersonal nature of the therapeutic relationship and about how to think more deeply about case conceptualization. It is also beneficial for students to seek out supervision in systems approaches or at least to gain education and training in systems theory. Students may find it helpful to work with a range of supervisors and orientations as they are beginning therapy and tailor their experiences more closely with their areas of interest as they go along.

Obviously, students should also establish relationships with supervisors who do work that interests them. If students want to work with anxious children, they should find a supervisor who works with anxious children. Seeking supervision from such a person will reap far greater benefit than seeking supervision from a "close match," such as a therapist who treats anxious adults. Students should see their supervisory experiences as an opportunity to get exposed to different populations and work environments that they think they might want to pursue in the future.

Additional Considerations in Selecting a Supervisor

Perhaps more important than orientation, population, and setting is finding a *good* supervisor. What does this mean? First, it is important to find someone who regularly supervises students. Supervision and teaching are skills and it is always best to work with someone who has these skills down pat!

Second, the supervisor should have time and be available. This means being on time to meetings, being available for the whole time allotted for the meeting with no interruptions, and coming to meetings prepared (i.e., having listened to tapes or reviewed session notes). It also means being available to students in the event of emergencies. Supervisors should provide all contact information, as well as alternative people to contact if they are unavailable. Ultimately, they are responsible for the clinical care of their supervisees' patients, and should behave as such. While it might be appealing to be supervised by the most well-known cognitive-behavioral therapists in the area, this is not always the best supervision. Often, very well-known people travel a lot and are overextended. This might mean *no* supervision, rather than great supervision.

Third, the supervisor should be a pleasant person with whom to work. As a new clinician, seeing patients can be stressful and difficult. Having a highly critical supervisor can only add to that stress. It is important that students feel comfortable with their supervisors and do not feel defensive. If students do not feel comfortable sharing their difficulties and challenges for fear of being criticized or reprimanded, they will not grow and develop their clinical skills. There are a lot of people around who can provide supervision, so there is no reason to work with someone unpleasant and unsupportive.

The best way to learn if a potential supervisor has these qualities is to ask around. Students should ask potential supervisors if they can speak to his or her former supervisees. Students can also ask former supervisors for suggestions of other people to work with. Word travels fast in the world of CBT and students can often learn a lot from talking to "people in the know."

The Purpose of Supervision

Supervision serves many purposes. The foremost purpose of supervision is to provide patients with the best possible treatment. Yet, supervision is also about teaching—it allows students or clinicians to learn about providing treatment. Students can read countless books and articles, watch hours of tapes of other people doing therapy, and can practice on friends, but the real learning begins when they start seeing patients.

Supervisors should ensure that students are practicing in an ethical, law-abiding way. They should educate students about the ethical codes for their profession, and the laws governing their work in their state or province. In addition to following rules, supervisors should be sure that students are treating their patients with respect, warmth, and empathy.

Beyond this, supervision depends greatly on the clinical experience that the student intends to get. Some clinical practica are focused on assessment. In these situations, the supervisor might help the student with such things as administering, scoring and interpreting assessment measures, establishing diagnoses, and writing reports.

For practica focusing on assessment and/or treatment, a major task of supervisors is to help students learn how to conceptualize cases. This often falls to the wayside, with focus being placed instead on the nuts and bolts of CBT. Placing undue focus on technique though can lead students to practice in a mindless way. As we discussed in Chapter 4, failing to form a case conceptualization prior to starting treatment is like leaving for a road trip without a map. Supervisors should help students to formulate case conceptualizations and should keep returning to the conceptualization throughout treatment to ensure that students are adjusting their understanding of the case as it progresses.

When a clinical practica focuses on treatment, supervisors teach students the nuts and bolts of actually doing a given treatment, like CBT for anxiety disorders. This might involve reading assignments, watching tapes of other therapists, and doing role-plays with the supervisor or peers. Students must learn how to decide what to do in a session, based on what has happened in a previous session. While treatment manuals provide a very good framework for therapy, they do not tell students what to do in each session with a given patient. Supervisors help students learn to use the ongoing case conceptualization to inform the treatment plan.

Obviously, working with psychologically ill people is not without challenges. A final purpose of supervision is to help students learn how to deal with these challenges. Supervisors should ensure that students know what to do when faced with suicidal or homicidal patients. They should also help students learn how to deal with difficult patients, like those who will not talk or those who get angry. Supervision can be used to teach students techniques for dealing with these situations, and for processing feelings that might be associated with them. While CBT supervision is typically focused on the content of the work the supervisee does with patients, a good CBT supervisor will also help the student process how she or he feels about conducting therapy and about their work with particular patients.

Methods of Supervision

After establishing a supervisory relationship, one of the most important things to discuss is how supervision will be carried out. A meeting time should be set and students should be sure they are getting the amount of supervision that they need for licensing requirements. These requirements aside, students should meet for at least one hour per week with their supervisors. They should have the option of extra meeting time when faced with particularly complex cases.

Once a meeting time is set, it is important to establish how supervision will actually be carried out. Many CBT therapists conduct supervision similarly to a therapy session in that an agenda is created and covered during the supervision meeting. For example, the supervisor may ask the supervisee what he or she would like to cover, and together they would create an agenda to focus on during the supervision session. Supervisors can model methods of returning to the agenda when the supervision goes astray and supervisees learn about the process of a CBT session and tools for handling some of the challenges (such as straying from the agenda) that can arise.

Some supervisors ask their supervisees to recount what occurred in each treatment session. This method of supervision is fine, but is of course reliant on the student's self-report. While few students want to "skew the data," it is difficult to describe the nuances of one's own behavior. Furthermore, so much can go on during a session that it might be hard to remember all the important details to share with the supervisor.

With that being said, the self-report method can be appropriate for more senior students, or for students who have worked with a particular supervisor for a sufficient amount of time that their style and handle on techniques is known. Students should come to their supervision meetings with notes on each session that they have had since the last meeting. For each patient, they should note which session they had, any pertinent data (e.g., scores on self-report measures), what material was covered, what the plan is for the next session, and questions that they would like to ask. This facilitates an efficient and productive supervision meeting.

Other methods of supervision should most certainly be used along with the self-report method, particularly for beginning therapists. There are a number of possibilities:

Co-therapy

It can be a wonderful experience to treat a patient with a supervisor. The supervisor can get things started, sharing psychoeducational material with the patient and doing the first exposure, for example. The student can then do a few exposures while being directly observed by the supervisor. And, finally, the students can finish up the treatment on his or her own. This can be a great way to treat one's first patient because it serves as a transition from watching someone else do therapy, to doing it completely independently.

Direct Observation

Supervisors can observe students either right in the room with patients, or through a one-way mirror. Supervisors can observe clinicians conducting intake evaluations and therapy sessions to provide specific feedback based on their observations. Supervision time can be set aside right after the treatment session when it is still fresh in both the student's and the supervisor's minds. While being observed can be anxiety provoking for *any* therapist, it can serve as a valuable learning experience.

Taping

Perhaps the most common method of supervision is to record (audio or video) sessions and have supervisors listen to or watch them. This is an excellent substitute for direct observation, which is often hard to orchestrate because of scheduling constraints. Tapes (particularly videotapes) allow the supervisor to pick up on the subtleties of both patient and therapist behavior that would never be accessible via self-report. The best videotapes are those that show both the therapist and the patient so supervisors can observe the therapist's nonverbal and verbal behaviors and the patient's reactions. Early in a supervisory experience, supervisors will often listen to entire treatment sessions. Later, it can be helpful to cue up segments where the student feels particularly in need of help. Segments can also be watched during supervision meetings, and role-plays can be used to help the student learn how they could differently explain a concept, process an exposure, or deal with a difficult clinical issue.

Peer Supervision

Peer supervision can be an excellent adjunct to a formal supervisory experience. A peer supervision group can be established with students at different levels of training. Cases can be discussed, and much as with formal supervisors, students can share ideas on how to best conceptualize cases and carry out treatment. An advantage of peer supervision is that peers can also be relied on to provide moral support. Students often feel inadequate and not confident when first treating patients and might not want to discuss these feelings with supervisors. Discussing these feelings with peers often shows students that they are not alone, and that confidence does develop with time and experience.

Provision of Supervision

Seasoned clinicians often enjoy providing supervision as a means of giving back, helping supervisees learn effective CBT, and maintaining a commitment to ongoing education, both for themselves and others. Clinicians often report learning more during the process of being a supervisor than they have in many other clinical situations. As supervisors, clinicians must stay on top of current research and read the literature on the topics about which they supervise. Supervisors are challenged to not only conceptualize cases appropriately, but to communicate well with others. Supervisors develop excellent skills in describing the process of CBT that they can use with their own patients as well as with their supervisees.

References

Barlow, D. H. (2002). *Anxiety and its disorders: The nature and treatment of anxiety and panic* (2nd ed.). New York: Guilford.

Beck, A. T. (1979). *Cognitive therapy and the emotional disorders* (reprint ed.). New York: Plume.

Beck, A. T., Rush, J., Shaw, B. F., & Emery, G. (1979). *Cognitive therapy of depression*. New York: Guilford.

Beck, J. S. (1995). *Cognitive therapy: Basics and beyond*. New York: Guilford.

CHAPTER 16

Clinician's Top 10 Concerns and Challenges with Treating Anxiety

In this final chapter, we will address the most common questions and difficulties that arise in the clinical treatment of patients with anxiety disorders. The topics and discussions in this chapter are compiled from our own experiences with patients, as well as those of our clinical supervisees. We also utilize the research and treatment experience of our colleagues that we have learned about through peer supervision.

"My Patient Won't Do the Exposures I Suggest"

It is a significant problem when patients do not complete their exposures. When patients do not complete exposures, they not only minimize the likelihood that treatment will be successful, but they likely reinforce avoidance behaviors. If clinicians find that their patients are not completing exposure homework assignments, they should ask a series of questions to determine the reason or reasons that it is difficult for them to complete homework assignments. Common issues include:

- Avoidance or procrastination because exposure brings up anxiety.
- Time management and scheduling difficulties.
- Lack of a belief that it will truly help them.
- Embarrassment or thinking that the assignment is strange or unusual.
- Confusion about how to properly do the exposure.

Huppert and Baker-Morissette (2003) recommend that clinicians remain firm about the importance of homework in order to ensure maximum treatment benefits. They recommend that clinicians ask about homework at the beginning of every treatment session to reinforce its significance. Missed homework can be completed during the session.

It is common for patients to find homework assignments to be more difficult than the exposure was in session. Because it can be tough to do homework, patients need to have the proper education and motivation to realize how necessary homework completion is. They need to be held accountable for completing all assignments. If an assignment is given but then never discussed, patients will assume it was not very important. When patients complete homework, clinicians can reinforce the behavior and point out the positive results that occur when the homework is completed.

Huppert and Baker-Morissette (2003) also point out that many patients do not want to complete exposures because they feel that the exposures are not "normal." Patients state that it is not something they would ordinarily do in life. "Why would I want to touch a garbage can, no one else does that!" a patient might say. Clinicians can reinforce the rationale for exposures and explain that the point of exposures is not to do what is normal, but it is to elicit and eventually reduce disturbing thoughts, feelings, and sensations.

A common response when clinicians ask why patients did not complete exposures is that patients did not have time. This explanation raises two areas of exploration. The first is that of priorities. Because people are more likely to find time for that which they deem important, clinicians can help patients to see how important homework practice is if indeed the patient is motivated to overcome anxiety. This point may lead to discussion about whether the patient has any reasons *not* to overcome anxiety. Giving up anxiety, for many patients, presents a whole set of unknowns, which are often more difficult for anxious individuals than the familiar albeit uncomfortable situation. The second area to explore is time management skills. Is the patient frequently behind and unable to accomplish important tasks? If so, the clinician can help the patient to problem solve and create a schedule that includes exposure homework.

Patients may also say that they did not do the exposures because they did not feel well. While it is certainly understandable if patients do not complete exposures while they have the flu, but many times patients simply do not feel 100 percent when they say they do not feel well. Because it is rare to feel 100 percent, patients could end up waiting a long time to do exposures and miss out on valuable learning opportunities. Huppert and Baker-Morissette (2003) suggest that patients be taught that exposures are best conducted in most situations, even when the patient is not feeling well or is tired. When the patient learns that the anxiety can be tolerated (or even useful) under difficult circumstances, he is less likely to attempt to avoid anxiety in the future. We do not want to send the message to patients that they can manage anxiety only when they feel perfect and the stars are aligned properly. We want patients to feel confident that they can manage their anxiety anywhere at any time.

"I Feel Badly Making My Patients Do This 'Hard' Stuff"

Working with patients with anxiety disorders in a structured format can be a different experience than other forms of therapy. When clinicians are used to working with patients primarily in a supportive, nondirective manner, the cognitive-behavioral treatment of anxiety disorders will feel very different. The clinician is, in fact, there to help the patients do the things they do not *want* to do. The clinician's role is to encourage and help the patient do the hard stuff that they would otherwise avoid.

Because patients know that they will probably face a challenging exposure when they go to their therapist's office, they may not like going to their appointments. The clinician can be seen as tough or even mean by some patients as they begin exposure therapy. Some of our child and adolescent patients have told their parents that they do not want to come to their treatment sessions or that they do not like us. Clinicians can learn to tolerate and invite these reactions because they know that patients will benefit. And patients typically like their therapists again by the end of treatment and are very thankful for the consistent approach.

This model is similar to a parent encouraging their child to choose healthy food options instead of candy. The child probably wants the candy and does not want the vegetables, but if they repeatedly choose the vegetables, they may actually begin to like them and they will definitely benefit from the nutrition they gain.

When clinicians gain more experience treating anxiety disorders, they acquire more confidence and success stories to show themselves and their patients that the treatment they provide works. A useful strategy is to educate patients at the beginning of therapy to the challenges that can arise in treatment and engage the patients' courage and strengths. Throughout the process of exposures, clinicians should be nonapologetic even if they feel badly watching their patients struggle. Clinicians should remember that if patients are anxious in session and during exposures, it means that we are helping them—after all, if exposures do not make patients anxious, it means that we have not targeted their fears. Furthermore, clinicians must remind themselves that the anxiety will habituate with repeated exposure.

Clinicians can also benefit from having the support of other clinicians, supervisors, consulting clinicians, or their own therapist to discuss the feelings that arise as they work with patients. Clinicians can work through their own needs to be liked and the discomfort they may experience if their clients are less than enthusiastic about coming in to some sessions. In supervision, clinicians can discuss their discomfort with being in the presence of negative affect or a need to help patients feel better rather than riding out their anxiety with them.

"My Patient's Anxiety is Not Habituating"

There are many reasons that a patient's anxiety does not habituate. The first area to explore is whether the patient has truly experienced prolonged and repeated exposures. Some exposures need to be conducted more frequently than others, and the duration of the exposures may need to be longer. If a patient does an exposure for a few minutes a couple times a week, it is unlikely that habituation would occur, and if it did, it would probably take a very long time. Clinicians should engage in an exposure with their patients for as long as needed for anxiety to habituate to show patients that habituation occurs when they stay with their anxiety and do no rituals. If the session is almost over, but the patient is still feeling anxious, she should be encouraged to continue the exposure on her own, and to repeat it everyday until the next session.

Another explanation for the lack of habituation is cognitive avoidance and safety behaviors. Patients may engage in subtle avoidance during the exposures. This avoidance may be safety behaviors, such as a patient with Social Phobia not making eye contact, or rituals, such as a patient with OCD washing her hands after an exposure to touching germs. The avoidance may also be cognitive avoidance and distraction. As patients are completing an exposure, they think about something else and do not truly engage in the exposure. Patients may also mentally reassure themselves during exposures, which is essentially a mental ritual. When a patient tells himself that it is not really a big deal or that he will be fine, he avoids experiencing anxiety, and habituation is not likely to occur. Clinicians should be sure to check for subtle safety behaviors and mental reassurance.

Another reason that habituation may not occur or may occur very slowly is comorbidity. Other disorders might interfere with the process of habituation. If a patient has an underlying untreated thought disorder, she may be so convinced that her feared consequence is 100 percent likely to happen that she cannot habituate. If a patient is severely depressed, he might not have the energy or the level of concentration necessary to do exposures. In such cases, it is sometimes necessary to abandon the anxiety disorder treatment temporarily and focus instead on the interfering comorbid disorder.

Patients who have a feared consequence that extends far out into the future may also have difficulty habituating during exposures. One patient was afraid that exposure to chemicals would cause her to get cancer in 20 years. It was difficult to disprove this fear during exposures. A useful approach is to help patients accept the uncertainty in life and learn to live with the fact that anything negative or dangerous *could* happen any day, but that the likelihood is low.

A lack of habituation during exposures can also signify an incorrect diagnosis. As a rule, when exposures are conducted in the way we have recommended, anxiety *does* habituate. In the absence of habituation, clinicians should return to the initial differential diagnosis to see if another disorder better fits the patient's current experiences.

"My Patient's Anxiety May Come Back When He is No Longer in Therapy"

As we discussed in Chapter 10, a patient's anxiety can return after the cessation of therapy. Clinicians can set up the end of treatment to minimize the likelihood of a relapse by beginning the process of termination early on, predicting difficulties that may arise and problem solving them, and scheduling ongoing maintenance sessions.

Clinicians should also remind themselves that a mild return in the patient's anxiety is not a treatment failure. If a patient's anxiety before treatment was a level 100, and after treatment the patient lived the rest of her life at a level 25, the patient probably considers that to be a tremendous success. Patients can be educated to discern normal from pathological anxiety. Normal levels of anxiety are to be expected, and the patient can learn to recognize these and feel good that she was able to prevent them from reaching a clinical level.

Clinicians can also offer patients the opportunity to call them to check in. If a patient is unsure whether what he is experiencing is the beginning of a relapse or a normal level of anxiety, he can have a brief telephone conversation with his therapist to discuss the situation. If the therapist thinks it is a good idea to engage in a maintenance session, they can schedule it during that phone conversation. The same process applies to parents calling to check in regarding their children's anxiety. Sometimes parents become hypersensitive to a resurgence of anxiety in the future and just need to be assured that their child's anxiety is normal and is not a part of their anxiety disorder. Most children and teenagers, for example, are going to be scared during a horror movie, nervous before a major test such as the SATs, or apprehensive about their first date.

"It Is Hard to Stick to the Agenda"

While there will be reasons that it would be advantageous to occasionally stray from the agenda, clinicians need to be careful that key agenda items are not regularly missed. There are times when clinicians make wise decisions to skip the agenda item and focus on an unforeseen topic that a patient brings in. One patient was working on social anxiety, but came in one day extremely distraught because a family member had died in an accident. The therapist made the wise and sensitive decision to put off the planned exposure session and instead discuss the patient's grief and feelings regarding the loss of her family member. The therapist realized that the patient needed assistance dealing with her sadness, that she would not have benefited from exposures that day, and that the therapeutic relationship would be best supported by showing flexibility and empathy for the situation. Earlier in this chapter, we emphasized the importance of doing exposures even when clients are not at their best. There are exceptions to every rule and crisis situations are often not an ideal time to do an exposure. Clinicians can assess the patient and ask how they feel about proceeding with the planned session.

Another reason that it can be difficult to stick to the assigned agenda is avoidance. Avoidance can exist on the part of the patient or the clinician. One way that patients avoid is by talking excessively. This is a stall tactic that reveals the way the patient typically responds to uncomfortable situations. Some patients come in with mini-crises or situations that they want to discuss in session. Clinicians need to determine whether these are situations worthy of modifying the agenda. Patients sometimes have situations that weigh heavily on their minds, but which are not directly related to their anxiety. Clinicians can consider providing a referral for these patients to address their issues with another professional and focus on the anxiety treatment in the current therapy. For example, a patient who frequently brings up marital difficulties could be given a referral for a couple's therapist for him and his spouse. A patient with significant career issues could be given a referral for a career coach.

When patients avoid session content by talking, the clinician can gently point out that it is difficult to stick to the agenda because the patient seems to have many other things to talk about. The clinician can then say, "I know that you are nervous about the session today because we are going to work on the exposure at the top of your hierarchy. Based on what you now know, what is the most common response to anxiety?" The patient would say, "Avoidance." The clinician can then respond, "Yes, you are absolutely right. I realize that the topic we are discussing is important to you; however, may it also be that talking about it is a way to avoid the difficult exposure?" The clinician can then ask the patient if she is willing to begin the exposure so there is time to complete it in session.

Clinicians also avoid. When a clinician is new to a structured treatment approach, it can be a lot easier to have a free-flowing conversation that does not address the agenda items. It is normal for clinicians to be nervous about interventions with which they have little or no experience, and be tempted to avoid these interventions. When a patient brings up a seemingly important topic, it can be easy for us to convince ourselves that we should be flexible about the agenda. Another reason that clinicians sometimes avoid is their discomfort with negative affect. It can be painful to watch a patient get overcome by intense fear or break down and cry because of the exposures we encourage them to do. Clinicians need to be convinced that the patient is benefiting from the anxiety and remind themselves how much the intervention is helping the patient. If clinicians have difficulty remembering or believing these points, they should pursue peer supervision or hire a supervisor or consultant. Clinicians must remember that patients are sensitive and perceptive, and if they pick up on the clinician's uncertainty, the exposure is less likely to be effective.

Clinicians can minimize avoidance by writing the session agenda on a dry erase board. To maximize patient investment in the agenda, clinicians can co-create it with patients at the beginning of the session. When patients become long-winded in their responses, clinicians can refer back to the agenda that they made with the patients.

Lateness to session can also make it difficult to stick to the agenda. If patients routinely arrive late for session, clinicians can ask them about it. For example, "I noticed that you've been about ten minutes late for the past few sessions and that we have had some difficulty accomplishing all the items on your agenda. Is this time of day a difficult one for you?" Patients may reveal that they always get stuck in rush-hour traffic or have a hard time getting out of the house with an infant in the morning. Clinicians can help patients to recognize the role of avoidance in coming in late to sessions or problem solve if time is the main factor.

"My Patient is Engaging in Therapy-Interfering Behaviors"

There are many behaviors that clinicians find interfere with treatment. Some common examples of therapy-interfering behaviors include arriving at sessions late, getting off topic during sessions, and not doing homework assignments. We have addressed several concerns in earlier parts of this chapter and will now reiterate a couple of important points.

In general, the most effective way to address these issues is in a straightforward, empathic, and unassuming manner. If, for example a clinician finds that her patient, Jennifer, has arrived to several sessions ten minutes late, she could say:

> Jennifer, I noticed that you have arrived to a few sessions late and that we've run out of time when doing the exposures. Let's take a minute to put our heads together about how to help you get here on time so we have the complete session time together. First, help me to understand what holds you up when you're on your way here.

Remember that the best approach is a Socratic one, which enables patients to see how their late arrivals negatively impact the process of treatment. If patients are unable to arrive at this conclusion, therapists can be direct and let patients know that the full treatment sessions are necessary for optimal treatment results. The clinician and patient can then collaboratively discuss a plan to ensure punctuality to sessions.

While lateness to sessions can be detrimental to the treatment process, clinicians should also remain flexible and be careful not to make a mountain out of a molehill that can negatively affect the therapeutic relationship. If, for example, a patient is a couple of minutes late, the clinician may astutely decide not to spend valuable session time discussing how the local bus system is unreliable.

One solution to running out of time during treatment sessions is to schedule double sessions. This means that the patient and clinician agree to do back-to-back sessions of 50 minutes each. The therapy session is, therefore, 100 minutes, allowing plenty of time to do exposures. Clinicians should keep in mind that insurance companies may not cover this arrangement. Patients should be informed of this and encouraged to check with their insurance companies before embarking on double sessions. If patients are not financially able to commit to a treatment plan of double sessions, then alternative arrangements should be discussed.

Another behavior that can interfere with treatment outcome is frequently getting off topic in session. There are several reasons that patients may divert the conversation, including avoidance of negative affect, embarrassment regarding lack of homework completion, and discomfort with exposures or other components of treatment.

It is, however, important to consider whether the patient's difficulty sticking to the agenda is a response to the clinician's behavior. A patient may attempt conversation or small talk as a way of building a relationship with the clinician. When this is the case, clinicians should be sensitive to the patient's needs and recognize that the best treatment outcomes will occur when a strong therapeutic alliance is present. The clinician should also consider whether the patient's desire to "chat" is representative of loneliness and a need for more social relationships outside of therapy. If this seems to be the case, establishing social relationships can become a target of treatment.

A patient may also get off topic when she is not clear on the session expectations. The patient may not realize that she is getting off topic if the agenda is not discussed and agreed upon. Clinicians, should therefore attempt to modify some of their own behaviors (i.e., by engaging in a couple of minutes of small talk or discussing session goals at the beginning of session) to see whether the patients' behaviors change.

"My Patient Refuses to Give up Safety Behaviors/Rituals/Subtle Avoidance Behaviors"

One of the most common reasons that patients do not give up safety behaviors, rituals, or subtle avoidance behaviors is that they do not realize how detrimental a seemingly "little thing" actually is. A patient with Panic Disorder thinks, "What's so bad about carrying around a pill bottle if I never take the pills?" A patient with OCD thinks, "What's the big deal about washing my hands before I eat dinner—everyone does that!"

The best way for a clinician to approach a patient's reluctance to give up avoidance behaviors is to return to the rationale for treatment and clarify any points that the patient may not have understood. Metaphors and analogies can be very helpful. For example, a clinician can say:

> I understand that it doesn't seem like a big deal to wash your hands three times a day because that is such a normal thing to do. Our work together, however, is not to do what's normal, it's to get rid of your OCD. You see, OCD is like a nagging child. If your child regularly bugs you to buy him candy in the supermarket line and you did, even just once, what do you think would happen? Would he ask you

for candy again? Sure he would! He would ask again because he'd think to himself, "I got the candy that one time, I should try again!" Washing your hands during the treatment is a ritual that is like feeding the OCD—it makes OCD stronger even if you only do it once in a while. So can we agree to do the ritual prevention in the way that we have discussed—and not wash your hands after an exposure until the treatment is completed and you've beaten OCD?

If a patient understands the treatment rationale but simply refuses to give up particular safety behaviors, rituals, or avoidances, then the clinician should discuss the potential impact on therapy outcome and alternative treatment options (such as medications) with the patient. It is often better for a patient to try a different treatment approach or hold off on therapy until he can fully engage in it than to do therapy in a way which is unlikely to be effective.

"I Am New to CBT and Want to Make Sure That I Don't Look Like a Novice"

Many clinicians treating anxiety disorders begin to experience anxiety themselves! This is because the treatments are more structured than many clinicians are used to, and therapists worry about appearing unprofessional or telling a patient the wrong thing to do.

Clinicians treating anxiety disorders do need to appear confident because they will recommend many ideas that sound "crazy" to patients and patients need to feel confident that they have a credible ally to help them overcome anxiety. Knowing that it is important to be confident can make clinicians feel even more nervous.

Novice clinicians do well to gain supervision and/or consultation as they are beginning to treat patients with anxiety. Supervision or consultation provides clinicians with additional confidence because they know that they have a second opinion and back up if they get into difficult situations.

Another important consideration is for clinicians to be careful that they do not engage in safety behaviors themselves as anxiety management strategies. Clinicians may be tempted to speak in an artificially secure tone of voice or use words that sound expert but actually end up confusing patients. Clinicians may also be tempted to overprepare for sessions. While it is important to be prepared for sessions, remember that overpreparation is a common safety behavior that can backfire, make you appear overrehearsed, and damaging your ability to connect with the patients if they feel they are being lectured to.

Clinicians may also try to see patients who are motivated and have a clear single diagnosis as their first CBT patients. In general (although definitely not always, as every patient is different), patients with comorbidity, lack of motivation, or other characteristics such as overvalued ideation (OVI) are more difficult. It can be beneficial, therefore, to selectively choose the first patients to see as one learns CBT. A patient with mild Panic Disorder without Agoraphobia, for example, is likely to be a better training case than a patient with severe Panic Disorder and severe Agoraphobia. A patient with mild to moderate OCD may be a better first choice than a patient with severe OCD and OVI. Keep in mind, however, that patients with only mild anxiety may be less motivated to overcome their anxiety, and therefore less dedicated to their treatment.

"What if Patients Aren't Able or Willing to Consider Other Ways of Thinking About a Situation?"

There is a difference between being unable and being unwilling. It is helpful if clinicians can ascertain which occurs for their patients because the way to respond may be slightly different for each.

There are patients who seem unable to accept that there are other explanations for a particular situation. Over the course of cognitive restructuring, these patients might not be able to generate alternatives at all. Or, they might be able to feed the clinician what they think he wants to hear, but discount all of the alternatives. There are a few ways to cope with these tricky patients. First, other cognitive tools can be used. A particularly helpful one is to ask the patient to put themselves in someone else's shoes. Consider a patient with Social Phobia who is convinced that he totally failed at making a presentation in class because he stumbled over a word. He is convinced that everyone noticed, and then took this behavior as an indication that he is clueless, stupid, and not deserving of being in school. After trying to generate other alternatives and failing, the clinician can ask, "What would you think of someone else in your class who stumbled over a word?" Often, patients will see that they hold themselves to much higher standards than they hold for others. And, they will see that a single behavior can have many possible interpretations. Patients can also be asked, "What would make a 'perfect' presentation?" After writing down all of the attributes of a perfect presentation, the patient could be asked if anyone in the class met these incredibly high standards. The clinician must get creative and move beyond simple cognitive restructuring to help patients see the errors inherent in their thoughts.

For some patients, even the cleverest cognitive techniques will not help! In these cases, the clinician is best advised to move on to exposures. Some patients simply learn better through experience than through verbal discourse.

Even with every trick in the book, some patients still hold on to their beliefs with 100 percent conviction. They seem to refuse to look at the world in a different way. In these situations, motivational interviewing techniques can be helpful (see Miller & Rollnick, 2002. The clinician can help the patient to weigh the pros and cons of retaining the *status quo* versus looking at things in a different way. In CBT, clinicians are on the side of change and their stance is to continually encourage the patient to think and behave differently. When clinicians push ambivalent patients, however, they often become even more entrenched in their current ways. The motivational interviewing stance is much less "judgmental." The clinician simply serves as a coach for considering different alternatives, but is careful not to voice a preference for one over another. This stance can be very helpful in getting patients "unstuck" and more ready for CBT. Henny Westra has been doing excellent work on integrating motivational interviewing with CBT for anxiety disorders (see Arkowitz & Westra, 2004; Westra, 2004).

"I Have a Lot of Experience with Anxiety Disorders, but I Am Stuck With This Particular Patient. What Should I Do?

Even the most seasoned CBT clinicians get stuck from time to time. First, clinicians should realize that this is completely normal and should not criticize themselves or doubt their clinical abilities because of difficulties with a particular patient. We have never met an anxiety disorder treatment expert who did not get stuck from time to time.

Second, clinicians must take some time to consider the reasons that they may be stuck with a particular patient. They should return to the case conceptualization to see if the initial diagnosis and treatment plan holds true after more information has been gathered and more time has been spent with the patient. If the patient has comorbid diagnoses, a secondary disorder may in fact be primary or may be contributing to the patient's inability to engage in the treatment. Clinicians should also consider whether a lack of motivation or lack of social support may play a role. When patients are children, clinicians should be mindful of family variables. For instance, if the parents are not involved in the treatment, the patient may not gain adequate practice between sessions or may not feel that the work is important. Consultation with other anxiety disorder experts can be invaluable in generating explanations for the patient's slow treatment progress.

Third, the clinicians should consider additional options. It can be very helpful to consult with a psychiatrist or refer the patient for a psychiatric evaluation to see if medications can be a helpful adjunct therapy or whether a change in current medications is needed. Asking a colleague to do a consultation with the patient for a second opinion can also be beneficial. Sometimes, an alternative type of therapy, such as supportive counseling, psychodynamic therapy, or skills training might be more appropriate than CBT. In these cases, clinicians should provide the patient with a referral.

While it can be hard to admit a poor fit, it can also be helpful to consider whether a different type of clinician (someone older, younger, male, female, soft in demeanor, bold in demeanor, stringent in approach, flexible in approach, etc.) may be a better match for the particular client.

Clinicians can also recommend that the patient terminate therapy if he is not engaging. It is always better for patients to come back when they are ready, than for them to spend a lot of time and money on a treatment that will likely not work.

References

Arkowitz, H., & Westra, H. A. (2004). Motivational interviewing as an adjunct to cognitive behavioral therapy for depression and anxiety. *Journal of Cognitive Psychotherapy, 18,* 337–350.

Huppert, J. D., & Baker-Morissette, S. L. (2003). Beyond the manual: The insider's guide to panic control treatment. *Cognitive and Behavioral Practice, 10,* 2–13.

Miller, W. R., & Rollnick, S. (2002). *Motivational interviewing: Preparing people for change.* New York: Guilford.

Westra, H. A. (2004). Managing resistance in cognitive behavioural therapy: The application of motivational interviewing in mixed anxiety and depression. *Cognitive Behaviour Therapy, 33,* 161–175.

Resources for Anxiety Treatment for Clinicians and Self-Help for Patients

Training and Supervision

Larina Kase and Deborah Ledley offer training for mental health professionals. They are available to speak at continuing education workshops and seminars. Individual and group supervision and consultation are useful for clinicians interested in building their expertise in the treatment of anxiety disorders. For more information, call 888-820-7325 (telephones are answered as "PAS Coaching") or email info@pascoaching.com.

Books

Antony, M., & McCabe, R. (2004). *10 simple solutions to panic: How to overcome panic attacks, calm physical symptoms, and reclaim your life.* Oakland, CA: New Harbinger Publications.

Antony, M., & Swinson, R. (2000). *The shyness and social anxiety workbook.* Oakland, CA: New Harbinger Publications.

Antony, M. M., Heimberg, R. G., & Ledley, D. R. (2005). *Improving outcomes and preventing relapse in cognitive-behavioral therapy.* New York: Guilford.

Barlow, D. (2004). *Anxiety and its disorders: The nature and treatment of anxiety and panic* (2nd ed.). New York: Guilford.

Beck, A. T., Emery, G., & Greenberg, R. L. (1990). *Anxiety disorders and phobias: A cognitive perspective.* New York: Basic Books.

Bourne, E. L. (2000). *The anxiety and phobia workbook* (3rd ed.). Oakland, CA: New Harbinger Publications.

Bourne, E. L. (2001). *Beyond anxiety and phobia.* (3rd ed.). Oakland, CA: New Harbinger Publications.

Foa, E., & Wilson, R. (1991). *Stop obsessing! How to overcome your obsessions and compulsions.* New York: Bantam.

Kase, L. (2006). *Anxious 9 to 5: How to beat worry, stop second guessing yourself, and work with confidence.* Oakland, CA: New Harbinger Publications.

Ledley, D. R., Marx, B., & Heimberg, R. G. (2005). *Making cognitive-behavioral therapy work: Clinical process for new practitioners.* New York: Guilford.

Paterson, R. J. (2000). *The assertiveness workbook.* Oakland, CA: New Harbinger Publications.

Ross, J. (1994). *Triumph over fear.* New York: Bantam.

Stein, M., & Walker, J. (2002). *Triumph over shyness: Conquering shyness and social anxiety.* New York: McGraw Hill.

Web Sites

The Anxiety Disorders Association of America (www.adaa.org)

A great source of information that includes a directory of anxiety specialists.

Association of Behavioral and Cognitive Therapies (www.aabt.org)

Search for a therapist near you with the *Find a Therapist* link.

The Anxiety Panic Internet Resource (www.algy.com/anxiety)

Provides self-help information for those with anxiety disorders.

Performance & Success Coaching, LLC (www.PAScoaching.com, www.anxious9to5.com)

Dr. Kase's consulting company web site which offers many free articles, assessments, and reports on overcoming anxiety and stress in the workplace.

PsychJourney (www.PsychJourney.com)

A web site that forms a bridge between health seekers and mental health professionals.

Obsessive Compulsive Foundation (www.ocfoundation.org)

A web site offering help for people and families affected by OCD.

The Center for the Treatment and Study of Anxiety (www.med.upenn.edu/ctsa)

Find information on treatment and training for professionals.

The Children's Center for OCD and Anxiety (www.worrywisekids.org)

A web site with dozens of resources for children and parents of children with anxiety.

AboutOurKids.Org (www.aboutourkids.org)

A web site run by the NYU Child Study Center with great resources for parents and families.

INDEX